25 N 03

Henry S. Jacoby

1597

ANDREW KLOMAN
OUT OF WHOSE LITTLE FORGE GREW THE CARNEGIE STEEL COMPANY

The Inside History
of the
Carnegie Steel Company

A Romance of Millions

By

JAMES HOWARD BRIDGE

NEW YORK
THE ALDINE BOOK COMPANY
32–34 LAFAYETTE PLACE
1903

TO RECALL THEIR FORGOTTEN SERVICES

This

History of a Great Business

is Dedicated

To the Memory of

the Men who Founded it, Saved it from early
Disaster, and won its First Successes:

ANDREW KLOMAN

DAVID McCANDLESS

WILLIAM COLEMAN

THOMAS MORRISON CARNEGIE

WILLIAM R. JONES

WILLIAM P. SHINN

DAVID A. STEWART

HENRY M. CURRY

PREFACE

THIS book is the outcome of a magazine article undertaken at an editor's request. Having spent a number of years in the closest intimacy with one of the owners of the great steel works, and enjoyed exceptional opportunities of becoming acquainted with the men who had wrought their success, I entertained little doubt as to my fitness for the task. So recalling the stories I had heard the partners tell, and adding a few I found in the writings of Andrew Carnegie, I wrote my article, and found I had enough material left for a couple more. These also were written, and in due time published.

To my surprise they brought an avalanche of dissent and protest. From distant Oregon and near-by Meadville, from Pittsburg and New York, came word from unknown correspondents that my conventional story was only a repetition of similar publishings, all faulty and all designed to glorify some individual at the expense of his associates. One letter contained an expression so vigorous that it has won a place for itself in this book: "They have filched their laurel wreaths from the tombs of the dead." Another assured me that what I had deemed honorable success was but the outcome of "Macchiavellian astuteness." I was told by one who had played an important part in the early history of the enterprise that "the bad faith, treachery, and chicanery that lie at the bottom of many great fortunes had their parallel in the history of the Carnegie interests." "Dear me!" sighed an unknown Pittsburg correspondent, "the humbug of greatness is so grotesque in the careers of those we know that it makes one wonder at the accidents which happen to men—accidents which elevate mediocrity and the commonplace to Olympian heights." In other letters were references to " porcine proclivities," " pachyderm entities," "a vainglorious medley of contradictions."

Under this interesting stimulus I determined to go to Pittsburg and stay there until I had got at the core of things Carnegian. My experience was at once a disappointment and an encouragement. With documentary proof before me I found that almost every man who had written a line about the events I was investigating had blundered; one in dates, another in sequence of happenings, a third in the placing of credit for inventions and improvements; and of them all I found Andrew Carnegie's own narrative the least trustworthy. Knowing how excellent is his verbal memory, it puzzled me to find him mistaking his own birth-year; claiming to have been the first in America to operate the Bessemer process of steel-making; to have originated iron railway bridges; to have been the founder of the business that bears his name; to have been ever on the alert to adopt new processes and mechanical improvements; to have maintained without a break the friendliest of relations with his partners; to have been the principal factor in the gigantic growth of the business; to have fervently tried to carry his high ideals concerning labor into his own works. Instead of this I everywhere found proof of the contrary; and when, finally, I was notified that I must agree to submit my manuscript to the usual Carnegie revision before I could count on any assistance of the present officers of the company, my disillusionment was complete.

But it made my work more interesting. To write a conventional history from the official records of the company, with the aid of the company's press agent and under the guidance of an official censor, was a thing any journalistic fledgling could do. To dig into the secrets of the great corporation, to expose its enormous profits, reveal its peculiar business methods, its ways of heading off competitors, its internal strife, to get its first annual reports and even its later balance sheets, and to do all this openly and without a bribe or the betrayal of a confidence, to involve no employee in a covert act or breach of faith—this was a task of no small difficulty. It is for the reader to judge of my success.

Thus disadvantaged, I have not hesitated to use personal letters and private documents as I might not otherwise have done. Whenever an interesting fact has come to my knowledge, properly authenticated, I have used it without regard to its implications. Yet I have stated nothing that cannot be verified. Often I have risked being tedious in order to quote a corroborative document. In other cases I have kept the proofs by me in case my accuracy should be called into question.

From this independence has resulted a narrative more truthful than it could otherwise have been. Had the official representatives of the Carnegie Steel Company revised this story, it is certain that many of the statements it contains would never have seen the light of day. More than once the company has accepted a large monetary loss rather than disclose its secrets in court. If, therefore, this book has any value it owes it to its frankness. While the author expects censure for some of his revelations, he is willing to accept it in the cause of truth. The conventional history of the concern, based on benevolent aphorisms and platitudinous maxims about thrift, industry, genius, and super-commercial morality, has been written a hundred times, and will probably be written again and again.

The Carnegie Steel Company, as will be seen from this narrative, is not the creation of any man, nor indeed of any set of men. It is a natural evolution; and the conditions of its growth are of the same general character as those of the " flower in the crannied wall." Andrew Carnegie has somewhere said, in effect: Take away all our money, our great works, ore-mines, and coke-ovens, but leave our organization, and in four years I shall have re-established myself. He might have gone a step further and eliminated himself and his organization; and in less than four years the steel industry would have recovered from

the loss. This is not the popular conception of industrial evolution, which demands captains, corporals, and other heroes;
but it accords with evolutionary conceptions in general.

This inevitableness of industrial growth is frankly recognized by the most far-seeing but least talkative member of the
group. "The demands of modern life," says Mr. Frick, "called
for such works as ours; and if we had not met the demands
others would have done so. Even without us the steel industry
of the country would have been just as great as it is, though
men would have used other names in speaking of its leaders."
This is a frank acknowledgment, from one of themselves, that
the kings of industrialism have no divine right.

Little is here said on the subject of the tariff. The book is
neither a protectionist's pleading nor a free-trader's argument.
It is simply the story of the growth of a great industry, and the
author deems his mission fulfilled in setting forth the facts as he
finds them, leaving the reader free to make his own deductions.

As this is not a political tract, neither is it an ethical trea-
tise; and the author considers it no part of his duty either to
extenuate or accentuate the lapses from a high moral plane
which may occasionally have been suffered by some of the individuals whose efforts are here described. The men who were
instrumental in building up this great business were, originally
at least, none of them philanthropists. There was hardly a
step in their progress which had not the impulse of unqualified
selfishness; and if, in the light of retrospection, some of their
actions seem inconsistent with a book morality, it must be
remembered that in the fight for industrial life, as in that earlier struggle for physical existence, the victory is not to the gentle and the tender-hearted, but to the others. No great business
has yet been built on the beatitudes; and it is not all cynicism
that condenses a negative decalogue into a positive exhortation
to be successful—"somehow!"

CONTENTS

CHAPTER I

The Humble Beginning

CHAPTER II

"A Most Hazardous Enterprise"

CHAPTER III

Early Struggles and Successes

CONTENTS

CHAPTER XII

The Capture of the Duquesne Steel Works

CHAPTER XIII

Labor Contests in Theory and Practice

CHAPTER XIV

The Homestead Battle

CHAPTER XV

Attempted Assassination of Mr. Frick

CHAPTER XVI

The Aftermath of War

CHAPTER XVII

A Reluctant Supremacy

CHAPTER XVIII

The Workings of the Corporate Mind

CHAPTER XIX

The Zenith of Prosperity

CHAPTER XX

Carnegie's Attempt to Depose Frick

CHAPTER XXI

The Failure of the Iron-Clad

CHAPTER XXII

THE ATLANTIC CITY COMPROMISE

CHAPTER XXIII

THE BILLION-DOLLAR FINALE

APPENDIX

THE HISTORY

OF THE

CARNEGIE STEEL COMPANY

CHAPTER I

THE HUMBLE BEGINNING

IN 1858 a small forge was started at Girty's Run in Millvale, Duquesne Borough, now a part of Allegheny. It stood on the edge of the straggling village, and a muddy road ran past it along the river-bank. Judged by modern standards it was an insignificant affair, with a little engine and a wooden trip-hammer—that first cumbrous mechanical substitute for the sledge-hammer. The building was a light wooden construction, about a hundred feet long and seventy wide; but even in these narrow limits the scanty machinery seemed at first lost. It had been brought from the basement of a near-by dwelling where the business was started five years before. In the course of time the vacant corners and empty spaces were gradually filled with axle-bars, small forgings, and iron scrap of various kinds, and the place took on a busy air.

The men who owned this little shop were typical blacksmiths, deep-chested, muscular fellows, who had grown up in the light of the smithy and the music of the anvil. They were Andrew Klowman and his brother Anton, who had come from

Treves in Prussia a few years before.   In time the superfluous "w" of their name was dropped, and Anton became Anthony.

This little place, which its owners valued, good-will and stock, at $4,800, was the beginning of one of the greatest industrial aggregates in the world, valued and bought, forty-three years later, for nearly five hundred million dollars!

In character the Kloman brothers were very different. Andrew was a steady, plodding man of preternatural gravity, earnest in his manner and watchful of every detail of cost and

A German trip-hammer.
From the American Manufacturer.

profit.   Anthony, although the elder, had no high sense of responsibility.   He was careless and free with both money and time; and the beer-can was often raised to his perspiring face. Andrew preferred water, not only as costing less, but as leaving him in better shape for bargaining.   And in little things he was a shrewd bargainer.   He had been trained in a school where a pfennig—the tenth of a cent—was the unit of expenditure and a mark the equivalent of a dollar.   Like the Prussian workmen among whom his youth had been spent, he was suspicious, and, at the outset of his career, more prone to insistence on his own rights than solicitous about those of others. Later, he outgrew this; but the trait led to great happenings.

The workmanship of Kloman Brothers, however, was faultless; and they soon won a reputation for a reliable product. Their specialty was axles, which they forged out of scrap-iron, and sold to railroads and car-builders in and around Pittsburg. The peculiarity of their product was caused by alternately reversing the direction of the fibres while forging the iron, which gave their axles a superiority soon recognized by the trade. The practice was original with Andrew Kloman.

Among their clients was the Pittsburg, Fort Wayne and Chicago Railway, then called the Ohio and Pennsylvania, which had shops and offices at Allegheny. The purchasing clerk of this company was Thomas N. Miller, who was born in Allegheny in 1835 and had grown up with a group of boys who were destined to leave a deep impress upon the industry of their town. Miller early recognized Andrew Kloman's abilities, and frequently put business in his way by introductions and recommendations to manufacturers using axles and forgings; and a certain intimacy was thus established between them.

In 1859 Kloman came to Miller, and told him that his business was growing so rapidly that, if he could get money to install a second trip-hammer, he could double his output and easily market it. He estimated the cost of this addition at $1,600; and he offered Miller a third of the profits of Kloman Brothers if he would put this sum into the business. As Miller was purchasing clerk for a company which dealt with the Kloman Brothers, he had some doubts about the propriety of directly associating himself with them; and he so expressed himself to Kloman. " But I have a young friend," he added, " who might represent me; and if you like I'll introduce him to you." Kloman consented; and Henry Phipps was brought into the negotiation."

Henry Phipps at this time was just twenty years of age, having been born in Philadelphia on September 27th, 1839. His father was a shoemaker who had moved during Henry's child-hood to Allegheny City, where he set up a little shop for him-self in Rebecca Street.   At the age of thirteen young Phipps was earning a dollar and a quarter a week as general utility boy with a jeweller named Barton, who had a small shop at the cor-

ner of Cherry Alley and Liberty Avenue, Pittsburg. In 1856 he entered the office of Dilworth & Bid-well, who had something to do with iron and iron spikes, and were also the local agents of the Dupont Powder Company. First he was office boy, and later became bookkeeper. In a few years the firm was dis-solved, Dilworth taking the spike-mill and Bidwell the powder business; and young Phipps was taken by

Young Phipps, trudging along the canal bank on his way to Kloman's.

the latter into partnership.   He was, however, still bookkeeper for Dilworth & Bidwell when Miller proposed that he should take an interest in the Kloman forge.

Young Phipps readily agreed to join Miller in the enterprise, and set out to raise his share of the $1,600 required by Kloman. The problem was not easy; and it was only temporarily solved when the elder Phipps agreed to mortgage his house for $800; for, not knowing that this $800 would grow into $50,000,000, he presently regretted his offer, and showed such distress that his son felt obliged to release him from his promise.   Finally it was arranged that Miller should pay the whole of the $1,600 required by Kloman, and that Phipps should refund half of this out of his profits in the business.   In return he was to have half of Miller's interest, which, for propriety's sake, was put in

Plate II.

HENRY PHIPPS

OF KLOMAN & CO.; KLOMAN & PHIPPS; CARNEGIE, PHIPPS & CO., LTD.;
THE CARNEGIE STEEL CO., LTD.

the name of Phipps. In addition, Phipps was to keep the Kloman books.

This arrangement proved very satisfactory to all parties; and, the second trip-hammer having been installed, the business grew rapidly. Miller secured the Klomans the preference of the Fort Wayne business, and recommended them to new firms building cars for the railroad, such as Whittaker & Phillips of Toledo, Haskell & Barker of Detroit, Jessup Kennedy & Co. of Chicago, Barney Parker & Co. of Dayton, and others, from whom the bulk of their trade was soon received. Phipps, with the energy which has always characterized him, walked three miles out to the Kloman shop after his day's work at Dilworth's, posted up the books, and then trudged back along the dark towing-path of the Pennsylvania canal to his father's house on Rebecca Street. And Kloman, with his sleeves rolled up, worked with his brother and half-a-dozen men in the forge.

Then the war broke out, and axles, which had been selling for two cents a pound, jumped to twelve cents a pound. And when it came to filling government orders for parts of gun-carriages, there was no limit to price for quick deliveries. The making of railway supplies dwindled; and soon the firm was working almost exclusively on high-priced government orders.

Under this stress of prosperity the primitive forge in Girty's Run was found inadequate before the war was a year old. A new and larger mill was therefore decided upon, and the firm was reorganized. Here are the articles of partnership:

Articles of agreement made and concluded this sixteenth day of November, A.D. 1861, by and between Andrew and Anthony Kloman, of Duquesne Borough, of the first part, and Henry Phipps, Jr., of Allegheny City, of the second part, all of Allegheny County and State of Pennsylvania, witnesseth:

That the said parties have agreed, and by these presents do agree, to associate together as equal copartners in the business of manufacturing, selling, and vending axles, iron forgings, and the rerolling of scrap into iron bar, and the general work of an iron-mill and all things pertaining thereto.

It is agreed that the style of the firm shall be Kloman and Company, of Pittsburg, Pa.

The capital stock shall be $80,000, to be paid in from time to time as the wants of the business may demand, in equal proportion by the said parties.

It is further agreed that a full and correct inventory shall be made of the machinery on hand at present in the buildings now occupied by Kloman and Co., of Duquesne Borough, and a fair valuation shall be made thereof after the removal of the same to the new establishment; and in case the said copartners shall not be able to agree on a valuation, then the same shall be adjusted by arbitrators, of whom the parties of the first part shall choose one, the party of the second part one, and the two so chosen shall select a third; and the valuation arrived at shall be binding, the amount so valued shall be allowed to the said Andrew and Anthony Kloman as cash invested in the new company, and six per cent. interest shall be allowed thereon to the said Andrew and Anthony Kloman, from time to time, until the accruing profits to the party of the second part shall equal his share of the excess so admitted to Andrew and Anthony Kloman.

It is further agreed that all purchases made after said appraisement of Andrew and Anthony Kloman's stock shall be made share and share alike individually in cash advancements, the said Andrew Kloman, the said Anthony Kloman, and the said Henry Phipps each advancing one-third of all the cash required for the business of the firm, up to the full amount of the capital stock aforementioned.

It is further agreed, and to these presents the parties do bind themselves, that the said Andrew and Anthony Kloman shall not engage in any other business whatever and shall give their undivided attention and time to the business of the said copartnership, without charge or compensation, unless when travelling on business of the company, when necessary travelling expenses shall be allowed.

The said Henry Phipps, Jr., shall keep the books of the firm, or exercise a supervision over them during such evenings as he can devote thereto, but he shall not be required to further exertions in the business than such time as he can consistently spare from his other engagements, and he shall lend his influence so far as he can towards forwarding the interests of said copartnership.

There shall be kept during the copartnership of said firm full, true, and correct books of account by double entry in regular sets, in which shall be entered all purchases, sales, accounts, and other transactions, and the same shall be neatly kept and posted by the party of the second part, or by his direction, and shall be open at all times to the inspection of the copartners.

A correct and true inventory shall be made and entered in the Stock Book on the first day of July or January of each year, and the profits and loss estimated.

No purchases or sales exceeding $1,000 shall be made by any one of the said copartners to any one person or firm, without due consultation and approval of all parties hereto.

No partner nor partners shall sign any Bond, Mortgage, Note, or any Obligation, or make any endorsement, or assume any liability, written or verbal, for the benefit of any other party, nor shall any money be loaned from the firm without the written consent of all the parties hereto.

And it is further agreed that neither of the parties hereto shall sell or assign his interest in said business without the consent of all the partners being first obtained in writing.

Neither party shall draw out more than his share of the profits, and the party drawing out the largest amount shall pay interest at the rate of six per cent. on the excess drawn.

It is agreed that in case of the death of any parties hereto, the business of the firm shall be carried on by the surviving partners until the first of January or July following, as the case may be, when an account of stock shall be taken and profits ascertained; and the one-third of the profits and stock, after allowance of capital stock paid in by each of the partners respectively, with interest, shall be paid over to the legal heirs of the deceased partner, one-third to be paid in cash and the remainder in equal instalments of one and two years.

Such copartnership shall commence on the first day of January, A.D. 1862, and embrace all contracts and business of the present firm of Kloman and Company except their debts, and it shall continue for and during the space of five years thereafter; and if the said Henry Phipps, Jr., shall see fit so to elect, he shall have the privilege of continuing for a further period of three or five years.

And it is further agreed that at the termination of this copartnership a valuation shall be had of the real and personal property of the firm, to be arrived at as in page one of this agreement, and one-third of the amount (after allowance of original capital with interest to each partner) shall be paid to the said Henry Phipps, Jr., by Andrew and Anthony Kloman in cash, if there be that amount of money available; if not, then so much as there is available, not less than one-third, and the balance in one and two years with interest.

And it is agreed that in the event of Henry Phipps, Jr., retiring January 1st, 1867, he hereby binds himself to execute and deliver to the said Andrew and Anthony Kloman a bond in the penal sum of $10,000, conditioned that he will not engage in a similar business for the space of three years from January 1st, 1867.

Witness the hands and seals of the parties aforesaid the day and year above written.

ANDREW KLOMAN, L.S.
ANTON KLOMAN, L.S.
HENRY PHIPPS, JR., L.S.

Signed, sealed, and delivered in presence of
As to Andrew Kloman and
   Henry Phipps, Jr.,
    A. LUDWIG KOETHEN.
As to Anthony Kloman,
   CHAS. A. BURROWS.

It is eloquent of hope and self-confidence that in the clause providing for the purchase of a deceased partner's interest, only profits are mentioned. No one entertained the possibility of losses; and the event justified their faith. This clause has a further interest as the precursor of similar provisions in later articles of association, finally elaborated into the so-called "iron-clad" agreement which became so famous in the annals of the Carnegie Steel Company.

An interesting annex to this document is the inventory of the first Kloman forge. It shows with indisputable exactness the humble beginnings of the business which afterwards grew to such impressive proportions. It is as follows: "One frame building situate in Duquesne Borough; one steam-engine; two hammers; one furnace; sundry tools and merchandise; one small frame house and lot."

The new mill was built on a large plot of ground at Twenty-ninth Street, Pittsburg, leased from the Denny estate at an annual rental of $324 for twenty years, with the right of renewal. It was a substantial affair, and provision was made for extensions. An inventory made after it had been a year and a half in operation shows that it then comprised four puddling-furnaces, four heating-furnaces, three boilers, one large steam-engine, four small engines, one steam-hammer, one trip-hammer, one tilt-hammer, one train of bar-rolls, one set of muck-rolls, one squeezer, three blacksmith's forges, four turning-lathes, one drilling-machine, one screw-cutting machine, one safe, shafting, pulleys and belting connected with the above machinery, sundry tools and merchandise, office furniture and fixtures. This list is dated April 16th, 1863. It tells the story of eighteen months of exceptional success, of progressive management, of the development of new lines of business, of earnings and profits put back into the business. Contrasted with the meagre resources of the little Duquesne shop, the Twenty-ninth Street mill, or the Iron City Forge as it was called, was a large and well-equipped establishment, with a large capacity for highly finished products worked up from the crudest forms.

An idea of the great profits of a rolling-mill at this period may be obtained from the fact that between 1860 and 1864 the price of rolled bar-iron advanced from $58 to $146 a ton, while the cost of pig-iron rose only from $22 to $59.

It will be noticed that, in the articles of partnership just quoted, the Miller-Phipps interest was again put in the name of Henry Phipps, the original objection to Miller's open association with the firm being still thought valid; although it was a matter of remark by the Klomans that Miller, when making purchases for the Fort Wayne Road, drove a closer bargain with them than did any other of their customers. The condition was nevertheless an unfortunate one; and, as might have been expected, it presently gave rise to disagreements which ended in a quarrel and rupture.

It is necessary to advert at some length to this quarrel because it had an important bearing on the subsequent history of the enterprise. Indeed, it may be said to have completely changed the current of events, giving them a shape contemplated by none at the outset, and bringing in new influences which in the end dominated the firm and gave it a new name.

In June, 1862, Miller went to England for a holiday. Incidentally he made large purchases of railway supplies for his road, which were shipped in haste in order to evade the war-tax of thirty-five per cent. which had just been imposed on such things. On his return in November he was met by Andrew Kloman, who made a statement to him. This meeting and the events which followed were so important that Miller at the time wrote an account of them. In this statement he says:

" When in Europe was written to by Phipps that my presence would be a source of relief to them (Kloman & Co.). . . . On my return I was soon approached by Mr. Kloman, who stated that the business was growing too great for him, that his brother was getting careless in business, and that he could not sleep at nights owing to his many cares, and desired to know if I would take an active interest in the concern and buy his brother out. Mr. Phipps also joined in urging me to take active part and buy out Anthony Kloman. I desired that if I did so I might be privileged to stay with the P. Ft. W. and C. RR. until January, 1865, but Mr. K. was very anxious that I should take hold as soon as possible. So I accordingly commenced negotiations with Anthony, assisted by Phipps and Kloman, and after considerable trouble induced him to sell at $20,000, which was then estimated to be more than interest conveyed was worth by two or three thousand dollars."

This transaction was closed on April 16th, 1863; and endorsement of it was made on the original articles of partnership, November 16th, 1861, quoted above. This endorsement reads as follows:

Having by articles of agreement taking effect the sixteenth day of April, 1863, bought the interest of Anton Kloman in the above firm of Kloman & Co. and paid for same in hand the sum of twenty thousand dollars (which sum covers other interests also), and having done this by the assistance in influence and by the desire and wish of the other two partners, and at a price set by Andrew Kloman, I do this the thirteenth day of June, 1863, on the original papers handed to me by Henry Phipps, Jr., accept and assume the partnership of Anton Kloman to all intents and purposes, to the full and complete responsibility involved.

Witness my hand and seal the day and year above written.

THOMAS N. MILLER.

Witness,

J. H. MILLER.

It appears, however, from Miller's written statement that before the actual transfer of Anthony's interest, Andrew Kloman betrayed great uneasiness at the passing of control into the hands of his partners. To reassure him, Miller gave Andrew Kloman a bill of sale of half the interest just acquired

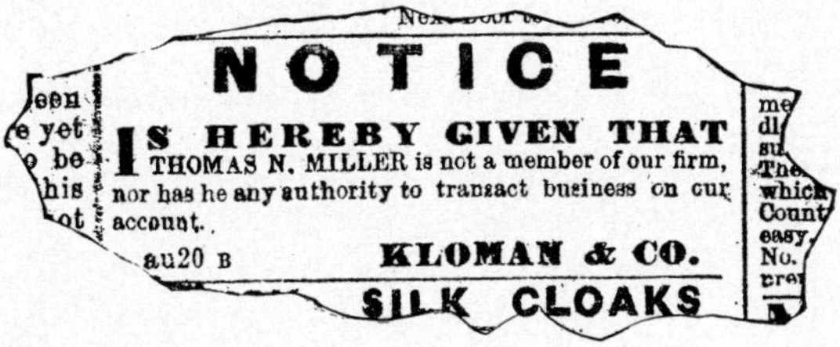
NOTICE

IS HEREBY GIVEN THAT THOMAS N. MILLER is not a member of our firm, nor has he any authority to transact business on our account.

au20 B KLOMAN & CO.

SILK CLOAKS

[Photographic Reproduction.]

from Anthony; and for a time Kloman seemed satisfied with this. Presently he realized that he still owned only half the stock of the company; and, to the surprise of Miller and the alarm of Phipps, he demanded that the latter sell out to him. Phipps naturally demurred to such summary ejection from a business which was daily becoming more valuable, and which he had helped to build up; and he set himself to resist the proposal. Then Kloman turned to Miller and asked him to sell; and presently all three were at odds. The situation was made worse when Kloman discovered that Phipps, at Miller's suggestion, had sold, some time before, a share of their first interest to William Cowley, who had enlisted in the war and had died of typhus fever contracted on the field of Fredericksburg. This share was now offered for sale by the young soldier's brother, who was his executor. It was bought back by Miller for $8,500; but Kloman was naturally alarmed to learn that any part of the business which bore his name should be sold without his knowledge and in contravention of the articles of partnership; and he became further incensed against Miller. The strain reached fracture-point when Miller, pending a satisfactory settlement, withheld, as agent of the Fort Wayne Road, certain payments due from it to the Kloman firm; and Phipps, who had tried to remain neutral, was forced to take sides against his old friend Miller.

It unfortunately happened about this time that a paragraph appeared in a local paper to the effect that Miller had bought an interest in the Kloman business, and that the style of the firm was to be changed to Kloman & Miller. It was probably one of those unauthorized statements which help to make up the local news of a paper; but it had the merit of truth. Nevertheless, by the advice of Ludwig Koethen, his lawyer, Kloman next day inserted an advertisement contradicting the statement. This appeared in the *Pittsburg Evening Chronicle* on Thursday, August 20th, 1863.

This was the condition of affairs when the services of Andrew Carnegie were sought as peacemaker, with results that recall the ancient fable of the lawyer and the oyster. As the world knows, each of the litigants got a shell.

"Each of the litigants got a shell."

CHAPTER II

"A MOST HAZARDOUS ENTERPRISE"

Carnegie's Birthplace.

ANDREW CARNEGIE was born in a little tile-roofed cottage in Moodie Street, Dunfermline, Scotland, on November 25th, 1835. His father was a weaver of fine damasks, taking the weft and warp from merchants and working them up on his own loom at home. The introduction of steam-looms and the extension of the factory system to the linen trade put Carnegie and other hand-weavers out of work; and in 1848 he migrated to America with his wife and two sons. Making their way to Pittsburg, where they had relatives, Carnegie found work in the old Blackstock cotton-mill on Robinson Street, Allegheny City; and young Andy presently joined him there as bobbin boy at $1.20 a week.

They lived in a little black frame house which stood in the rear of what is now 336 Rebecca Street, Allegheny—a district then known as Slabtown and later as Barefoot Square. The mother eked out her husband's earnings by taking in washing; and her evenings were spent in binding boots for the father of Henry Phipps, who lived next door but one.

A little later, when young Andy was fourteen, he got a position in the bobbin-turning shop of John H. Hayes, on Lacock Street, at $3 a week. His duties were to fire a furnace in the cellar with wooden chips and to assist in running a small engine. Later he was made bill clerk of the factory, and

13

left when he was fifteen to become a messenger boy for the Ohio Telegraph Company. Here he learned telegraphy, became an operator, and was taken in 1854, when he was nineteen, into the service of Thomas A. Scott, then superintendent of the western division of the Pennsylvania Railway Company.

A year later, in September, 1855, the father died. His unmarked grave is in Uniondale Cemetery, Allegheny. The house in Rebecca Street in which he lived had been purchased out of his savings; and this he left to his wife, who afterward sold it for $1,500.

During the next few years young Carnegie engaged in various outside enterprises, and through the aid of his chief, Mr. Scott, often made money in them. Indeed, during this fruitful period of his career, before he learned that "pioneering don't pay," he appears to have been ready to go into any scheme that was brought to his notice. Besides the Woodruff Sleeping Car Company and the Columbia Oil Company, in both of which Mr. Scott gave him an interest, and which are known to have been the basis of his fortune, he had interests in a scheme for building telegraph-lines along the Pennsylvania Railroad, in a construction company, in a project for establishing a sutler's business in soldiers' camps, in a horse-trading concern in connection with General Eagan for the supply of cavalry mounts to the Government, in a bridge-building company, in a locomotive works, in the Duck Creek Oil Company, in the Birmingham Passenger [horse-car] Railroad, the Third National Bank, the Pittsburg Grain Elevator, the Citizens' Passenger Railroad, the Dutton Oil Company, and probably other ventures forgotten by himself and all who knew him. By 1863, the date of his entry into this story, when he was twenty-eight, he had made quite a little money, and had been promoted to Scott's position as local superintendent, with offices at the Outer Depot, Pittsburg. His brother Tom, some nine years his junior, was his assistant.

As boys, Andrew Carnegie and Thomas N. Miller had belonged to a group which called itself The Original Six. This also included William Cowley, who has been mentioned, James R. Wilson, who reappears later, James Smith, and John Phipps. The last-named was Henry Phipps' brother, who died in youth. The Original Six took walks in the country together, met at each other's homes, and some of them belonged to a singing-class conducted by Ludwig Koethen, the lawyer, choir-master, and assistant pastor of the Swedenborgian Church, of which all the Carnegies were members. Henry Phipps, being four years younger, belonged to another group, which included Tom Carnegie, Henry W. Oliver, and Robert Pitcairn.

Andy, as he was generally called, was looked up to by the rest of the boys because he was older than any except Miller, who was three months his senior, and because of an assertiveness in his man-

"Some of them belonged to a Singing-Class."

ner which the boys interpreted as evidence of fitness for leadership. It was therefore not unnatural that both Miller and his young friend Phipps should submit to him their difficulties with Kloman. Miller, in particular, left his interests in the hands of Carnegie, whom he held as his dearest friend. They had been the previous year in Europe together, where Miller had tended him in a long and dangerous illness. He had also tried to induce Kloman to admit Carnegie into their partnership; but Kloman would not hear of it. So that in many ways Carnegie's selection as peacemaker was appropriate. It was in this strange guise that Dame Fortune, having already gently tapped several times at Carnegie's door, now began a regular tattoo; but so busy was he with his little schemes that many years passed before he realized the meaning of the noise.

Carnegie's efforts in the interests of harmony produced nothing but fresh discord, until at length he decided upon the

ANDREW CARNEGIE.   GEORGE LAUDER.   THOMAS N. MILLER.

Taken in Glasgow, 1862. This is one of the few portraits showing Andrew Carnegie without a beard.

elimination of the chief cause of trouble by ousting Miller himself. This was not his avowed intention; but it was the result of his method of restoring peace. A new partnership agreement was drawn up, dated September 1st, 1863, in which

Miller, in lieu of four-ninths, was given one-sixth, and made a special partner. The capital of the company, now known as Kloman & Phipps, was to be $60,000, and was to run for six years and four months; but there was a clause reading:

"But if at any time during the term aforesaid the said Kloman and Phipps shall desire to terminate the same as to the said special partner, then upon the said Kloman and Phipps giving to the said Thomas N. Miller sixty days' notice in writing, and jointly signed, of their desire to that effect, the interest of him, the said Thomas N. Miller, shall at the end of said sixty days, and upon the payment to him of the capital invested by him and share of profits coming to him, or, in case of loss, of the total amount of capital still remaining due to him, retire from said firm, and his interest therein shall at that time wholly cease, and the same shall in such case accrue to the said Henry Phipps, Jr., as having a pre-emption right thereto, upon his paying in the capital for the purchase thereof."

This agreement was signed by all the parties, Miller adding to his signature a protest "against the sixty days."

In the course of a few months fresh disputes occurred, and Miller was served with the sixty days' notice of expulsion.

Upon this Andrew Carnegie and his brother Thomas M. Carnegie both drew up written and signed statements of their connection with the quarrel; and in these appears for the first time the fact that Tom Carnegie had been admitted into the partnership with money which his brother had furnished, and that, in addition, to quote from Andrew's statement: "In the event of Miller's ejecture one-half of this interest would fall to my brother." This was the way in which the Carnegies first went into the iron business.

In regard to the merits of the dispute itself, it is impossible after this lapse of time to unravel the tangled evidence. The suspicions and vacillation of Kloman seem to have contributed more than anything else to the quarrel. First he wished to be rid of his brother. Succeeding in this, he became desirous of sacrificing Phipps in order to regain the lost balance of power.

Finally, he preferred to force out Miller, probably realizing that his greater financial strength made Miller more dangerous than Phipps, who, beyond his small salary, had nothing but his interest in this firm.   The elder Carnegie says in his statement that Kloman was alarmed lest Miller and Phipps should have a controlling interest.   "A violent quarrel ensued, and the parties were embittered toward one another.   Finding Miller obstinate and determined Mr. Klowman eventually thought Phipps would be more desirable as a member of the firm; and they became friendly disposed as the breach widened between Miller and Klowman. For some weeks," adds Carnegie, "scarcely a day passed that I did not see one or more of the parties. Hearing both sides, I was fully satisfied I could not establish harmony upon the basis of a common partnership. I finally got all three together in my office and proposed that Miller should have his one-third interest

THOMAS N. MILLER.

First partner of Kloman and Phipps, and with them the founder of what afterwards became the Carnegie Steel Company.

and be a silent (not special) member, Phipps and Klowman transacting the business. This was agreed to; but unfortunately ill feeling was created about a trifle, the result aimed at was lost, and the conference separated under angrier feelings than ever.   Time only served to increase the violence of the quarrel."   After making reference to Miller's having stopped the Fort Wayne payments, Carnegie continues : "But I considered it so essential to Miller's standing that the notice [*i.e.*, the advertisement denying his partnership] be recalled, as enemies were not wanting who began circulating slanderous reports about his clandestine arrangement with Klowman while acting as agent of the Fort Wayne Road, that I insisted upon Miller agreeing to anything that would reinstate him in the eyes of the public as a legitimate member of the Klowman concern."

This was the weakness of Miller's position; but it need not have been fatal to it, since he had bought Anthony Kloman's interest openly and in his own name. It is, indeed, impossible to resist the thought that Andrew Carnegie compromised his friend by giving serious attention to the puerile objections of Kloman. Some of these, as quoted by Carnegie himself, are so childish that one is astonished at their influence on Carnegie. Kloman "told me," he writes, that he "found such a [special] partner might possibly create trouble by insisting upon coming into the mill, sitting in the office, talking to the men, etc., but more especially he was afraid Miller might involve the firm in some way, or attempt to do so, for revenge, or might insist upon withdrawing his share of the profits at inconvenient times, etc. To cover these objections I suggested that Miller's good behavior might be secured by a clause giving the other partners the right to eject him upon notice, provided the fears expressed were realized. This was accepted and the present papers executed."

Having reached this extraordinary settlement with Kloman, Carnegie telegraphed his brother to write Miller that he must accept it, as otherwise "the position in which I [Andrew Carnegie] would be placed would be that of an agent whose acts were disavowed by his principal, and this would be the first time during my life in which I had been so placed."

Miller therefore accepted the settlement under protest, and allowed his interest to be cut down to what it was before the purchase of Anthony's stock, and to hold even this interest only on sufferance of his partners.

THE TWENTY-NINTH STREET MILL IN 1886.

The incident closed for the time being, after Miller had accepted his expulsion and allowed his capital to be put in the name of T. M. Carnegie as trustee. Thenceforward it was a partnership between Kloman, Phipps, and the younger Carnegie.

Even before the narratives of this quarrel were written— August 5th, 1864—Miller had quietly paid $400 to a gardener named Cumming, as compensation for five acres of half-grown cabbages which he destroyed to make room for a rival mill at Thirty-third Street, Pittsburg, only four blocks from the Kloman-Phipps Iron City Forges. The lease bears date of July 1st, 1864. In this venture Andrew Carnegie, despite his brother's interest in the Kloman mill, had a large share. The list of organizers also included the names of Aaron G. Shiffler and J. L. Piper, who had bridge-building works near, which were to be supplied with iron from the new mill. There were also the names of John C. Matthews and Thomas Pyeatte on the association papers when these were published on October 14th, 1864. Pyeatte was the bookkeeper of the concern, and Matthews was manager. The Cyclops Iron Company was the name given to the new organization; and the mill was designed to be the best in Pittsburg. None of the men, however, except Matthews, had had any practical experience; and Matthews was handicapped by the ambitious plans of his associates, who, he used to complain, "wanted him to build a $400,000 mill on a $100,000 capital." The principal construction was 230 feet long and 80 feet wide. The building and equipment of the works occupied all winter; and when, in the spring, the machinery was started, the structure was found too weak for its safe operation.

Tom Carnegie had watched with grave concern his brother's connection with this enterprise; and when his forebodings of disaster seemed about to be realized he urged Andrew to seek a union with the Kloman firm, so as to have the benefit of the German's mechanical experience and skill in remodelling the Cyclops Mill. Andrew, as was his wont when facing trouble,

Photographic reproduction of Andrew Carnegie's letter reproaching Thomas N. Miller with having induced him to go into the iron business, which he here calls a "most hazardous enterprise."

laughed at his brother's anxiety, but decided to follow his advice. Overcoming Miller's objection to an alliance with his recent opponents, Carnegie authorized his brother to open negotiations with Kloman and Phipps for a consolidation of interests.

In the meantime the Twenty-ninth Street mill had been successful beyond all expectation; and at the beginning of 1865 its capital was raised, to keep pace with its earning power, from $60,000 to $150,000. The proposal for union with the discredited Cyclops concern was naturally received by Kloman and Phipps with coldness; but Tom Carnegie had a persuasive manner, and he made liberal offers. Finally it was agreed that Andrew Carnegie and his group should turn over the Cyclops Mill and a lump sum of $50,000, to be divided among the Kloman partners, in return for a little less than half of the shares of a new company, of which Andrew Kloman was to be manager. This was done; and on May 1st, 1865, the Union Iron Mills Company was organized with a capital of half a million dollars. Thenceforward the two mills were known as the Upper and Lower Union Mills, and are so known to-day.

Andrew Carnegie's disappointment at the outcome of this venture was carefully concealed at the time; but he gave expression to it a couple of years later in a letter full of reproaches which he sent to Miller. "I knew you had previously been wronged," he wrote, "and felt you could not forget it. I did what I could at the time to redress the wrong and went into the most hazardous enterprise I ever expect to have any connection with again, the building of a rival mill." And so, regarding it as a "most hazardous enterprise," Andrew Carnegie found himself fortuitously and complainingly thrust upon a road which was to lead him to a fortune of $250,000,000.

The Cyclops Mill was built on five acres of land leased from the Denny estate, which paid $5,000 to recover the leases held by the market-gardener whose cabbages Miller dug up to make room for his foundations. The annual rental was $2,000 for twenty-one years, with a right of renewal for a similar term at the rate which should be found current in the neighborhood. In 1884 the Dennys ascertained that rentals of adjoining property had increased fifteen-fold in twenty years. So they demanded $25,000 a year for the old-time cabbage-patch, but finally accepted $12,000. Additions have been made from time to time to the original five-acre tract by purchase and by filling in the river front, until the Upper Union Mills now cover eight acres.

PITTSBURG.

The Allegheny River on the reader's left, the Monongahela on the right. They form the Ohio at their junction. The first Kloman forge was at the (left) end of the furthest bridge up the Allegheny, seen in the above illustration. The second Kloman forge was almost opposite, on the Pittsburg side of the river.

Plate III.

HENRY PHIPPS, ANDREW CARNEGIE AND JOHN VANDEVORT
TAKEN IN 1865 DURING A WALKING TOUR IN ENGLAND

CHAPTER III

EARLY STRUGGLES AND SUCCESSES

THE war of the rebellion was drawing to a close when the consolidation of the two mills took place. At once the demand for government supplies ceased; and it became necessary not only to find new markets, but to make other kinds of goods than the Kloman mill had been producing. This was no easy matter; and the difficulty was increased by the need for finding an outlet for the products of the new mill. Mr. Phipps says that business runs wonderfully easily when it gets in a groove. But in the beginning there are no grooves; and the paths of trade for the Union Iron Mills had to be created.

With the carelessness of youth Phipps gave little thought to the making of trade-grooves for the new company; but having just received his first large sum of money, he thought the time had come for a great and glorious holiday. Andrew Carnegie shared the idea; and, accompanied by John Vandevort, they went to Europe on a nine months' walking tour, leaving Kloman in charge of the Lower Mill, with Matthews, under his supervision, to manage the Upper Mill. Tom Carnegie was to help in such ways as he could. Miller, who was now the largest individual owner, took no active part in the direction of affairs; but he occasionally made the firm an advance of ready money. For it soon became evident to these young men, venturing in untried fields and with conditions of trade undergoing a sudden and radical change, that the financing of their operations was going to be difficult. Recalling this time, Miller long afterward used to express his wonder, not only at their audacity, but at their luck. "It is no credit to any of us that we did not 'bust' twenty times," he used to say.

As the weeks grew into months the ever-increasing financial pressure developed in Tom Carnegie a resourcefulness which he himself had never suspected, and was a constant surprise to those who had known him only as his brother's assistant. He had a winning personality, and made friends even when asking a favor. His nature was broadly human; and he found a point of sympathetic contact in everybody he touched. The conviviality which his more austere brother afterwards so freely condemned had a positive monetary value during these trying times, when the tourists in Europe were discuss-

"Discussing cathedral architecture."

ing cathedral architecture and falling into bewildered rapture over the beauties of the blossoming heather. If the situation was saved for the Union Iron Mills Company, it was due to Kloman's mechanical genius and Tom Carnegie's ability to make friends and then promptly to convert them into cash.

Despite all this, it is doubtful if the firm had survived the return of the holiday-makers had it not been for the lucky speculation in oil which Miller had made in 1862, the returns from which enabled him repeatedly to come to the company's rescue. "A friend in need is a friend indeed," Tom would say to Miller by way of preface when asking for a couple of thousands to meet the wage-roll on Saturdays.

Then Kloman had his troubles. The new mill was even more faulty in construction than he had supposed; and large sums were needed for alterations. Mr. Phipps says it had almost to be rebuilt. Andrew Carnegie, in his reproachful letter to Miller, says: "We had to spend at least $30,000 on the Upper Mills to remedy blunders." Rarely, indeed, has a great enterprise been started under such hopeless conditions; and had it been known how hopeless they were, it is likely that the partners would have given up the struggle in despair and gone back to their bookkeeping and their telegraph instruments.

Presently the tide turned. The railroads throughout the South were being rebuilt, the West was opening up, the Union Pacific was under way, and a general revival of the iron trade took place. Tom Carnegie had the benefit of the ripe experience and solid judgment of William Coleman, a pioneer in the Pittsburg iron business, whose daughter he was hoping to wed. Under Mr. Coleman's direction the energies of the firm were directed into the channels which Kloman had partially known before the war; and the boom in railroad-building came in time to save the Union Mills. In addition, a new outlet for their product was opened through the connection which Andrew Carnegie had formed with the bridge-building firm of Piper & Shiffler, afterwards known as the Keystone Bridge Company. This concern now bought all its shapes and most of its structural material from the Union Iron Mills; and soon the alterations which Kloman made in the Upper Mills enabled him to roll beams large enough for bridge purposes.

In the spring of 1866 Phipps and the elder Carnegie returned from their European trip; and the former at once assumed financial management of the company, thereby taking upon himself a burden which never left him for twenty years. In these days of mammoth financial operations we are so accustomed to see tens and even hundreds of millions raised for this, that, or the other purpose, that it is difficult to conceive of the greatest constituent company of a billion-dollar organization having trouble to find money to pay the wages of its workmen. But Phipps had years of such experiences; and more than once the men were obliged to accept, in lieu of wages, orders for groceries on a local store.   An amusing circumstance is recalled to illustrate the chronic nature of this effort to do business without adequate capital.

Mr. Phipps had an old black mare, Gypsy, which he used to drive from one bank to another.   This old horse made the rounds so often that it would stop of its own accord whenever it came to a bank; and it would make a diagonal line across Wood Street from the Citizens' National to the First National, and then on to the Third National, stopping before each bank and quietly waiting until Mr. Phipps

"A diagonal line across Wood Street."

had arranged for the day's necessities.   It was impossible to drive this old horse in a straight line on Wood Street.

The president of one of the old Pittsburg banks recently said to the present writer concerning those times: "What we used to admire in young Phipps was the skilful way in which he could keep a check in the air for two or three days."

For a while financial conditions became easier; but before Mr. Phipps had grown accustomed to the change a fresh stringency arose through an unwise incursion into a new field.

There was a pipe-works adjoining the Lower Mill, and some one suggested to Andrew Carnegie that it would be a good thing to buy this property; it would round out their holdings, besides providing them with a new market for their iron.   The plan commended itself to the elder Carnegie, who was always on the alert for new uses for the product of the mill; but Tom, who often served as a balance-wheel to his brother's over-sanguine temperament, and who, moreover, had had some personal experience of the difficulty of financing a growing business with a stationary capital, strongly opposed it, and showed that the sort of iron used in the pipe-works was not the kind the Union Mills produced. His opposition was nevertheless overruled. "Tom was born tired," Andy used to say in excuse of what he considered his brother's lack of enterprise. So the pipe-works were acquired at a cost of $36,000; and soon afterwards they were burned down while only partially insured. The loss in cash amounted to $25,000; but Mr. Phipps used to say that this was offset by the advantage of being rid of a white elephant, and by the comfort of $11,000 insurance money in the till.

Despite the prosperous condition of the iron trade at this time—the difference between pig-iron and rolled bars was still about $50 a ton—the loss on the pipe-works, joined to that resulting from the faulty construction of the Upper Mill, gave a very discouraging aspect to the balance-sheet of the company. Indeed, the scanty profits of the first three years hardly redeemed the enterprise from failure. While there was no actual deficit there was practically no profit—none at all, in fact, if due allowance be made for depreciation of the plant; and Andrew Carnegie expressed a desire to get out of the business at any price. Writing to Miller on September 4th, 1867, he says: "I want to get out of them [the Union Iron Mills], and will do so before long. Even if I can't sell my stock it can go." And he adds that "$27.40 per share will be very gladly received." As he then held 1,600 shares, he would thus have received $43,840 for his entire interest.

It is proper to state that the letter from which this quotation is made was part of an effort to get Miller to sell out of the Union Iron Mills Company. In the fall of 1867 the old

quarrel had broken out afresh.   Indeed, Miller, from the date
of the consolidation, had consistently refused to sit on the
board of directors with his former opponents; and against
Phipps in particular he cherished grievances that hampered the
harmonious working of the new organization.   And now, to
make matters worse, a dispute occurred between him and the
elder Carnegie, concerning some shares in the Columbia Oil
Company which the latter had sold him " at cost," but which
Miller had reason to believe had yielded Carnegie a profit of
over three hundred per cent.   The actual facts of this transaction have never been ascertained; but in 1896, when Miller
officially came into possession of the old books of the Columbia
Oil Company, he found on the minutes the original record of
Andrew Carnegie's purchase of some treasury stock at $2 a
share, and a protest of other shareholders against it.   As Miller
paid Carnegie $6. 37 ½ a share for similar stock—probably not
the same—he felt that he had been justified in his criticisms
of Carnegie.   He later sold this stock, which had cost him
$637.50, for $72,000, after receiving many large dividends
which enabled him to make the loans to Tom Carnegie for the
Union Iron Mills Company.

Naturally this double dispute made Miller's position in the
company untenable; and he set out to find some one to buy him
out.   Carnegie offered to help him; and the letters he then
wrote show the poor regard in which he held the enterprise.
In one he states that on his return from Europe he had "found
the Union Iron Mills, in my opinion, going as fast as they could
into bankruptcy"; and he estimates (1867) " the mills as worth
(or as costing exclusive of the large sums paid to repair defective mill) $300,000.   When we pay off $37,602.29 of debt,"
adds Carnegie, " they will be worth that."   A month later he
writes: " Profits are not quite $30,000 "—after running two
years and five months.   " Our whole thing to-day could be replaced for $250,000, and we still owe a good deal upon it.   I
could not recommend the purchaser to pay more than $27.50 for

it per share. I would like to get rid of my own at that figure."

The purchaser here referred to was supposed by Miller to be David A. Stewart; but when the sale was finally made the buyer proved to be Andrew Carnegie himself. The price paid was $32 a share for 2,300 shares. These included the holdings of Matthews which Miller had previously bought. In this way Andrew Carnegie increased his holdings to thirty-nine per cent of the total number of outstanding shares.

The lack of harmony in the council-chambers of the Union Iron Mills was reflected at the works; for about this time a strike occurred among the puddlers. In an unexpected, and even a romantic, way this strike brought about changes that, in the end, benefited the firm to the extent of millions of dollars, and did much to put it in the van of progressive iron-workers.

"A large number of foreigners were brought over."

At this date the Amalgamated Union did not exist; but there were separate trade associations for each class of labor. The puddlers were strongly organized under the title of the Sons of Vulcan. By reason of falling prices a demand had been made on the puddlers in the Pittsburg district to accept a reduction of wages. This being refused, a lockout resulted; and the firm had its first fight with labor. It was not a very serious one, for sympathetic strikes were then unknown; and the rest of the men in the mills continued to work as long as the material on hand lasted or fresh supplies could be had.

During the summer of 1867 the manufacturers affected by the strike raised a fund and sent to Europe for workmen to take the places of the refractory puddlers. There being no contract labor law to prevent it, a large number of foreigners were engaged and brought over. They were of all kinds and many nationalities. Some Germans who could not speak English were allotted to the Union Iron Mills because Andrew Kloman, being a German himself, could easily control and direct them. It is interesting to note that it was not these drastic measures that broke the strike; for the increasing boom in the iron trade soon absorbed the labor of all, at wages even higher than before.

Among the Germans sent to Kloman was one named John Zimmer, a bright, capable fellow, who knew not only his own business but that of the next man. After he had been a little time in the works, he described to Mr. Kloman a mill that he had worked on in Germany, on which it was possible to roll plates of various widths having well-finished rolled edges. Such plates were unknown in America. The mill described by Zimmer consisted of a pair of horizontal rolls similar to the ordinary plate-mill then in use, but having in addition two movable vertical rolls that could be opened or closed at the will of the operator. Mr. Kloman was at once struck with the value of the improvement, especially for rolling material for bridge orders; and with Zimmer's aid he erected the first German mill in the country. This is the machine now known in the trade as the Universal Mill. It was capable of rolling plates from seven to twenty-four inches wide, and from three-six-teenths to two inches in thickness, with rolled edges. From the first day this mill was a mechanical success, and was the forerunner of several improved mills of the same character afterwards erected at the Upper Mill and at Homestead. Indeed, the great slabbing-mill which was erected at Homestead in 1888 was a lineal descendant of the little Zimmer mill built in 1867–68 at Kloman's. This slabbing-mill now turns out thirty thousand tons of steel slabs a month; and, as it has steadily increased its production from year to year, it seems probable that its limit has not been reached even yet. Before its erection the average weight of an ingot that could be used to make plates direct was about one ton; whereas ten- and fifteen-ton ingots are now rolled down to a thickness of four to six inches, then cut while red-hot into the lengths needed at the plate-mill.

This little idea of the German workman has been worth millions of dollars to the firm that imported him to take the place of a striker. As for Zimmer himself, his reward was a well-paid position as foreman of the mill he erected and of its improved successors. He accumulated a competence, and was believed to be possessed of upwards of one hundred thousand dollars before he died.

Despite the vaunted progressiveness of the American manufacturer, these machines, open to the inspection of anybody who passed through the Union Mills, were but slowly adopted by other firms. Even Andrew Carnegie, after twenty years' experience of the excellencies of the German mill, in consonance with his dictum, " Pioneering don't pay," opposed the erection of the slabbing-mill at Homestead; although he afterwards became an enthusiastic admirer of its work. The Carnegie works to-day have still the most perfect-running Universal mills in the country; and there is not another slabbing-mill in the world to compare in power, size, and efficiency with that at Homestead. Within five miles of Homestead, one of the largest plate-mills in the country is producing, from the ingots which it necessarily uses, not more than one-third the product of a similar mill at Homestead, which works up the slabs made on the giant descendant of the little Zimmer mill.

In the larger sphere now open to it Kloman's inventive

3

genius found free scope.   Even in the early days of the Lower
Mill he perfected many devices that resulted in improved
output and increased economies.   Here he invented a machine
for "upsetting" the ends of eye-bars, which had previously
been made by forging and welding.   At the Upper works he
put in a twenty-inch beam-mill, the first ever built in Pittsburg
that was planed and fitted complete, the rough casting style
having been the rule; and on this were rolled the first beams
made in Pittsburg.   He also erected the first Siemens regenerative gas-heating furnace in Pittsburg.   He invented a
machine for straightening and bending beams, channels, etc.,
cold; and the disc-saw for cutting beams, etc., cold, was first
introduced by him.   In designing rolls for unusual shapes he
showed a rare capacity.   Indeed, his ingenuity in this line of
work was unequalled by any master mechanic in the country,
and made his connection with the Union Mills valuable beyond
compute.   Naturally he won the admiration of the men under
him, who were well qualified to recognize his powers; and his
associates reposed entire confidence in his ability, gave him a
free hand in the works, and cordially sustained him in his progressive methods.

As financial director of the Union Iron Mills Company Mr.
Phipps did not limit his duties to supervising accounts, banking transactions, and the mere routine work of the office.   He
went into the mill and watched the men at work, studied the
machinery, and familiarized himself with all the details of manufacture.   Then he wandered into other works, and, comparing
methods and results, suggested improvements and economies in
his own.   The spirit of enterprise that sanctioned the Zimmer
experiment led him to institute scientific tests of structural
material; and he was one of the first in his line of business to
call in the aid of the chemist.   He was ever seeking to get
the cost-line of mill productions to the lowest point consistent
with the quality required by the structural engineer.   To his
never-ceasing watchfulness are largely due the great economies

in production which placed his firm always beyond the reach of competition.

On one of his trips abroad Mr. Phipps was passing through a mill in Germany when he noticed that the piles made ready for the heating-furnace, to be used for rolling " I " beams, contained more than double the amount of scrap-iron rails used in Pittsburg. He quietly made a sketch of the pile, and on his return gave orders to change the piles at the Union Iron Mills to correspond with his sketch. He then had the resultant product tested, and, finding that the economy still left the factor of safety unimpaired, made the change permanent. The cost of this trip to Europe was saved almost daily thereafter to his firm.

Another great economy was effected by Mr. Phipps in 1872–1873. In the quiet, unobtrusive manner in which he habitually worked, he made a long series of observations at the two mills and then did a little careful figuring. After cautiously verifying his conclusions, he announced to his partners that at a cost of one-third the price for which he believed he could sell the Lower Mill, he could enlarge the Upper Mill so as to make its product equal to that of both. The saving in cost of management and in the handling of material he reckoned would exceed $25,000 a year, a sum equal to five per cent. on their capital. His partners, who had learned to trust his instinct for economies, offered no objection to the plan except the difficulty of finding a purchaser for the Lower Mill. This difficulty Mr. Phipps solved with his habitual originality: he got up a company to buy it! At the same time he brought in a new influence which eventually became of great value to the concern. This was his brother-in-law, Mr. John Walker.

At this time Mr. Walker was entirely without experience in the iron trade; but he had had a good commercial training under his father. Endowed with an extraordinary memory, he quickly mastered the details of his new business, and in the course of time he became a compendium of facts and dates, to

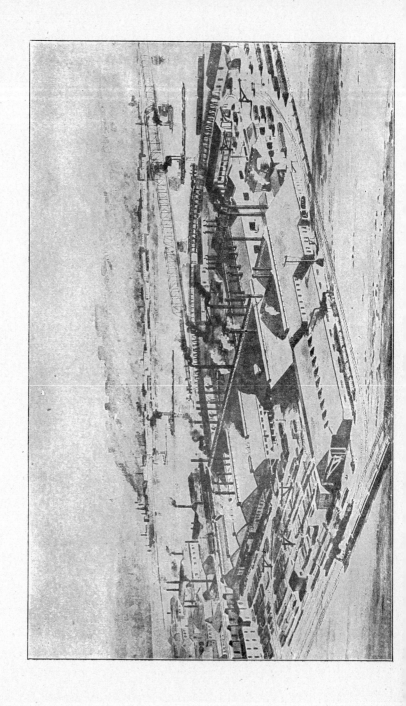

whom his colleagues referred for information of all kinds bearing on their business. Cautious in his undertakings and conservative in his methods, he had the confidence of the local bankers; and his financial connections were invaluable to his firm and to Carnegie, Phipps & Co. when he afterwards became chairman of that concern. Of studious habits and logical cast of mind, he showed his independence and intellectual honesty by openly combatting the protectionist theory at a time when this was held by his associates as the rankest treason. The same frank spirit was shown in all the relations of his business life; and he had, in an exceptional degree, the confidence and even affection of his partners and others with whom he was associated.

With Mr. Walker as a consenting nucleus, Mr. Phipps proceeded with the creation of a company to buy the Lower Union Mill. The firm of Berry, Courtney & Wilson, which had been a large purchaser of iron from Mr. Phipps' company, was on the eve of dissolution; and no difficulty was found in persuading its most active member, Mr. John T. Wilson, to join Mr. Walker. The firm of Wilson, Walker & Co. was thus formed; and at once it bought the business and patents of Berry, Courtney & Wilson for $50,000. Half of this sum coming to Mr. Wilson, he put his $25,000 into the new company. Andrew Carnegie added $60,000 as a silent member of the firm; and the rest of the $200,000 capital was subscribed by John Walker, Alexander Leggate, and Howard Morton. The two last named soon withdrew from the firm. The old Kloman Iron City Forge, with its little Zimmer mill, the four puddling-furnaces, now increased to fifteen, its six heating-furnaces, four hammers, and five trains of rolls, was now turned over to Wilson, Walker & Co., and the Union Iron Mills Company concentrated itself upon the Upper Union Mills. As makers of bar-iron, railroad-car forgings and plates, the firm of Wilson, Walker & Co. ran as an independent concern until 1886, when it once more became part of the Phipps organization by inclusion in the firm of Carnegie,

Phipps & Co., Limited, at a valuation of $340,000 above $87,000 mortgage.

In regard to the Upper Mill, even greater economies than those foreseen by Mr. Phipps resulted from the change described. When the additions were made they were prudently designed for heavy work; and soon the company was rolling all sizes of beams up to fifteen inches for structural purposes, all kinds of channels up to fifteen inches, almost innumerable sizes of angles, tees, Z bars, and other structural shapes, and universal plates on two large and improved Zimmer mills, of which the enterprising German was placed in charge. By 1881, when the Union Iron Mills were taken into the consolidation of various properties under the name of Carnegie Brothers & Co., Limited, the original long building had been surrounded by nine others, some almost equal to it in length. They contained one eight-inch train of rolls, one twelve-inch train, an eighteen-inch muck-train, an eighteen-inch scrap-train, a rotary squeezer, all operated by five large horizontal engines. There were, moreover, nine Siemens furnaces, one Swindell furnace, twenty-one puddling-furnaces, two reverberatory furnaces, besides extensive machine-shops full of costly tools. The plant was taken into the consolidation at a valuation of $630,000. As the Lower Mill was sold to Wilson, Walker & Co. for $230,000, it thus appears that the plant had increased in value seventy-two per cent. in sixteen years.

CHAPTER IV

IRON RAILWAY BRIDGES

THE Keystone Bridge Company, to which reference has been made, was formed on April 25th, 1865, with a capital of $300,000. The list of organizers included the names of Aaron G. Shiffler, J. L. Piper, Andrew Carnegie, Walter Katte, and James Stewart.

Its purpose, as stated in its prospectus, was "the prosecution on an extensive scale" of the business of manufacturing and erecting patent iron bridges "for railways, canals, common roads, streets, &c., &c. Also wire suspension bridges, ornamental bridges for parks and cities, pivot and draw bridges for roads, canals and railways, . . . built according to plans and specifications, as may be desired."

The company is said further to have "purchased the extensive Bridge Works of Messrs. Piper and Shiffler, located in the Ninth Ward of the City of Pittsburgh, Pa., with the right for the United States to manufacture and erect the celebrated Iron Railway Bridges under the 'Linville & Piper' Patents, and 'Piper's Patent' Wooden Bridges and Roof Frames."

The works are described as having ample facilities "for the extensive contracts now in progress, and will be increased as rapidly as found expedient, in order to complete promptly the most extensive structures."

"The officers who superintend the manufacture and erection of all structures" are said to be "practical men, with extensive and varied experience, acquired in pursuing successfully, for many years, the business of constructing and erecting Iron and Wooden Railway Bridges, Roofs and Buildings.

39

"These Iron Bridges have been in constant use on the Great Pennsylvania Central Rail Road and its dependencies and connections, for many years. The great Iron Railway Bridge over the Ohio River at Steubenville, Ohio, with spans varying from 210 feet to 320 feet was erected by this Bridge Company, in accordance with the prescribed plans and specifications. . . . .

"The success of the 'Linville & Piper' Patent Bridges has been unprecedented; for many years they have borne without visible defect or deterioration, the immense traffic of the Pennsylvania Central Rail Road, Philadelphia and Erie Rail Road, Northern Central Railway, Junction Rail Road, and others. Miles of wooden bridge superstructure have been replaced by permanent iron structures, by the superintending officers of this Company, without detention to the business of the roads. No single instance of failure, either in materials or workmanship, has yet been reported."

Mr. W. H. Wilson, chief engineer of the Pennsylvania Railroad, writing from Altoona on July 21st, 1865, says:

"Messrs. J. L. Piper and A. G. Shiffler have been engaged for the last eight years under my personal observation, and for some years previously, in erecting bridges for the Pennsylvania Rail Road Company. The wooden bridges have generally been on the 'Howe' plan; the iron bridges have been constructed in the shops of the Company, from plans prepared by the Engineer Department, some of them of boiler plate, but most of them on the 'Pratt' plan of truss, with modifications introduced at various times. All the work of raising and completing these bridges has been performed by Messrs. Piper and Shiffler in the most satisfactory manner. It affords me pleasure to recommend them as unsurpassed for promptness, energy and skill by any builders with whom I have had business relations."

It thus appears that Piper and Shiffler had been extensively engaged in building bridges of wood and iron for at least eight years prior to the formation of the Keystone Bridge Company. Andrew Carnegie, however, in his account of the business, speaks as though it originated with the Keystone Bridge Com-

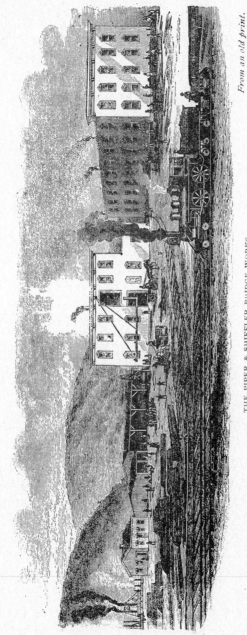

From an old print.

THE PIPER & SHIFFLER BRIDGE WORKS,
At Twenty-ninth Street, Pittsburg, in 1863.
In 1865 they became the Keystone Bridge Works.

pany, which he represents as his personal creation. In a short biography which he recently published through the S. S. McClure Newspaper Syndicate, he says:

"There were so many delays on railroads in those days from burned or broken wooden bridges that I felt the day of wooden bridges must end soon, just as the day of wood-burning locomotives was ended. Cast iron bridges, I thought, ought to replace them, so I organized a company, principally from railroad men I knew to make these iron bridges, and we called it the Keystone Bridge Company. Development of this company required my time, so I resigned from the railroad service in 1867."

Mr. Carnegie has an excellent verbal memory; but he is especially prone to error when recalling events. He is, in fact, constantly mistaking impressions for occurrences, as in this case. That it is his memory which is here at fault is shown by a further error in the same biography. Speaking of his entry upon the manufacture of Bessemer steel he says:

"On my return from England [he is speaking of the year 1868] I built at Pittsburg a plant for the Bessemer process of steel-making, which had not until then been operated in this country, and started in to make steel rails for American railroads."

First noting that the construction of the first Carnegie Bessemer steel plant was not commenced until April, 1873, and was not in operation until the end of August, 1875, it may be seen by reference to any cyclopedia that the first Bessemer steel produced in America was made at Wyandotte, Michigan, in 1864, and that the first Bessemer steel rails made in America were rolled at the North Chicago Rolling Mill in presence of the American Iron and Steel Institute in May, 1865, from ingots made at Wyandotte. Some of these rails were laid in the track of one of the railroads running out of Chicago; and were still in use ten years afterwards when the Carnegie firm made its first Bessemer steel. Even if Mr. Carnegie's recollection had been correct as to the date of this visit to England, it would still be at fault in respect to the beginnings of Bessemer steel rails in America; for there were produced no less than 7,225 tons of such rails in America in 1868. The prosaic fact is that the earliest of the Carnegie steel enterprises was the eleventh in America instead of the first to use the Bessemer process.

In themselves these discrepancies are of little moment. It is probable that not one reader in a hundred would notice them; but the author deems it his duty to the exceptional reader to set forth the facts as he finds them.*

The Keystone Bridge Company, then, was simply the incorporated business of Messrs. Piper and Shiffler. Carnegie, through his official position on the railroad, had long been familiar with their work; and he had known Piper since 1858, when the latter was employed for a time in the car shops at Altoona, where Carnegie then lived.

Piper was a mechanical genius who was always inventing

---

* The author has taken such pains, by reference to original documents, to establish the dates of every salient event in the history of the Carnegie Steel Company, that he ventures, even at the risk of being thought unduly insistent, to point out a further error of fact into which Mr. Carnegie has fallen through overconfidence in his memory. In itself the matter is trivial; but it may have a value in the determination of other questions of fact which may arise.

In the same biography Mr. Carnegie says: " For my father, who had been naturalized as an American citizen in 1853, had died soon afterwards. . . . At the age of sixteen I was the family mainstay."

The facts, as shown by the Allegheny county records on file in the Pittsburg Court House, are as follows:—On September 14th, 1855, the father of Andrew Carnegie made a will, bequeathing a house and lot in Allegheny City to Margaret Carnegie, his wife. Andrew was then within ten weeks of being twenty years of age. This will was recorded on March 30th, 1858, when Andrew was in his twenty-third year.

As regards " the family mainstay," the facts are as follows: During the first of young Andy's working years, his wages were $1.20 a week, or $62.40 for the year. At Lacock's he got $3 a week, or $156 for the year. Next he earned $3.50, or $182 a year. Thus, at sixteen years of age, his total earnings had amounted to about $400, or one-quarter as much as his father had invested in the little home at the time of his death.

But the elder Carnegie did not die until Andrew had almost reached his twenty-first birthday; and he worked until within a few weeks of his death. In the year of his father's death Andrew Carnegie's salary was $35 a month; but he lived away from home and had hardly more than sufficed for his own necessities. Even after this his mother kept a railway lodging-house near Twenty-Eighth Street, Pittsburg, where Robert Pitcairn, his successor on the Pennsylvania Railroad, was one of her lodgers.

things. One of his patents, still remembered by his associates of that day, was a turn-table for locomotives; and he afterwards embodied some of the ideas it contained in a drawbridge. He also devised an improved bridge-post which was extensively used; and there were other things invented in conjunction with Linville, who was bridge engineer for the Pennsylvania Railroad, and later became president of the Keystone Bridge Company. He was a man of impressive appearance, a physical giant, and earnest and convincing in manner. At the same time he was of singular trustfulness. One of the stories still current of Tom Carnegie's ready wit bears on this trait of Piper's.

The Keystone Bridge Company enjoyed certain rebates or discounts from the card rates of the Union Iron Mills Company, from which it bought most of its material. One time when the price of iron had risen, the discounts were omitted from the bill rendered to the Keystone Company, and the word "net" appeared in their place. "What does that mean, Tom?" asked Piper as he indicated the word "net." Piper, like most simple characters, loved a bargain; and Tom, knowing this, hesitated to mention the withdrawal of discounts. So he answered with his characteristic readiness, "Oh that? That's 'nit.' It means that there's nothing to be added!" The reply satisfied Piper, and he made no objection to the payment of the bill.

Shiffler, the other founder of the business, had worked with Piper in a contractor's gang under the firm of Stone, Quigley & Co. on the Pennsylvania lines prior to 1857. This was the period referred to by Chief Engineer Wilson, when he said he had known them "for some years" prior to 1857 while "erecting bridges for the Pennsylvania Rail Road." Here they got the experience which made their firm so successful, and qualified them for the direction of the Keystone Bridge Company when that was formed. But neither of them originated the use of iron in bridges; for this material had been so used from the earliest days.

From an old print.

THE KEYSTONE BRIDGE WORKS,

At Fifty-first Street, Pittsburg, in 1866.

The first iron bridge ever attempted was at Lyons, France, in 1755. It was to have been an arch; but the work was abandoned, after a portion of the iron had been made, because of its great cost. In 1777–79 the first iron bridge was built by Abraham Darby, over the Severn near Colebrookdale, in Shropshire, the place taking the name Ironbridge. Its form is that of an arch of 120-foot span and 45-foot rise. The next iron bridge was built at Wearmouth in Devonshire. It was in the form of a segmental arch of no less than 236-foot span; and it cost £27,000. In Sunderland, also in England, a bridge was built in 1796, of large segments of cast iron. It was justly considered a wonderful achievement. Affixed to it was the motto *Nil desperandum auspice Deo ;* and Sir Lowthian Bell says that every traveller to the north of England considered himself bound to visit what then was regarded as a most daring example of metallic engineering. In France the iron foot-bridge across the Seine near the Louvre was built in 1803; and during the ensuing fifty years many other iron bridges were constructed in Europe.

With these examples before them it is not surprising that American engineers adopted iron for railroad bridges early in the history of steam transportation. As early as 1841 Squire Whipple, called the father of American iron railroad bridges, patented an iron truss-bridge; though even he was not the first in the field. It is said that Tom Paine built an iron truss-bridge. Be this as it may, there were iron bridges spanning the Erie canal as early as 1840; and by 1847 a company—the New York Iron Bridge Company—had been formed for the exclusive manufacture of such structures. A bridge built by this company on the Harlem Railroad is described in the *American Railroad Journal* for November 27th, 1847; and an iron Howe railroad bridge was already in existence on the North Adams branch of the Boston and Albany Railroad, a few miles north of Pittsfield, in April, 1847, where it was examined by Squire Whipple. In 1848 Whipple built two iron bridges on the Erie

Railroad; in 1849 he built two more near the Chester junction of the Newburgh branch of the Erie. In 1852–53 the first iron railroad bridge of considerable span, being 150 feet to centre of bearings, was erected on the Albany Northern Railroad at the crossing of the Erie canal between the cities of Troy and

J. L. PIPER,
Who, with Aaron G. Shiffler, founded the Keystone Bridge Works.

Cohoes. It stood for thirty years, and was removed in good condition to make way for a double-track bridge. A bridge of the same description was built in 1854 for the Black River and Utica Railroad at Utica. In 1855 one was built for the same road at Boonville, Oneida County. During the decade between 1850 and 1860, which brings us to the time of Piper and

Shiffler, the firm of S. & J. M. Whipple alone built over a hundred iron bridges of all kinds and shapes.   In 1863 the Detroit Iron Bridge Works was organized into a joint stock company; and its prospectus states that its manager had "for some years previous been engaged in the construction of iron bridges for railways."

Thus, so far from being the pioneer in the iron railroad bridge business, Mr. Carnegie occupied a position a long way down the list.   When he finally did become interested with Piper and Shiffler it was not, as he alleges, in "cast-iron bridges." When cast iron was in vogue for bridge structures in England, wood was used in America; and when wood was replaced with iron it was wrought iron, and later Bessemer steel, that was used.   The only parts of Piper & Shiffler's bridges that were of cast iron were Piper's patent posts; and these were a very small part of the whole, which, of course, was of wrought iron.

It is also worthy of mention that Andrew Carnegie's principal interest in the Keystone Bridge Company was given to him in return for services rendered in its promotion.   He paid no cash for any of his shares; but desiring to have a larger holding than that gratuitously assigned to him, he gave his note to the company in payment of the increased interest, and the first four dividends sufficed to liquidate the debt.

It is possible that the standards of commercial morality were as high forty years ago as they are to-day.   Business men of that period aver that they were higher.   It is none the less certain that the ethics of railroad management in early days were formed after other standards than those of modern times; else had there been more general condemnation of the fault which Andrew Carnegie discovered in Miller's "clandestine arangement with Klowman while acting as agent of the Fort Wayne Road."   Such arrangements, not always clandestine, seem to have been the rule in those days, and the early history of the Carnegie enterprises affords many examples.   Despite

the fact that the principal business of the most important of
these enterprises was the manufacture of rails, railway structures, and railway material of various kinds, it was from the
salaried officials of railways that much of their first financial
support was received.   Miller did not sever his connection with
the Fort Wayne road when he built the Cyclops Mill; nor did
Andrew Carnegie resign from the Pennsylvania when he joined
him.   Indeed, it was not an uncommon thing for the president
and vice-president of a railroad to own shares in a corporation
which obtained most of its business from such road.   No doubt
the business was contracted for by faithful subordinates, and
was honestly and properly carried out by the contracting companies; and while it is possible that no question of morals is
involved in the dual allegiance of such important officials, modern opinion would unhesitatingly condemn it as a breach of propriety and good taste.

In the formation of the Keystone Bridge Company this in-
fraction of modern standards was especially conspicuous; although the matter-of-fact way in which Mr. Carnegie speaks of
organizing a company "principally from railroad men" shows
that he, at least, had no idea that the propriety of such a proceeding might be questioned.   President J. Edgar Thomson,
however, had his interest appear on the company's books in
the name of his wife.   Besides Colonel Scott, vice-president, the
Pennsylvania Railroad officials who became stockholders in
the Keystone Bridge Company included the chief engineer, the
assistant general superintendent, the superintendent of motive
power and machinery, and Andrew Carnegie, the superintendent of the Pittsburg division of the line.   There were also the
president of another road, two chief engineers, and a general
superintendent.   Carnegie says he did not resign his position
on the Pennsylvania Railroad until 1867, two years after the
formation of the Keystone Bridge Company;* and Mr. Pitcairn,

---

* Another error.   He left the Pennsylvania Railroad in 1865, in his thirtieth
year.

4

his successor on the railway, afterwards joined the Keystone board of directors.

It is deserving of notice that most of these gentlemen wrote letters of recommendation to the Keystone Bridge Company, in which the work of Piper and Shiffler was spoken of in the most flattering terms; and these were published by the company as an advertisement. Here for example are those from Mr. J. Edgar Thomson and Colonel Scott:

PENNSYLVANIA RAIL ROAD COMPANY
President's Office
Philadelphia, Sept. 25th, 1865.

Messrs. Piper and Shiffler, who will hereafter conduct their business of Bridge Builders under the name of the "Keystone Bridge Company," have for many years been engaged, both as employees and contractors, in erecting bridges of wood and iron on the Pennsylvania Rail Road and its connections. From the uniform success that has attended their plans, and the character of the work executed, I have no hesitation in recommending them to the patronage of the officers of rail road companies, for the erection of these structures, either upon the well tested plans they have been building, or upon such as may be prepared for them. Their facilities at Pittsburgh for building bridges will enable them to execute work with dispatch.

J. EDGAR THOMSON,
President.

PENNSYLVANIA RAIL ROAD COMPANY
Office of the Vice President
Philadelphia, July 28th, 1865.

The Keystone Bridge Company for several years past have been engaged in erecting iron and wooden bridges, &c., for the Pennsylvania Rail Road Company and its connecting roads.

I have had ample opportunities for observing the character of their structures, and can cheerfully testify to the responsibility and skill of the Company. I consider the iron rail road bridges as constructed at their extensive works, in Pittsburgh, Penn'a., the best that I am acquainted with.

THOMAS A. SCOTT,
Vice President Penn'a. R. R. Co.

With such powerful backing the Keystone Bridge Company soon became one of the most important factors in the business of bridge-building in the country. The extent of the work it accomplished was officially set forth in 1883, when it was stated that the bridges built by it, if placed end to end, would measure over thirty miles in length, and that their cost exceeded $23,000,000.

The most prominent of these structures, containing in each

Copyright, 1902.

THOMAS A. SCOTT,
Who gave Andrew Carnegie his start and many a subsequent lift.

case the longest span of its kind then in existence, are the following:

Steel Arch.—The Mississippi River bridge at St. Louis, Mo.; one span of 520 feet and two spans of 502 feet. Double-track and double deck railway and highway bridge.

Steel Truss.—The Missouri River bridge at Plattsmouth, Neb.; two spans of 402 feet each. Single-track railway bridge for the Burlington and Missouri River Railway. Also, the Ohio River bridge at Point Pleasant, W. Va., 3,805 feet long; channel span, 420 feet.   Single-track railway bridge for the Ohio Central Railway.

Iron Truss.—The Ohio River bridge at Cincinnati, O.; channel span, 519 feet.   Single-track railway bridge for the Cincinnati Southern Railway.

Iron Swing Bridge.—One span of 472 feet, over Raritan Bay.   Single-track railway bridge for the New York and Long Branch Railway.

A description of the Keystone Bridge Works published by the company at this time shows that they "are exclusively devoted to the manufacture of bridge and structural material, finished ready for erection.   The shop buildings are fireproof, and cover more than three acres of ground, and the capital invested exceeds $1,000,000.   The company employs over six hundred men at these works and over three hundred and fifty in the field, engaged in the erection of bridges, so that the total number of men on its pay rolls is about one thousand.   The works are equipped in the most comprehensive manner with special machines and tools of the most approved type, among which may be mentioned hydraulic, pneumatic and power riveting machines, a 150-foot multiple punch, shears, planers, lathes, steam hammers, drilling and boring mills, rivet and bolt making machines, and a 300-ton hydraulic testing machine.   The works are operated day and night, being lighted by the electric light after dark.   The company has lately made extensive and costly additions to its plant, designed solely for the successful and economical working of steel, it having become evident that this material, in the near future, is destined altogether to take the place of iron.   These additions consist in a gas heating furnace and [Kloman's] upsetting machine for the manufacture of steel eye-bars, a gas annealing furnace 54 feet long, the only furnace of this kind so far built, and a multiple reaming machine."

The growth of the plant is thus seen to have been great, though not phenomenal.   The position of the company at the

beginning of 1885 is shown in the following abstract from its
balance sheet:

Resources.

Real Estate.......................................$100,650.00		
Shop Equipment account............... 272,267.36		
Construction account................... 345,942.43		
Sharpsburg and Lawrence Br. stock...... 1,100.00		$719,959.79
Available accounts.....................$229,724.39		
Overdue account (Pt. Pleasant Br)....... 152,752.61		
Doubtful accounts.................. ...... 2,964.48		
Amount Inventory account............. 299,098.33		
Cash..................................... 24,947.08		$709,486.89
Total Effects...............................		$1,429,446.68

Liabilities.

Due Maury Heirs on Mortgage $50,000.00		
" Union Iron Mills (C. Bros. & Co)... 409,129.11		
" Sundry accounts 134,423.37		
Stock account $447,200.00		
Profit and Loss a/c...... 388,694.20		
	835,894.20	
		$1,429,446.68

Fourteen years later, just before the Keystone Bridge Company became part of the United States Steel Corporation, its
balance sheet for 1899 showed a loss of over $67,000 on con-
tracts. Its principal gains came from castings and rivets; and,
by a skilful manipulation of its "inventory adjustment," the
statement was made to show a slight profit.

Although one of the most talked-about branches of the Carnegie business, the Keystone Bridge Works was one of the least
profitable, and, when stripped of its false character as a pioneer,
the least interesting of them all.

CHAPTER V

A RIVALRY OF GREAT FURNACES

THE Civil War, and the great demand for iron which a year or two later followed it, gave a great impulse to the chief industry of Pittsburg; and during the years 1866 to 1870 many schemes were laid to meet the great local demand for pig-iron. Up to that time the lack of ore at convenient distances had handicapped the smelting industry; but when organized transportation made the ores of Lake Superior accessible, a more promising aspect was given to schemes for smelting iron in Pittsburg on a large scale.

In the fall of 1870 two of these projects assumed a definite shape, and the owners of the Union Iron Mills were invited to join one of them. This was the project of a number of iron manufacturers, including Lewis Dalzell & Co., J. Painter & Sons, Graff Bennett & Co., Spang, Chalfant & Co., Henry W. Oliver of Oliver Brothers & Phillips, and William Smith, owner of a large pipe-foundry. At this time there were only seven small blast-furnaces in the Pittsburg district with a total product of some seventy thousand tons a year; and pig-iron was selling at $40 a ton.

The Union Iron Mills were large consumers of pig-iron, and the scheme was not without attractions to Phipps and his associates, especially when presented by the most important firms in the business; and after consultation among themselves, the partners went to Mr. William Coleman for his advice. No one was more fitted to give the young men wise counsel, for no one had a closer knowledge of the iron trade or better business judgment. Mr. Coleman considered the matter gravely, as was his habit, and then unhesitatingly advised against joining the combination. He pointed out that if the members of the Union Iron Mills Company wanted to go into the manufacture of pig-iron, it would be better for them to build one furnace themselves than to own one-seventh of two furnaces which would not be under their control or management. This advice was accepted, and the decision communicated to the gentlemen named, who at once formed the Isabella Furnace Company, and started to build two furnaces. Later they added a third.

On December 1st, 1870, Messrs. Kloman, Phipps, and the two Carnegies organized the firm of Kloman, Carnegie & Co.; and when the winter was over they began the construction of a blast-furnace at Fifty-first Street, Pittsburg. This was the first Lucy furnace, so called after the wife of Thomas M. Carnegie, the daughter of Mr. Coleman, as the Isabella plant was called after Mrs. Herron, the sister of one of the members of the firm of Spang, Chalfant & Co. Important departures were made from established usages in American blast-furnace construction, and many English ideas were utilized. The Clinton furnace of 1859, the two Eliza furnaces of 1861, and the two Superior furnaces of 1862–63 were all forty-five feet high and twelve feet in diameter at the boshes; and owing to the ill-success of the fifteen-foot furnaces first erected, the twelve-foot bosh continued to be the favorite dimension. The Struthers furnace in Ohio, however, was fifty-five feet high, with sixteen feet diameter of bosh; and its large output—over sixteen hundred tons of iron in one month—made it much talked about in Pittsburg, especially as this result was achieved with raw coal. The English idea of furnaces of large capacity thus came into favor; and both the Lucy and Isabella furnaces were made seventy-five feet high, the former with twenty feet diameter of bosh, and the latter with eighteen, afterwards changed to twenty feet.

A spirit of rivalry sprang up between the two concerns from the outset. Isabella No. 1 and the Lucy went into blast about the same time in the early summer of 1872; and each started out by making 50 tons of pig-iron a day, which was a fair average at that time. Within a few weeks both furnaces increased their output; and by the end of the year the Lucy had made 13,361 tons, an average of nearly 500 tons a week, notwithstanding a chill experienced in December. The Isabella followed closely and produced 498 tons in a single week. The next year the Lucy made 87 tons in a day and 578 tons in a week. During the early part of 1874 the Lucy kept ahead, and in February produced 593 tons; but by August she was overtaken by the Isabella's 612 tons. In October the Lucy shot ahead with 642 tons, and by the 24th of that month the Isabella had almost caught up, with 651 against the Lucy's 653. On that day the Lucy for the first time produced over a hundred tons; and the achievement was greeted with loud hurrahs at the works, and heard of with incredulity by the iron trade. On November 2d the Isabella's output for the week was 672 tons, and the following week she broke all records with 702 tons. On December 24th she made 112 tons. Next year the contest between Manager Skelding of the Lucy and Manager Crowther of the Isabella was continued as fiercely as ever; and in October the former passed his rival with 762 tons. In the same month Isabella No. 2 crept up with 714 tons, and the following month shot ahead of the Lucy with 771½ tons. The 800 mark was not crossed until 1878, when the Lucy made 804 tons in a single week. In March, 1880, she made 945 tons, and this was beaten by the Isabella, February, 1881, with 1,000 tons. The trade gasped with astonishment, and editors asked: "What will these Titans do next?" On March 30th the same furnace made 215 tons, and next day 217½ tons, bringing her average for the week up to 1,130 tons. In April she made 1,282 tons, and in October

THE LUCY FURNACE IN 1873.

1,438 tons, the Lucy dragging behind with an average weekly output of about 1,000. Mr. Kennedy then joined the struggle with a new furnace at Braddock and ran the Isabella very close. In 1883, as related elsewhere, he shot so far ahead that neither the Lucy nor the Isabella was in the race until he himself took the management of the Lucy and brought her daily output to over 300 tons. But even this record was beaten again and again by the same firm, as new furnaces were put in operation, and the lessons learned by earlier experience showed managers what to avoid and what to practise.

An interesting account of the Lucy Furnace in 1873 was given in the *Iron Age* of that date, which is worth quoting. It is as follows:

To one accustomed to the methods of blast-furnace construction as practised east of the Allegheny Mountains, the Lucy Furnace possesses much interest. It may be said to embody the best features of the Western practise, both in construction and management, and will well repay a visit from any Eastern iron master who may find himself in Pittsburg, either on business or pleasure. The furnace is located on the bank of the Allegheny River, about four [two] and a half miles from the centre of the city. The location is attractive as well as convenient. From the top of the stack one overlooks a little valley of unusual beauty on the one side, with the Isabella furnaces in the distance and a pretty river between; and on the other the suburbs of the Iron City, overhung with its cloud of black smoke —not beautiful, indeed, but busy, prosperous, and progressive. Switches connect the stock-house and cast-house with the Allegheny Valley Railroad, which affords easy facilities of connection with the Pittsburg market and with the termini of the various lines of transportation by which ores and fuel are received. The Lucy Furnace was built by Messrs. E. J. Bird and William Tate, and went into blast in May, 1872. It is seventy-five feet high by twenty feet diameter of bosh. Like most Western furnaces, it is an iron cylinder lined with fire-brick, with an independent iron gas-flue, around which winds an iron stairway, by means of which access is had to the top of the furnace. The fuel and ores are carried to the tunnel head in barrows by means of a pneumatic lift, from which they are run under cover of an iron roof to the top of the stack and dumped by hand. In its external appearance the furnace is neater and more attractive than the stone stacks of the East, and in many respects more convenient.

The machinery of the works is of the best quality, though of a very different character from that usually seen in the East. There are three excellent blowing engines by Messrs. Macintosh, Hemphill & Co. of Pittsburg, and four pumping engines to raise from the Allegheny the water needed about the furnace, by Messrs. Epping, Carpenter & Co., Keystone Pump Works, Pittsburg. The locomotive used about the works is by Messrs. Porter, Bell & Co. of Pittsburg. All the machinery is in the best condition, being comparatively new and having only the most careful and intelligent management. Steam is raised by a battery of eight boilers, each sixty feet long by forty-three inches in diameter.

The capacity of the furnace is about 550 tons a week, taking the average of the seasons. The ores used are mostly Lake Superior, specular and hematite. During the present season the furnace will have received about twenty-five thousand tons from the Kloman mine, the property of the company near Negaunee, Mich. [This is an error.] Some Iron Mountain ores have been smelted in the furnace; but they were found more costly than profitable, and their use has been abandoned. The fuel is a coke made from the slack of the bituminous mine near Pittsburg —at ovens located at Carpenter's station on the Pennsylvania Railroad, about nineteen miles distant. The fuel costs but $3.60 per ton at the furnace, and we are informed that the consumption in the stack is only about one and a half tons to the ton of pig-iron made.

Among the novelties to be seen at these works is a very simple and practical machine for cooling slag, invented by Mr. Andrew Kloman, one of the proprietors. Its object is simply to cool the slag quickly in blocks of convenient size for removal, thereby saving both time and labor. It consists of an annular water trough, with supply and waste pipes, in which, by suitable appliances, a series of cinder boxes are made to rotate so that they may be brought successively under the slag spout. The boxes taper slightly toward the bottom so as to admit of the easy withdrawal of the slag cakes when sufficiently cool. On the bottom of each box is placed an iron wedge with a broad, flat head, upon which it stands upright, and with a hole in the taper end by which it may be lifted out. The slag runs around these wedges which stand up in the middle of the boxes and project for some inches above the upper crust. Around, under, and between the boxes water flows continuously, and their inner surfaces are kept so cool that in a few minutes the slag is sufficiently solid to be removed in carts. The transfer is effected by means of a small hydraulic crane. The hook at the end of the chain is fastened in the hole in the taper end of the wedge, and the cake is lifted out of the box and deposited on the floor of the cart, which has a square hole in its bottom to facilitate the removal of the wedge. The slag cake is so placed that the head of the wedge comes over the hole, and a smart blow with a hammer causes it to drop out on the ground. The cake is then carried off and dumped. In construction and operation this machine is perfectly simple, and it may be worked so rapidly as to dispose of the slag as fast as it can be run from the spout. There are seventeen cinder boxes; and by the time the last has been filled the slag cake in the first is ready to be lifted out and removed. The proprietors of the Lucy Furnace consider it altogether the cheapest and best method of disposing of the cinder they have ever tried, and we have no hesitation in pronouncing it the most practical device of its kind we have ever seen in use.

Some months ago the furnace got a chill, and but for the ingenious manner in which it was cleared the company would have suffered a heavy loss in consequence. The following account of the means employed, which we take from a paper lately read by E. C. Pechin before the American Institute of Mining Engineers at Philadelphia, will be read with interest: "She had been working well on low-grade ores of about fifty per cent., producing daily sixty-eight to seventy-five tons. There was on stack five hundred tons of Republic ore—one of the purest and best of the Lake Superior ores, averaging over sixty-eight per cent. of iron—which had been procured for the purpose of making a trial for Bessemer iron. This was charged by itself, and Mr. Skelding, the founder, reports that he did not succeed in getting a single cast when it came down, before the furnace chilled from the hearth to the top of the bosh, some twenty-five feet. Every effort was made to save her, but without avail; and the disagreeable duty of cleaning her out was begun. The hearth was dug out some five or six, or perhaps eight, feet up, when Mr. Skelding remarked, in the hearing of one of the proprietors, that he wished he had a cannon. A mortar was forthwith procured from the arsenal, and they commenced firing shots into the chilled mass. A large number of shots were fired and with considerable success, bringing down from time to time portions of the chill. But by and by the mass became pasty, and the cannon balls, of which they only had three, stuck fast. Mr. Skelding put in a large charge of powder, and then, to the amusement of the bystanders, rammed the mortar full of cotton waste, and on top of this placed a lump of hard ore weighing about fifty pounds. This novel shot brought down the scaffold and cannon balls, and the furnace is again running and doing exceedingly well." As far as the writer knows no patent has been taken out for this process (for a wonder!), so that it is available for any furnace man who is so unfortunate as to have a scaffold.

Another experiment is shortly to be tried at this furnace which is novel, at least in this country. It is proposed to use two tiers of tuyeres, one eighteen inches above the other—seven below and five above. There is a theory that by elevating the zone of fusion a larger product of superior metal would result. The Lucy Furnace will test this theory on a large scale and under the most favorable circumstances, and the result will not be without interest to all in the business.

This naïve description gives a better idea of the primitive methods of furnace practice then in vogue than could possibly be obtained from any modern authority.

Much of the excellent work of the Lucy Furnace in early years was due to the skill and enterprising management of H. M. Curry, who remained an important factor in the success of the Carnegie enterprises until his death in 1899. Mr. Curry was born on January 30th, 1847, at Wilkinsburg, a suburb of Pittsburg, where he spent his early years. At sixteen he joined the army as a private, and served in the Fifth Army Corps as a member of Company F, 155th Pennsylvania Volunteers, for three years, and was mustered out of service as a sergeant. He was slightly wounded at the battle of Five Forks, but only spent a few days in the hospital. His first position on returning from the war was with the firm of Haleman & Caughey, pig-iron brokers, where he attracted the attention of Mr. Phipps, who, towards the close of 1870, gave him a position as pay and bill clerk in the Upper Union Mill. In 1871 he was transferred to the Lucy Furnace, where he was given charge of the record department of furnace burdens. His simple cordiality won the devotion of the men, while his thoroughness and conscientious attention to duty gained the confidence of his employers; and when, after two or three years, certain structural changes in the furnace were decided upon, Mr. Curry was put in charge of them. On the retirement of the first superintendent, William Skelding, Mr. Curry, at the urgent recommendation of Mr. Phipps, was put in his place, and under his management the

"The experiment was repeated."

Lucy Furnace won the records just described.

Of course such results were not entirely due to any one man's skill. Many of the improvements made were suggested by others; but Mr. Curry was so free from conceit that he was just as ready to cherish the ideas coming from outside as he was to fondle his own.

Another man to whom no small part of the credit of the improvement is due was Mr. Whitwell, the inventor of the famous stoves that bear his name. In 1873 this gentleman came to Mr. Phipps, and showed him that if he would shape the bell of the furnace so that the contents would be thrown toward the sides, it would not only preserve the lining of the furnace and save the great cost of frequent renewals, but it would result in such a segregation of the contents as to make a better draught, with resulting increase of output. The proposition was so revolutionary that Mr. Phipps naturally hesitated to make the change; and Mr. Whitwell had a glass model of the improved furnace made and erected in the Lucy yards. At once the beneficial effect of the change could be seen through the glass as the miniature loads of ore, lime, and coke were poured into the model. It was a bitterly cold day when the demonstration was made; but the event was so important that the partners endured the icy blasts for hours, and the experiment was repeated again and again. All the partners conceded that it was eminently successful—but next day most of them were laid up with colds, and Andrew Carnegie did not reappear at the works for a week. When the change was made in the furnace the results predicted by Mr. Whitwell were surpassed, and again a new furnace record was made for the world.

In 1877 the second Lucy furnace was built, and "blown in" on September 27th of that year. Its general dimensions were those of the first Lucy furnace. By 1878 it made a monthly output of 3,286 tons on a coke consumption of 2,973 pounds per ton of iron, and in a single week it made 821 tons. In twelve consecutive months the output was 33,931 tons on a coke consumption of 2,850 pounds, a remarkable achievement at that time.

The first Isabella furnace also made a wonderful record, when it ran continuously from January, 1876, until May, 1880, making a total output of 117,575 tons of pig-iron, an average of 2,264 tons a month. The coke consumption averaged about 3,000 pounds.

The Lucy furnaces during all this time were the especial care of Mr. Phipps. For months he almost lived in their vicinity, and sat up with them at night when they were ailing as he would have watched by the sick-bed of a favorite child. As he had earlier watched the machinery at work at the Union Mills, he now attended the operation of the furnaces night and day, thinking, scheming, and studying them in every aspect. An example of the ingenuity he displayed in his never-ending quest of economies is here recalled.

One of the products of the furnace was known as mill-iron.

This was the iron resulting from a mixture in the furnace of seventy-five to eighty per cent. of Lake Superior ore and twenty to twenty-five per cent. of puddle-furnace cinder. The cost of this cinder per unit of iron was less than one-tenth the cost per unit of iron made of ore; but the cinder contained more than three times the phosphorus that was in the same amount of ore, which limited the use of the cheaper mixture. Mr. Phipps knew that the Union Iron Mills, in common with all similar works, made a large amount of heating-furnace or flue cinder, which was considered a waste product and thrown out on the river-banks. He quietly had some of this cinder analyzed, and found it as rich in iron as the puddle-cinder. It also worked equally well in the furnace, and carried less than one-fifth the amount of phosphorus contained in the puddle-cinder. He therefore changed the furnace mixture to sixty per cent. of flue-cinder and forty per cent. of Lake Superior ore; and, despite this great economy, a better pig-iron was produced than before. This was kept a trade secret for years, during which thousands of tons of flue-cinder were bought at prices much below the cost of puddle-cinder. Indeed, the firm for years sold its puddle-cinder through brokers at $1 and $1.50 per ton, which found its way into the hands of a competitor, and in the same way bought this competitor's flue-cinder for fifty cents a ton. Naturally the Lucy Furnace was prosperous and making money when rival concerns, thus disadvantaged, were running behind.

This incident, one of many that might be cited, fairly illustrates the character of the services which Mr. Phipps was constantly rendering his firm; for of course his discovery was only used to benefit the company. It also recalls the fact that not all the partners took the same broad view of their obligations to the common interest; for one of them, a protégé and cousin of the Carnegies, who had recently been admitted into the partnership, engaged in a private speculation on the strength of Mr. Phipps' discovery. He bought up all the flue-cinder he could hear of; but, lacking a knowledge of the correct percentages, or being estopped by partnership obligations from making them known, he could find no market for his cinder-heaps, and he made a large loss.

Mr. Phipps acquired a reputation for close trading at this time which is still remembered. In buying scrap-iron he had to bargain with all sorts of odd characters, one of whom would insist in the strongest brogue that "divil a cint was left to a harrd wurrking man afther a thrade with Harry Phipps, bad cess to him!" Another was detected in an ingenious method of evening things up. He had two carts shaped and painted exactly alike, but one weighed about five hundred pounds more than the other. On delivering his first load of scrap at the furnace he would use the light wagon, which was weighed both before and after unloading, and the difference constituted the net weight of scrap for which he was paid. On subsequent trips, however, he used the heavier cart, and failed to weigh it after unloading. The clerk, believing that it was the same cart as had previously been weighed empty, credited him every trip with five hundred pounds more than had been delivered.

"Bad cess to him!"

It was at the Lucy Furnaces that Mr. Phipps first employed a chemist with excellent results. The Pennsylvania Steel Company at Harrisburg were large buyers of Bessemer pig-iron, and their requirements were stated in chemical terms, the principal one being that the metal should not contain more than ten hundredths of one per cent. of phosphorus; and twenty-five cents a ton was deducted from the price for every increase of one-hundredth of one per cent. In this way it was early impressed upon Mr. Phipps, who was the pocket-nerve of the concern, that a practical chemist was a necessary member of their staff; and it is believed that this company was the first not directly connected with Bessemer steel production to benefit by the services of an expert chemist.

It is unfortunate that the disagreements of partners should occupy so large a place in this history; but as these invariably had a more or less important bearing on the subsequent development of the enterprise, by eliminating some members and elevating others, they must rank with other factors in the evolution of this great business. This time it is the story of Kloman's withdrawal from the firm; and in view of the many erroneous statements which have been made concerning this event, it is especially desirable that the facts should at last be set forth.

Shortly after the construction of the Lucy Furnace was started Mr. Kloman was persuaded to join a group of enthusiasts for the purpose of mining and smelting ore in Michigan. Joseph Kirkpatrick, the leader of the group, was a flighty individual of the Colonel Sellers type, who is described by an acquaintance as being able to "talk the buttons off your coat." The mining company was known as the Cascade Iron Company, and the smelting concern was called the Escanaba Furnace Company. None of the other Carnegie partners would have anything to do with the enterprise.

The Cascade Company, having a large body of ore in sight, made special exertions to get a contract to supply the Lucy Furnace; and it is told of Kirkpatrick that, having found a specially rich specimen, he had it analyzed, and, on the strength of its high metallic contents, he undertook to supply ores "equal to any Lake Superior ores, Columbia ore only excepted." With this guarantee a contract was made with the Lucy Furnace Company; but when the Cascade mineral was worked in the furnace it developed only forty-five to fifty per cent. of metallic iron instead of sixty-two to sixty-six per cent. as had been expected. By this time new mines in the Lake Superior region had developed ore bodies which approached very closely in value to the Columbia ore; and, under the guarantee, the owners of the Lucy Furnace felt that they had a claim against the Cascade people for damages. The claim was made, and was met

THE LUCY FURNACES IN 1886.

by denials and counter-claims; and after some unpleasant correspondence the Carnegies entered suit for $200,000 damages. Before this came into court, Jay Cooke & Co. failed and the panic of '73 ensued. The Cascade and Escanaba companies, having used up most of their funds and all of their credit—which was exceptionally good at the outset—found themselves in no position to meet panic conditions while burdened with this great suit. They therefore deemed it prudent to compromise with the Lucy Furnace owners for $100,000, to be paid in instalments. Few payments were made under this settlement before both the Cascade and the Escanaba companies failed; and the members found themselves personally responsible for the companies' debts. Mr. Kloman, who had imagined the concerns to be limited liability companies, was a shining mark for the creditors, and he was pushed to the verge of bankruptcy.

Fearing that such a catastrophe, if forced by Kloman's creditors, would involve the other concerns with which he was connected and entail a dissolution of them, Andrew Carnegie made a written offer to Kloman to restore him to full partnership if he would make a voluntary assignment and get a judicial discharge. This Kloman agreed to do; and a committee of the creditors was formed to appraise his interests, which the Carnegies bought. Kloman was thus enabled to make a settlement of fifty cents on the dollar.

The disaster shook the Carnegie concern to its foundations; and for a time it seemed as if they all would be overwhelmed in a common ruin. But the high financial standing of McCandless, Stewart and Scott, with whom the Carnegies had just made an alliance, as will be told elsewhere, and the ingenuity of Mr. Phipps, enabled them to weather the storm.

The disentanglement of Kloman's affairs occupied three or four years, during which he worked with the Carnegies, and received a salary of $5,000 a year. When he was free to hold property again, Andrew Carnegie offered him an interest of

$100,000 in the various enterprises, to be paid for out of profits. This did not satisfy Kloman, who valued his interest at several times one hundred thousand dollars; and he demanded complete reinstatement in all the Carnegie companies, in accordance with the previous understanding. As he had no binding contract—the written offer and its acceptance had carried no legal consideration—he was unable to enforce his demand, and he withdrew from the Carnegie group in bitterness and anger.

The later history of the Lucy Furnaces as a separate organization can be told in a few sentences. In June, 1881, a two-thirds interest was sold to Wilson, Walker & Co.; and James R. Wilson of that firm, one of the Original Six of Andrew Carnegie's boy-friends, was made chairman of the Lucy Furnace Company, Ltd., which was now organized. The purpose of this change was to release Mr. Phipps and Mr. T. M. Carnegie from the close attention which they had been giving the furnaces, that they might concentrate their efforts on the business of the Edgar Thomson plant at Braddock. Mr. Wilson was in poor health at the time of his accession to power at the furnaces; and his new duties and responsibilities aggravated his trouble. He died in 1883 and was succeeded by E. A. McCrum. Later Mr. Julian Kennedy had charge of the furnaces; and, with the same skill as he has applied to all his work, he soon won back for the Lucy the laurels she had lost to the newer furnaces at Braddock.

On January 1st, 1886, the Lucy Furnaces, the Upper and Lower Union Mills, and the Pittsburg Bessemer plant at Homestead were all brought together in one organization, Carnegie, Phipps & Co., Limited, of which Mr. John Walker became chairman.

The complete record of these furnaces, on which the attention of the iron-making world was riveted for many years, will be found on the following page.

LUCY FURNACES.

	No. 1. Tons per annum.	No. 2. Tons per annum
1872	13,361	......
1873	21,674	......
1874	24,543	......
1875	22,984	......
1876	16,174	......
1877	28,918	6,644
1878	33,980	28,151
1879	25,942	31,668
1880	20,910	33,931
1881	.38,186	30,978
1882	22,385	35,453
1883	44,317	24,235
1884	Rebuilding.	58,416
1885	68,047	47,498
1886	56,209	64,266
1887	64,259	57,099
1888	63,970	55,834
1889	60,447	70,749
1890	76,019	72,155
1891	72,128	53,186 { No iron April '91 —Coke strike.
1892	66,203 Relining.	71,289
1893	59,413	48,787 6 months only.
1894	81,395	82,419
1895	102,867	87,542
1896	102,341	104,411
1897	113,060	104,963
1898	62,967 Relining.	61,186 Relining.
1899	88,777	37,102
1900	62,231 Relining.	57,895 Relining.
1901	82,677	41,251
1902	73,537	38,575

CHAPTER VI

BEGINNINGS AND GROWTH OF THE STEEL BUSINESS

Fort Pitt.

MANY accounts of the beginnings of the Carnegie Bessemer steel business have appeared from time to time in magazines and other periodicals, some unwittingly fanciful, others obviously unfair, and most of them contradictory. Indeed, so far as the author knows, the actual facts concerning this important event have never been correctly set forth in any of the numerous historical sketches of the enterprise which have been written, nor in the many published biographical notices of the men associated with it. Even the more carefully compiled books which occasionally have been published on the subject have contained more romance than fact. This is equally true of all the other branches of the Carnegie business.

The reason of this ever-increasing accumulation of misstatement is not far to seek. Hitherto no documentary history of the constituent companies of the Carnegie Steel Company has been attempted. No independent effort has been made to go back to the beginnings of things—to trace to their source the tiny, separate rivulets which, later, came together and formed such a great and impressive stream. Having no authoritative data before them, early writers were led into errors and misstatements of facts which have been transmitted from one generation of historians and biographers to another, until now it is hardly possible for the chance investigator to disinter even an occasional truth from the mass of error under which it is buried.

71

Another thing has contributed to give these fictions the semblance of fact: they have been tacitly accepted as true by those who knew better. The Carnegie Company grew to such vast proportions as practically to dominate the steel industry of America; and the honor of founding and guiding it to success was very flattering to the vanity of those to whom it was ascribed. During the later history of the concern, when the trade-grooves of which Mr. Phipps so aptly speaks had been made, and the business was running smoothly, there came into prominence a group of "young geniuses," as Andrew Carnegie calls them, whose achievements have overshadowed those of the men who did the first hard work and made the grooves. Many of these being dead, the credit which was rightly theirs has been given to the living, and generally accepted without disclaimer. Many laurel wreaths are being proudly worn to-day which, in all honor, should deck the graves of Andrew Kloman, William Coleman, Thomas M. Carnegie, David A. Stewart, William P. Shinn, David McCandless, Henry M. Curry and others who have long since joined the silent and unprotesting majority.

The important part which William Coleman had in the origin of the Lucy furnaces has already been mentioned. To him also is due the honor of founding the Carnegie Bessemer steel business.

Early in 1871 Mr. Coleman, who had been a manufacturer of iron rails,* visited the various steel works throughout the

---

* The first steel rails used in the United States were imported from England in 1862 by the firm of Philip S. Justice & Co. of Philadelphia and London. Mr. J. Howard Mitchell of that firm reported the transaction to the editor of *Iron Age* in 1882. Steel rails were then used to a limited extent in England; and so enthusiastic in their praises of these rails were the managers of the lines on which they were used that the firm in question endeavored to have American railroads make some experiments with steel. But the Philadelphia firm were looked upon as fanatics, if not swindlers, when they talked about steel rails to American railroad managers ; and it was seldom that they could obtain the earnest attention of the proper officers. "The rule was," Mr. Mitchell says, "to bow us out of the office and end the annoyance of being talked to by a dreamer."

In 1862, however, after many efforts in this and other directions, J. Edgar

Plate IV.

THOMAS M. CARNEGIE
AT THE AGE OF NINETEEN

country—at Johnstown, Cleveland, Harrisburg, Spuyten Duy-
vil and Troy—in order to observe the operation of the Bessemer converters which had been installed at these places during the preceding four years. He was then sixty-five years
old, but full of energy, and enterprising and far-sighted beyond
most of his contemporaries.

The first result of his observations was to secure a site for
a steel works. In this he got his son-in-law, Thomas M. Carnegie, to join him; and together they obtained the option of
purchasing a tract of one hundred and seven acres of farm land
called Braddock's Field, being the identical site of the defeat
of General Braddock in 1755, on the Monongahela River, a
dozen miles above Pittsburg. Bounded on the north by the
Pennsylvania Railroad, traversed through its centre by the Baltimore and Ohio, with the Monongahela affording water transportation on its southern boundary, it was an ideal spot for the
purpose.

Mr. Coleman resided at this time in the old homestead of
Judge Wilkins on Penn Avenue, Homewood; and young Car-

Thomson, then president of the Pennsylvania Railroad Company, was induced to
give steel rails a trial; and he ordered one hundred tons at $150 per ton in gold—
equivalent at that time to something like $300 per ton in currency. But unfortu-
nately the trial lot of rails was made of crucible steel, which proved to be very high
in carbon, though made to resist wear. They were put in the tracks of the company in yards and at other points where the greatest wear took place; and during
the following winter, which was a very severe one, many of them broke. Such a
result might have been a crushing blow to the use of steel rails if it had happened
under the management of a less sagacious man than Mr. Thomson. He saw,
however, that if he could get rails that would not break, yet would endure the
great traffic on his railroad with as little wear as this lot had shown, it would be
extremely desirable; and he therefore gave further orders, first for five hundred
and then for one thousand tons, which at that time were looked upon as wonderfully large orders.

In 1867 Messrs. Philip S. Justice & Co. sold to the old Beaver Meadow Railroad Company, now part of the Lehigh Valley Railroad Company, one hundred
tons of steel rails for $162.50 per ton in gold, or about $250 per ton in currency,
and other lots at $135 per ton gold. These rails were still in the tracks in 1883,
and Mr. Lloyd Chamberlin, then treasurer of the Lehigh Valley road, told Mr.
Mitchell that they were excellent rails and were still in use. Very slowly did the
use of steel rails grow from these humble beginnings. (*Vide Iron Age*, August
16th, 1883.)

negie lived in a smaller place adjoining.   Coleman and his son-in-law used to drive to town together; and the plans of the new steel works were developed during these drives.   Their nearest neighbors were David A. Stewart and his brother-in-law, John Scott, both railway men, the former being also president of the Pittsburg Locomotive Works, while the latter was a director of the Allegheny Valley Railroad.   Mr. Stewart was also president of the Columbia Oil Company, of which Mr. Coleman had been one of the original organizers; but making over his stock to Andrew Carnegie, Mr. Coleman did not materially benefit by the fabulous dividends which made Andrew Carnegie rich.

WILLIAM COLEMAN,
Who, with his son-in-law, Thomas M. Carnegie, founded the Edgar Thomson Steel Works.

On mentioning the scheme to his neighbors, whose connections with the railroads made their co-operation especially desirable, Coleman readily obtained the adhesion of both Stewart and Scott.   At the same time young Carnegie brought the project to the attention of his brother, who lived in New York and was engaged in various construction companies and similar schemes. The elder Carnegie strongly opposed it, and refused to connect himself with it in any way.   It conflicted with his theory about the unprofitableness of pioneering.   Tom then sought the co-operation of Mr. David McCandless, one of the most prominent merchants of Pittsburg, and vice-president of the Exchange National Bank.   Mr. McCandless had known the younger Carnegie since childhood through his connection with the Swedenborgian Church, of which all the Carnegies were members; and being familiar with the excellent work he had done during the early struggles of the Union Iron Mills, he consented to join him and Coleman in the new venture, provided that his friend William P. Shinn was taken into the firm and made treasurer of it.

In the spring of 1872 Colonel Scott, who was ever seeking to put profitable things in the way of Andrew Carnegie, had him commissioned by President J. Edgar Thomson, of the Pennsylvania Railroad, to go to Europe to market a block of the bonds of a new railroad which was to run to Davenport, Iowa. Carnegie sailed in April, and was successful in selling $6,000,-000 of the bonds. His aggregate commissions—for he was fortunate enough to get them from both sides—amounted to $150,000. Incidentally the loss to the purchasers of the bonds was $6,000,000—every cent they put in; and a futile effort was afterwards made to hold Carnegie responsible for the loss.

During this European trip Carnegie made a study of the Bessemer steel situation there. In England the industry was firmly established; and Bessemer steel rails were being made in ever-increasing quantities at good prices. At Derby visitors were shown a double-headed Bessemer rail which had been laid down in 1857—at a point on the Midland Railway where previously iron rails had sometimes to be renewed within three months—and which after fifteen years' constant use was still in good shape. In the presence of exhibits of this kind Carnegie was readily convinced that Coleman's Pittsburg scheme was not only practicable, but likely to be extremely profitable. This conviction was strengthened by the prospect of an additional outlet for the product of the Lucy Furnace; and on his return he was found to be an enthusiastic supporter of the Bessemer project. Indeed, he volunteered to put into the venture the whole of his European profits, in addition to a commission of $75,000 which he had made the previous October on the sale

of a block of Gilman bonds, also a commission won through the
friendship of Colonel Scott.

Andrew Carnegie had sailed on this mission in April, 1872.
During the same month Coleman, Scott, McCandless and the
younger Carnegie entered upon a real-estate speculation.   They
bought the Mowry homestead tract in Pittsburg and subdivided
it into building lots.   The venture resulted in a large profit,
and left the partners in good financial shape to enter upon their
steel enterprise.   On Andrew Carnegie's return with his golden
sheaves and his new enthusiasm, the project was at once put
into execution.   On January 1st, 1873, Mr. Coleman took up
the option on Braddock's Field for himself and associates, paying the sum of $59,003.30 for the entire tract, subject to a
mortgage of $160,000; and on the 13th of the same month the
firm of Carnegie, McCandless & Co. was organized with a capital of $700,000.   Coleman himself put $100,000 into the firm,
Messrs. Kloman, Phipps, McCandless, Scott, Stewart, Shinn,
and the younger Carnegie each subscribed $50,000, and An-
drew Carnegie added $25,000 to his European profits and put
$250,000 into the venture.   For by this time his ambition to
own the largest individual interest in all the enterprises with
which he connected himself had become definite, although it
was not yet the absorbing passion it became later.   Thus was
started the great enterprise which afterwards became famous as
the Edgar Thomson Steel Works.

In 1874 the legislature of Pennsylvania, prompted by the
widespread ruin of the panic, passed an act authorizing the
formation of limited liability companies; and Kloman's failure
having brought home to the other members of his firm the
danger of partnership agreements, they took advantage of the
new law, and on October 12th, 1874, the firm of Carnegie, Mc-
Candless & Co. was dissolved, and the Edgar Thomson Steel
Company, Limited, was incorporated with a capital of $1,000,-
000 to take its place.   On October 31st the unfinished works
at Braddock were transferred to the latter corporation, the con-

sideration being $631,250.43, subject to a mortgage now amounting to $201,000.

The works were laid out under the supervision of A. L. Holley, the well-known Bessemer engineer, who offered a guarantee that the plant would have a capacity of seventy-five thou-

A. L. HOLLEY,
Builder of the principal Bessemer Steel Works in America.

sand tons of ingots a year. Ground was broken on April 13th, 1873. Before the work was more than well started, however, the panic involved the firm in great financial difficulty; and but for the high standing of McCandless, Stewart, and Scott, the infant industry would have suffered an early death. As it was, an issue of bonds was found necessary. These conferred on holders the right to exchange them within three years for paid-up stock in the company. J. Edgar Thomson took a hundred of these bonds; and Colonel Scott, true to his traditional helpfulness, took fifty. This gave the firm $150,000 at a time when it was worth double that amount; and Gardiner McCandless, son of the chairman of the company, bought about $70,000 of the bonds for himself and friends. Besides tiding it over a period of difficulty and danger, this bond issue brought to the company the prestige and favor of President Thomson and Colonel Scott, as was found as soon as it entered the market with its rails.

While the works were in course of construction a curious development took place at Johnstown, which greatly benefited the Edgar Thomson Company. In the spring of 1873 a labor dispute took place at the Cambria Iron Works. The trouble grew out of an extraordinary situation. Foreseeing difficulty with the local labor union, the Cambria Company induced its principal men in all departments to become members of the organization; hoping that in this way they would get control of it and manage it in the company's interest. For some reason these men failed to get control, and a strike being ordered by the union they had no alternative but to obey, at least for the time. Hoist by their own petard, the company's officials capped their blunder by telling these foremen that their situations would be forfeited unless they brought the dispute to an end. In those days, as we have seen in the case of the puddlers' strike at the Union Iron Mills, labor disputes with capital were in an elemental stage; and it is barely possible that the simple measures of the Cambria officials might have ended the trouble. But Andrew Carnegie, hearing in New York of the dispute, returned hastily to Pittsburg, and proposed to his firm that these heads of the Cambria departments be invited to join the new works at Braddock. This was done; and Capt. William R. Jones having accepted the invitation, the leading men in every department hastened to follow his example. In this way

Carnegie, McCandless & Co. secured a corps of trained men who had gone through the costly apprenticeship of Bessemer steel-making at the expense of a rival concern. It was a master stroke, and at once carried the embryo business past the experimental stage.* Among the men thus secured, in addition to Captain Jones, who was without a peer, were Captain Lapsley, superintendent of the rail mill, John Rinard, superintendent of the converting works, Thomas James, superintendent of machinery, Thomas Addenbrook, head furnace builder, F. L. Bridges, superintendent of transportation, and C. C. Teeter, chief clerk. Later, scores of others followed. Indeed, there was hardly a skilled workman in the whole of the Cambria plant that did not want to join his beloved " Bill " Jones; and when the Edgar Thomson mill was ready to open, many of them did so. During the panic the first arrivals were put on board wages, and kept about the place until the trouble was passed, and the work of construction resumed.

Captain Jones, who was made superintendent of the works, was probably the greatest mechanical genius that ever entered the Carnegie shops. He had passed, moreover, through every branch of the iron and steel manufacture ; and there was nothing in the works of which he had not that intimate knowledge which comes through the hand alone. His power to manage men, joined to his inventiveness and thorough practical training, made him the most conspicuous personal element in the phenomenal success which attended the enterprise from the very first. He gave many valuable suggestions to Mr. Holley while the plant was being erected, which were frankly adopted; and his later inventions added enormously to the profits of the firm every year of his life, and long after. Even in 1903 the United States Steel Corporation filed a bill in equity to restrain the

---

* " Its [the Edgar Thomson plant] successful operation is greatly due to the large experience in Bessemer manufacture of Capt. William R. Jones, general superintendent of the works and of Capt. Thomas H. Lapsley, superintendent of the rolling mill, who have a force under them largely composed of men experienced in the manufacture of rails."—*American Manufacturer*, November 18th, 1875.

Jones & Laughlin Steel Company from using the famous metal mixer which Captain Jones invented for the Edgar Thomson

Pouring hot metal into the Jones Mixer.

Company; and this one device, used as it is in every Bessemer department of the great steel corporation, is still the means of saving it millions of dollars every year. At the same time no detail was too small for Captain Jones' personal attention. This indeed was one of the secrets of his success with workmen. He was ever on the lookout for their comfort. He personally attended to the ventilation of the shops; and, as another little illustration of his care, may be mentioned a generous supply of oatmeal and water for drinking purposes. To Captain Jones is also due the system of rewards for exceptional service which afterwards characterized the administration of all the Carnegie properties, and which has since been extended, with beneficial effects, to all the constituent parts of the United States Steel Corporation.

Molten metal flowing from the Jones Mixer.

In illustration of the wise and broad views held by Captain Jones in regard to labor, an interesting letter written by him at this time may here be quoted. It also gives some data concerning profits which are worth preserving. It is as follows:

WORKS, Feb. 25, '75.

E. V. McCandless, Esq.

DEAR SIR: I wrote you somewhat hastily last night. In regard to the figures I gave you of cost of mixture, I gave you the Cambria figures, viz. mixture at $35 which of course includes spiegel metal which is (a) great deal more than it really cost them. A friend of mine who has gone over their estimates carefully gives as the cost of one ton of steel rails $44. Now allow for at least 15% on half they pay for labor as profit they derive from their store, and you will readily see that the profits of the Cambria works on steel are simply enormous.

I will give you their figures again in a more intelligent manner :—

Cost of mixture : pig-iron and spiegel	$35
Credit allowed converting department per ton of ingots....	9
" " blooming mill per ton of blooms	3
" " rail mill " " " rails	10
Total cost of producing a ton of rails	$57

Now in order to show you how much more above the actual cost they put their figures, I know of plenty of men who will take their rail mill at $4.00 a ton and find everything.

Now I know that the profits in manufacturing steel rails are enormous. If such works as the Pa. Steel Co. and Newburgh, Ohio can manufacture rails and make money these works can certainly yield very handsome profits.

Now I will give you my views as to the proper way of conducting these works.

1st. We must be careful of what class of men we collect. We must steer clear of the West where men are accustomed to infernal high wages. We must steer clear as far as we can of Englishmen who are great sticklers for high wages, small production and strikes. My experience has shown that Germans and Irish, Swedes and what I denominate " Buckwheats "— young American country boys, judiciously mixed, make the most effective and tractable force you can find. Scotsmen do very well, are honest and faithful. Welsh can be used in limited numbers. But mark me, Englishmen have been the worst class of men I have had anything to do with; and this is the opinion of Mr. Holley, George and John Fritz.

2nd. It should be the aim of the firm to keep the works running steadily. This is one of the secrets of Cambria low wages. The workmen, taking year in and year out, do better at Cambria than elsewhere. On steady work you can calculate on low wages.

3rd. The company should endeavor to make the cost of living as low as possible. This is one bad feature at present but it can be easily remedied.

These are the salient points. The men should be made to feel that the company are interested in their welfare. Make the works a pleasant place for them. I have always found it best to treat men well, and I find that my men are anxious to retain my good will by working steadily and honestly, and instead of dodging are anxious to show me what a good day's work they have done. All haughty and disdainful treatment of men has a very decided and bad effect on them.

Now I have voluntarily given you my views. I have felt this to be a necessity on my part; for I am afraid that unless the policy I have marked out is followed we need not expect the great success that is obtainable. These suggestions are the results of twenty-five years' experience obtained in the most successful iron works in this country :—Crane and Thomas Iron Works, Port Richmond Iron Works, and the Cambria works.

You are at liberty to show this letter to your father and Mr. Coleman; otherwise regard it as a confidential letter.

Yours truly

W. R. JONES.

The converting works were completed in August, 1875; and on the 22d of that month the first blow was made. On September 1st the first rail was made, and a piece of it, made into a paper weight and stamped with this date, presses on this page as it is written.

At this date Bessemer steel production in America had progressed to important proportions, the output of the country for 1875 being 375,517 tons. Of this amount 290,863 tons were rolled into rails. The business had grown from 3,000 tons in 1867. In England Bessemer steel rails had been known since 1857; so that in no sense was the Edgar Thomson Company a pioneer. It is indeed noteworthy that in anticipation of the change from iron to Bessemer steel which every railroad man foresaw, the production of iron rails in the United States fell from 900,000 tons in 1872 to 500,000 tons in 1875. In this

one decade the output of steel rails multiplied nearly thirty
times—from 34,000 tons in 1870 to 954,460 tons in 1880.
The subsequent advance has also been great; for from less than
a million tons of steel rails produced in 1880, the output rose
to 3,000,000 tons in 1902, while the price had fallen from $106
a ton in 1870 to $17 a ton in 1898.

Many things combined to make the Edgar Thomson enterprise a success from the start; and in so far as these were foreseen and planned, they serve as evidence of the consummate
skill of its projectors. Coleman must be credited with the
great advantage which resulted from the intimate relations the

The Edgar Thomson steel works in 1875.

firm had with the chief officials of the Pennsylvania Railroad.
It was he who induced Stewart and Scott to join the scheme.
To him also was due the exceptional pains taken to educate
Andrew Carnegie in the merits of the enterprise, and thus indirectly to reach Carnegie's late associates, Mr. J. Edgar Thomson
and Colonel Scott. That these important men favored the
company which bore the name of one of them is evidenced by
the fact that some of the directors of the railroad, who were
interested in rival concerns, presently insisted upon a fair division of the Pennsylvania's patronage, so that a portion of their
orders for rails afterwards went to the steel works at Johnstown
and Harrisburg.

In regard to the charges of preferential treatment in the
matter of freight rates which have often been made in this con-

nection, it can be said in all frankness that, while they were not unfounded, they were greatly exaggerated. The Edgar Thomson Company got exactly the rates and rebates that other shippers of equal importance had. Full local rates were paid; but, owing to the saving to the railroads resulting from the steel company's system of loading cars, and even at times making up the train, it was only fair that the latter should share in the results of this economy. So there was established a system of rebates. A monthly statement of the sums paid for freight and due in rebates was made out; and the rebates were paid almost as soon as the statements were presented to the railway company. While these sums were considerable, and probably inured to the injury of competing iron-rail makers, in the same district, they were no greater than those received by other manufacturers of steel rails who loaded their own shipments.

"There goes that bookkeeper."

At first this rebate system was confined to the Pennsylvania lines ; but presently President Garrett, of the Baltimore and Ohio Railroad, who had some suspicion of the facts, sent representatives to Pittsburg to learn the reason of the apparent discrimination against his road. As a result of their report Mr. Shinn, general manager of the Edgar Thomson works, received an invitation to visit Mr. Garrett in Baltimore, when an arrangement similar to that in force with the Pennsylvania company was made, and the traffic was then divided between the two roads.

Another factor which contributed in no small degree to the success of the firm was the voucher system of accounting which Mr. Shinn introduced. This had long been used by railroads, and the Standard Oil Company's accounts were thus kept; but it was not in general use in manufacturing concerns, and the Edgar Thomson Company was the first to adopt it in Pittsburg. No order for rails was ever accepted until there had first been ascertained the actual cost of every element entering into their manufacture, and options obtained on the pig-iron of which they were to be made. An eloquent testimony to the efficiency of this method of accounting was given by a workman engaged in building a heating-furnace: "There goes that —— book-keeper. If I use a dozen bricks more than I did last month, he knows it and comes round to ask why!" This was no exaggeration. The minutest details of cost of materials and labor in every department appeared from day to day and week to week in the accounts; and soon every man about the place was made to realize it. The men felt and often remarked that the eyes of the company were always on them through the books. If the workmanship was exceptionally good, or the output beyond the high average which was insisted upon, the head of the department received a letter of congratulation and perhaps a present at Christmas. If it fell behind in either quality or output, the fact was promptly brought to his notice, and Captain Jones himself would see if the fault lay in the machinery. If it did, he generally knew how to remedy it. If the defect was in the human machine, and reproof did not suffice to correct it, the man was replaced by the understudy which Jones usually had trained in view of such a contingency.*

In 1877 it was found that more steel ingots were being

---

* Dr. Frank Cowan has written a unique poem on the contrast presented by the actual condition of Braddock's Field with that of the day of the battle on July 9th, 1755. Here are a couple of verses:

> Where the cannon of Braddock were wheeled into line,
>   And swept through the forest with shot and with shell—
> But woe to the Britons! In vain they combine
>   The thunder of heaven and the lightning of hell!
> There the turning converter, while roaring with flame,
>   Pours out cascades of comets and showers of stars,
> While the pulpit-boy, goggled, looks into the same—
>   Thinking little of Braddock and nothing of Mars.

made than the rail-mill could roll; and an attempt was made to capture the local market for merchant steel. Some billets of high-carbon steel were made and submitted to a firm of buggy-spring makers. To their astonishment the material was satisfactory; and they gave a large order for billets at three cents a pound. Then some samples of axle steel for cars were submitted to the Pennsylvania Railroad Company, and subjected to tests by experts who did not know that they were not the crucible steel usually employed for car-axles. Again the tests were satisfactory, and large orders resulted. Next came the more difficult test of making steel for plow-shares, which required a soft ductile metal capable of being welded to sheets of crucible steel. Even these severe conditions were met. Finally the firm made steel capable of being rolled cold down to a paper thinness for use as stove-pipe, roofing-channels and cartridge cases stamped out of the sheet. So that, two years after the realization of his dreams, Tom Carnegie had the satisfaction of showing to his brother as many varieties of excellent steel made at the Edgar Thomson works as he had previously seen in England. But by this time the elder Carnegie was the most enthusiastic member of the company and needed no such reminders.

The profits of this line of business were very great; but the capacity of the rail-mill having been enlarged, and the demands of the railroads ever increasing, the company abandoned the manufacture of merchant steel for the time being and returned to the exclusive production of rails. The demand that had thus been created, suddenly found itself shut off from supplies; and

> Where the guns of the foe were revealed by a flash—
>   A report—and the fall of the killed and the wounded,
> Till the woods were ablaze, and a deafening crash
>   With the wail of the wounded and dying resounded;
> There the ingot aglow is drawn out to a rail,
>   While the coffee-mill crusher booms, rattles and groans,
> And the water-boy hurries along with his pail,
>   Saying, Braddock be blowed! he's a slouch to Bill Jones.

an interesting development resulted. This was the establishment of a rival converting plant at Homestead by the group of manufacturers who had been educated in the use of Bessemer steel in place of the more costly crucible steel which they had previously used. Pending the erection of the new plant, an enterprising firm of Pittsburg brokers got Mr. McCandless, the former bookkeeper of the Edgar Thomson Company, to go to England to buy the merchant steel necessary to fill local demands. In two years this firm sold nearly two million dollars' worth of English steel at a profit of $5 to $15 a ton, after paying forty-five per cent. duty and both ocean and railroad freights. At the end of two years the Edgar Thomson Company sought to head off the independent manufacturers at Homestead and resumed the manufacture of merchant steel. The import business suddenly ceased; and these profits with others went into the erection of a series of blast-furnaces which became the wonder of the iron-making world.

Up to this time the Lucy furnaces had been supplying most of the pig-iron used by the Edgar Thomson Company; but as the members of the latter corporation were not all interested in the furnaces, there arose differences among them as to the proper price that should be paid for pig-iron. Although these differences were finally adjusted by a sliding scale based on the price of steel, the discussion developed in Shinn, McCandless, Stewart, and Scott a desire to own their own blast furnace. The desire was strengthened by the phenomenal profits of the Lucy plant, which had paid for its construction in a single year. Eventually an agreement was reached, and furnace A was erected at Braddock.

This furnace was a part of the Kloman wreck, namely, the little charcoal furnace which he had built at Escanaba. It was bought for a mere song—a little over $16,000—and such parts as could be transported were brought down and installed at the Edgar Thomson works. This was in 1879. Mr. Julian Kennedy was put in charge of its erection, and afterwards of its

operation.   It was "blown in " in January, 1880, and yielded
442 tons of pig-iron the first week.   In view of the fact that its
cubical capacity was but 6,396 feet compared with 15,000 feet
in the Lucy Furnace, this large product excited great astonishment.   The fourth week, however, it made 537 tons; and during the following month (March) its output reached a total of

JULIAN KENNEDY.

2,760 tons, while the coke consumption was reduced by May to
1,945 pounds per ton of iron produced.   Later the output of a
single week ran up to 671 tons, and the iron-making world
regarded the achievement with wonder.

In April, 1880, a second furnace, constructed by Mr. Kennedy, was put in blast, which in its third month showed an
output of 4,318 tons, and at the end of the first half year was
making the marvellous total of 4,722 tons in a single month.

During the first twelve months this furnace produced 48,179 tons. In 1883 a third furnace was put in, and in its second month passed all previous records by a yield of 6,045 tons; and in the first twelve months made 65,947 tons of pig-iron. During the next three years two other furnaces were erected; and in December, 1885, one of them yielded 6,451 tons, the total for twelve months being 74,475 tons. In October, 1886, still another furnace was "blown in," and in January, 1887, three months afterwards, it produced 8,398 tons on a coke consumption of 1,935 pounds per ton of pig-iron. Its total output for twelve months was 88,940 tons. These were the world records at the time; but changes in the construction of one of the other furnaces, made under the supervision of Mr. James Gayley, one of the ablest of the so-called "young geniuses," brought the monthly record in December, 1889, to 10,603 tons on a coke consumption of only 1,756 pounds! These figures indicate at once the rapid growth of the business of the Edgar Thomson Steel Company and the proportionate advance made by its superintendents in the art of iron production. Both records, at that time incomparable even in this great land of rapid growth, have since been repeatedly broken by the same firm.

Here this great evolution may be seen at a glance:

FIRST FURNACE.

Years and months.	Tons produced.	Pounds of coke per ton of iron.
1880—April	2,723	2,536
May	3,718	2,574
June	4,318	2,344
July	4,345	2,706
August	4,601	2,811
September	4,221	2,757
October	4,722	2,736

SECOND FURNACE.

1882—Second month	6,045	2,617
Average for twelve months	5,495	2,570
Best month	6,131	2,387

THIRD FURNACE.

Years and months.	Tons produced.	Pounds of coke per ton of iron.
1885—October	6,320	2,396
November	6,306	2,396
December	6,451	2,172
1886—January and February	Shut down.	
March	6,352	2,105

FOURTH FURNACE.*

1886—November	6,735	2,128
December	7,494	2,105
1887—January	8,398	1,935
1889—October	6,512	2,450
November	9,097	1,897
December	10,603	1,756
1890—January	10,536	1,736
February	8,954	1,859
March	9,941	1,845
April	10,075	1,847
May	10,035	1,884

Hardly less remarkable were the results achieved in the con.
verting and rail departments. In the four months ending December, 1875, 6,555 tons of rails were produced, although,
through a scarcity of spiegel, the works lost two weeks. At
this time a thousand tons a month was considered a good average for the first year of a two five-ton converter plant. In the
twenty-six working days of January, 1876, the product of 433
blows was 2,550 tons of ingots, or 2,055 tons of rails. In a
single week in February 119 heats gave 707 tons of ingots,
while the blooming-mill passed 709 tons, and 560 tons of rails
were rolled. During the first full year of its operation (1876)
the mill produced 45,563 tons of steel. The tonnage of rails
was 32,228. In January, 1877, the product of a week was
more than double the extraordinary record of the preceding February; the output being 1,543 tons of ingots and 1,129 tons of
rails. The way this was done is naïvely explained by a local

---

* Twelve years later one of the above furnaces produced in one month,
December, 1902, a total of 17,449 tons of pig-iron on an average coke consumption of 1,875 pounds.

journalist of that day: " Mr. Campbell, a roller, ten days or two weeks ago, rolled 540 rails in eleven and a half hours, which is 108 more than the usual run for twelve hours. This put John Little, another roller, on his mettle, and last Thursday night he rolled 600 thirty-foot rails in eleven and a half hours —thus beating his competitor by 60 rails and the usual run by 168 rails. John may be Little, but the Edgar Thomson wants that Little here below, and wants that Little long !" In the twenty-four working days of the following February, 915 blows produced 5,993 tons of ingots; 4,474 tons of rails were rolled and 182 tons of billets. On the 26th of February the day's product was 383 tons of ingots—half as much as was produced in a week the year before. The product for March was 8,002 tons of ingots.

A little less than two years before this Mr. A. L. Holley, then managing the Rensselaer Steel Works at Troy, wagered the Hon. John A. Griswold, one of the proprietors, that their Bessemer plant (two converters) could produce in one month 1,500 tons of ingots. He won his bet, of course; and the figures 1,500 and 8,000 mark the advance of American steel-making at this time in twenty-three months.

This rate of progress was maintained during the next two years. In September, 1879, the Edgar Thomson beat all the records of two-converter plants by producing 10,788 tons of ingots. The tonnage of a single day was 519, of a week, 2,536. The output for the year (1879) was 107,877 tons of ingots, of which 76,043 tons were rolled into rails. In November the two converters produced 13,116 tons of ingots, and the mill 10,037 tons of rails. The total rails for the working year, nine months and twenty-nine days, was 100,094 tons. Incidentally the profit of the Edgar Thomson works for 1880 amounted to $1,625,000; and there were orders booked for 80,000 tons for the following year.

The known facts—of course no outsider knew the profits, which are now made public for the first time—produced surprise and chagrin in competing plants. In England the news was received with doubt. "An almost incredible statement," said E. Windsor Richards, the British steel manufacturer; and when Captain Jones, in a paper read before the British Iron and Steel Institute, gave details and dates, incredulity gave way to consternation, for it was plainly to be seen that England's supremacy in steel was at an end. Here is the amazing record in detail:

NOVEMBER, 1880.

Number of vessels, 2.   Blows, 1,746.

Average charge, 7½ tons.

Tons of Ingots .. .. 13,116$\frac{1040}{2240}$
Blooms............... .... 12,168$\frac{1770}{2240}$
Rails................................ ...... 11,037$\frac{1587}{2240}$
Billets................................ 68$\frac{291}{2240}$
Merchant blooms .... 4$\frac{268}{2240}$

Total finished product 11,100

At this date the Edgar Thomson had held the record for nearly three years. During the next six months it beat this record out of shape. In the first six months of 1881 the two converters produced 76,756 tons of ingots as against 55,428

A train of rolls.

tons for the corresponding period of 1880—an increase of thirty-eight per cent. The best twenty-four hours' work was 623 tons. The product of a week was 3,433 tons; the best month, 14,033 tons—more than nine times the tonnage of Holley's bet six years before! The rail-mill in the same time produced 65,087 tons as against 43,372 tons in the corresponding half of 1880—an increase of a fraction over fifty per cent. The average weekly yield of rails was 2,503 tons as compared with 1,664 tons in 1880.

These newer facts were again presented by Captain Jones to the British Iron and Steel Institute; and before the astonished Englishmen had time fully to digest them, he sent a fresh record:

November, 1881—Ingots................	16,193 tons.
Rails....................	13,646 "
Best 24 hours' work—Ingots....................	700 "
" " " " Rails....................	608 "
Best week's work—Ingots....................	3,902 "
" " " Rails....................	3,202 " *

Soon afterwards the works were enlarged and the direct metal process was introduced; but the product was not proportionately great, and the record passed from Captain Jones to Mr. Julian Kennedy, who by this time had been put in charge of the Homestead works. Captain Jones' great and noteworthy triumph forms one of the most picturesque episodes in the history of the Carnegie organization.

---

* For purposes of comparison a few details of the product of the earlier steel works in America may here be given. These were, like the Edgar Thomson, all two five-ton converter plants, working eleven turns or five and one-half days a week.

	Heats, 24 hours.	Heats, week.	Tons Ingots, 24 hours.	Tons Ingots, week.	Tons Ingots, month.
1868	....	....	....	....	500
					Cambria. Harrisburg.
1870, Troy and Harrisburg...	....	....	....	....	1,700
1872, Harrisburg	....	....	...	640	2,000
		Harrisburg			
1873	25 to 30	180	....	890	
		Cambria			
1874, Harrisburg	46	189	....	956	
" Troy.................	50	....	267	....	2,899
" Troy.................	....	195	....	972	
" North Chicago	....	....	....	....	3,526
" Cambria.............	....	211			

These were all two five-ton converter plants working eleven turns or five and one-half days a week.

CHAPTER VII

SOME INSIDE FINANCIAL HISTORY

THE striking achievements just set forth formed a legitimate source of pride and exultation in the firm; and the gratification of every member was increased by the wondering comments of the trade and the public, whose attention was invited to these mechanical victories by officially verified newspaper notices and by papers and speeches before the iron and steel associations in England and America. Braddock became the Mecca of iron and steel manufacturers from all over the world.

On the subject of profits there was naturally no disposition to take the public into the confidence of the firm. The protection of infant industries was a subject on which there was divided opinion in the council-chambers of the nation; and manufacturers showed a proper caution in concealing the extent of their gains. Indeed, the Carnegies at this time accepted what seemed to them a large monetary loss rather than produce the books of the Edgar Thomson Steel Company in court in response to a judicial order. Now, however, that the golden harvest is safely garnered and beyond the reach of legislators and others who might "break through and steal," there is no reason why the gratifying results of the government's wise policy of protection should not be set forth.

The admirable system of accounting introduced by Mr. Shinn enabled the Edgar Thomson managers to see at a glance the exact cost of every one of the many operations entering into the manufacture of a ton of ingots, blooms, or rails. Every month cost sheets were made out in which these items were given to the hundredth part of a cent. These statements were marvels of ingenuity and careful accounting.

The first was issued on October 1st, 1875. It gave in detail the output and cost of the first month's run, together with the name of the purchasing railroads and the prices received. It was a gratifying document to the anxious partners. The output for September, 1875, was $1,119\frac{62}{2240}$ tons of rails. Their cost was exactly $57 a ton, including all charges, even to office expenses and maintenance of the plant. The prices received averaged $66.50 a ton at the works, thus leaving a clear profit of $9.50 a ton, and a total of over $10,000 on the month's work. In the second month the output was $1,817\frac{1523}{2240}$ tons, which cost $57.20 and sold for $66.32. At the end of the year the average of four months' operations showed that ingots had cost $44.33 a ton, blooms $47.17, and rails $58.45. The average price at which they sold was a fraction under $66 a ton, giving a total profit on rails of $41,970.06. The percentage of rails from pig-iron and spiegel was eighty and fifty-six hundredths; and this was afterwards used as a basis on which to figure the making of contracts.

During the following year the improvements in processes made by Captain Jones, already referred to, greatly increased the output and reduced the cost. On the other hand, prices also fell. Andrew Carnegie wrote this year to one of his colleagues:

" We must not loose sight of the fact that the great products now made must effect prices. I look for Cost to be reached for a short time say 50^{50} at mills with us. Some concerns must stop. therefore any orders we can take netting above 52^{50} had better be taken—55$ at mills is a tall price.—Penna steel [i.e. Pennsylvania Steel Co.] has offered 60$ Balto to Georgia RR. but I hope to get a small order—"

In the same letter, however, he waxes enthusiastic over the future :

" What do you really figure we can put rails at cost—running double 4000 Tons per Mo. on this basis—Cant we shade 50$ If so where is there such a business—"

And so alluring is the picture in his mind that in the next sentence he says:

"I want to buy Mr. Coleman out & hope to do so.—"

But that is another part of the story.

Concerning his great expectations at this time, the following extract from a letter of his to Shinn, dated April 13th, 1876, is interesting. He estimates future profits at forty per cent. per annum, or $300,000 net on a capital of $750,000.

Harry Tom & I must give entire time
have only two anxieties to be able to feel
You are enlisted thoroughly in the work.
This is a great one & means 40 000$ a year
profit on 100 000$ - on an average.
say 750.000 - Cash - $300.000
Intr on loan 25
50000 Tons at 7$ $325 000
The profit will not stand permanently below
that tons - say price rails at Works average
55$ Cost 48$ - some years we shall do far

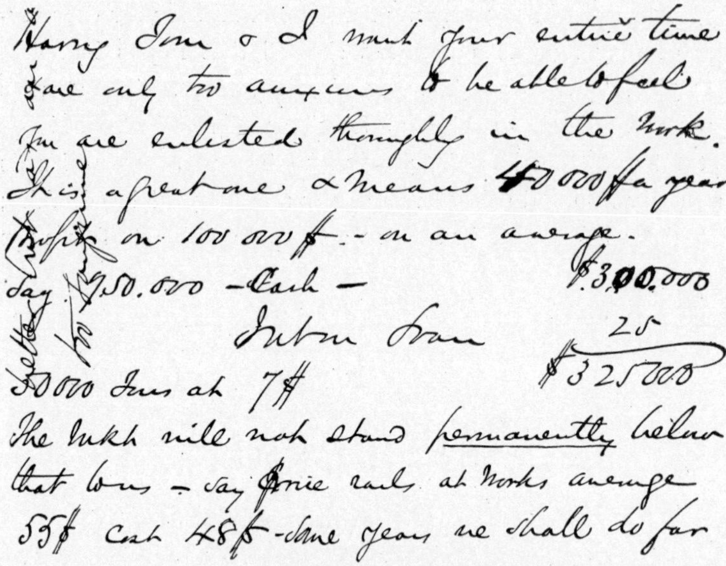

[Photographic reproduction.]

The price of rails this year (1876) dropped steadily from $67 in January to $52 in December; but the average price received by the Edgar Thomson Company for the sixteen months ending December 31st, 1876, was $60.61[6]. The product for the year was 32,228 tons, and for sixteen months $38,284\frac{573}{2240}$

tons. The cost of manufacture, which averaged $56.98[5] for the first seven months, had dropped to $53.19 for the second seven months. The net earnings for the year amounted to $181,007.18 on a capital issue of $731,500.

The Edgar Thomson Steel Works in 1890.

The output of rails for 1877 was $42,826\frac{978}{2240}$ tons. Both prices and cost of manufacture show a remarkable decline. They are as follows:

	Cost at E. T. works.	Price at mills.		Cost at E. T. works.	Price at mills.
January	$46.67[75]	$49.00	July	$44.87[50]	$45.25
February	44.89	49.00	August	42.55[54]	44.75
March	44.10[28]	49.00	September	43.83[02]	44.00
April	43.58[5]	49.00	October	42.00[48]	42.25
May	45.63[35]	47.25	November	40.13[14]	40.50
June	42.28[03]	46.50	December	40.35[88]	40.50

It must not be inferred from this that during the later months of the year the company was running at a loss; for the rails made in November and December had been sold at prices prevailing nine or twelve months earlier. At the same time

7

Office of The Edgar Thomson Steel Company Limited

Pittsburgh January 26th 1877.

To the members of The Edgar Thomson Steel Company Limited

The undersigned submits this, his first Annual Report, upon the financial condition of your Association, on December 31st 1876, and of the operation thereof to that date.

The Balance Sheet of the Association on December 31st 1876, showed as follows

Assets

Cost of Works	$1,096,432.84	
Real Estate Costs	259,625.93	
Tenements	33,072.40	
Discount on Bonds Sold,	12,100.00	
Total Capital invested		$1,401,231.17
Stock on hand.		
Manufactured Product	$29,641.62	
Materials for use	117,379.96	
Scrap	102,806.25	
		249,827.83
Available Assets		
Cash	$26,880.92	
Bills Receivable	64,828.45	
Book Accounts	171,728.20	
		263,437.57
Total Assets		$1,914,496.57

profits were greatly diminished, and the year's balance sheet showed only a net gain of $36,673.33. But about $115,000 had been spent on the works and some $20,000 of indebtedness had been paid off. As a matter of fact, the profits of all the Carnegie works this year aggregated $190,379.33.

In February of this year the first dividend was declared, being twenty-five per cent. in scrip. In August a second dividend of fourteen per cent. was declared, part of which was applied on stock and part paid in cash. In this way the capital was raised to $1,000,000. In October dividend No. 3, of two and three-fourths per cent., was declared; making a total for the year in cash and stock of forty-one and three-fourths per cent.

At the beginning of 1878 Andrew Carnegie indulged again in his habit of prophecy, and scribbled for the benefit of one of his partners his great expectations for the year. This rough memorandum is not very clear in its details, but it shows that further reductions in cost to $38 were expected, while the price to be received was put at $42.50, with an allotment by the steel rail pool of 60,000 tons. This would give a profit of $240,000 from rails, and other additions not now traceable were expected to bring the total net profit to $250,000. Well might he exclaim, "Where is there such a business!"

Let us see how the prophecy turned out. By March, 1878, thanks to Captain Jones' excellent practice at the works, the monthly product of rails had reached $7,383\frac{1316}{2400}$ tons. The cost of ingots had been reduced to $29.50 and that of rails to $37.77. During the year the cost of making rails did not go more than a few mills above $38. In April it was $38.06[6]; in May, $36.81; in June, $37.92[5]; in July, $38.01[3]; in August, $37.82[9]; in September, $36.98[7]; in October, $36.11[4]; in November, $36.41[5]; and in December, $36.52[5]. The average price at which they were sold was $42.50, exactly corresponding with Carnegie's guess. The net profits of a single month (November) amounted to a fraction over $52,000; and Andrew Carnegie, *à propos* of lofty heights, writes from Sorrento:

"Pyramids & Mt Etna & Vesuvius have been our last climbs —Mt E of course we did only from the base, Tell Capt Jones there was a proud little stout man who gave a wild hurrah when he saw E T ahead. Was nt it a close race with C I. Co. but they had a start. besides we had to go through the measles you know"

The earnings of the Edgar Thomson works this year were $401,800—over thirty-one per cent. on its capital, which had been increased to $1,250,000. Andrew Carnegie, by the way, subscribed for the whole of this increase; and a year later was

---

THEORY.

"We are creatures of the tariff, and if ever the steel manufacturers here attempt to control or have any general understanding among them the tariff would not exist one session of Congress. The theory of protection is that home competition will soon reduce the price of the product so it will yield only the usual profit. Any understanding among us would simply attempt to defeat this. There never has been or ever will be such an understanding."— *Andrew Carnegie, in American Manufacturer, July 25th, 1884.*

---

shown by the balance sheet to owe the company $175,000 on account of stock subscription—a simple and easy method of becoming a "majority stockholder."

The next year the price of rails took a sharp upward spurt, reaching $67 a ton in December and $85 by February, 1880. In the same period the cost of manufacture was slightly reduced. In January, 1879, rails cost $38.60[6] a ton to make, and in May, $35.84[5]. During the first six months of this year the Edgar Thomson works made $252,854. The second half of the year the gains were even greater. In August, with rails selling at $48, there was a clear profit of $10.50 a ton (pig-iron had gone up $12.50); in October a fraction under $15, and by December over $22 a ton net profit. The monthly output of ingots now exceeded 10,000 tons, and of rails five to six thousand tons. "Where is there such a business!"

These golden times continued throughout the following year. In January the difference between the selling price of rails and the cost of pig-iron was $53 a ton, the former being $75 and the latter $22 a ton. The next month it was $65, and of this something like $40 a ton was clear profit to the Edgar Thomson Steel Company, who were running day and night and

---

PRACTICE.

		Profit.	Loss.
EDGAR THOMSON STEEL WORKS.			
On rails, payment by rail pool.		$123,983.28	
HOMESTEAD STEEL WORKS.			
Axles,	pool assessments..		$22,345.32
Beams,	" " ..		29,392.84
Channels,	" " ..		13,002.74
Armor plate pool		100,842.59	
UPPER UNION MILLS.			
Zees,	pool assessment...		5,518.70
Angles,	" " ..		57,755.08
Tees,	" " ..		4,456.32
Beams,	" " ..		351.32
Channels,	" " ..		366.97

—From Profit and Loss account of Carnegie Steel Company for 1899.

---

had orders for 80,000 tons of rails. Without burdening this narrative with further details of costs and prices, it may be briefly stated that in this twelve months the Edgar Thomson works made a profit of $1,625,000. For an infant industry not out of its swaddling-clothes that was a very fair showing; and was certainly as legitimate a cause of exultation on the part of the members of the firm as those more public triumphs in mechanics already spoken of. The highest price of rails reached this year was $85 a ton. Who shall say in presence of these facts that protection is not synonymous with prosperity?

To the Carnegies the tariff was specially helpful at this

time, when an extraordinary demand arose for iron and steel in all its forms. The American manufacturers were unable to meet this demand, and prices rose to a point at which importations of foreign steel could be made despite the high duties. From $19,000,000 in 1879 these importations rose to over $71,000,000 in 1880, $60,500,000 in 1881, and $68,000,000 in 1882. Simultaneously the profits of the Carnegie companies rose from $512,068.46 in 1879 to $2,000,377.42 in 1881, and $2,128,422.91 in 1882; for while the cost of rails was between $34 and $38.50, the average price received during these years was $56.26. It is obvious that but for the tariff these enormous gains would have been impossible; and the magnificent series of blast-furnaces, into the construction of which these profits went, would never have been built. Of course, the railroads of the country paid the difference; but they eventually got it back, and more, out of the enormous tonnage of ore, coke, and lime needed by the furnaces. Here, however, we are trenching upon debatable ground; and that is neither necessary nor desirable in a work of this kind, which aims only to set out the facts and leave the reader free to draw his own conclusions.

During the following years, before Mr. Frick came into supreme power and multiplied the Carnegie profits elevenfold in eleven years, the net earnings of all the properties whose history we are tracing reached the following annual totals. The average price of steel rails for these years is also given.

1883	$1,019,233.04	$37.75
4	1,301,180.28	30.75
5	1,191,993.54	28.50
6	2,925,350.08	34.50
7	3,441,887.29	37.08
8	1,941,555.44	29.83

The causes of this abundant prosperity were not confined to the tariff, however. Some of them have been briefly adverted to in the course of this narrative; others have not been mentioned. A general review of this interesting division of the subject is therefore not out of place at this point in our story.

First and foremost among the causes of the extraordinary success of the Edgar Thomson works is the fact that they were planned and constructed under the immediate direction of the late A. L. Holley. In his day—he died in 1882—Mr. Holley was the most experienced Bessemer steel man on the continent. It was he who negotiated the purchase of the American patents in 1864, and who built the experimental works at Troy. He developed them into a commercial success, and was in charge of their management until 1867. In this year he built the Harrisburg Bessemer plant and superintended it until 1869. Then he rebuilt and enlarged the Troy works, which had been destroyed by fire. He next planned the Bessemer works at Chicago. All this was before the Edgar Thomson works were even thought of; and so completely had he identified himself with the English process of steel-making and the erection of Bessemer converting works, that when the Edgar Thomson scheme was first mooted Mr. Holley was the only man in the country to whom a prudent manufacturer would confide the construction of a new steel plant. There were, moreover, certain inventions and improvements of his without which no converting plant was complete. In a history of the Bessemer Steel Industry in America, Mr. Robert W. Hunt thus speaks of the Edgar Thomson works :

" In arranging these works, Mr. Holley made many improvements over any of his previous efforts, and, assisted as he was (by Mr. P. Barnes, resident engineer, and Mr. W. R. Jones), the works stand to-day as a fit monument of the progress of the Bessemer process in this country." *

---

* It is a little singular in view of these well-known facts that Andrew Carnegie should claim that he " built at Pittsburg a plant for the Bessemer process of steel-making, *which had not until then been operated in this country.*" Mr. Weeks, editor of the *American Manufacturer*, commenting on the completion of the Edgar Thomson works remarked [September 9th, 1875]: " We [in Pittsburg] have been slow to take advantage of the Bessemer process, though one at least of the owners of the Bessemer patents for this country is a prominent steel manufacturer of this city [James Park, Jr.]. This dilatoriness is the more remarkable as there has not been the least doubt as to its success and value both

In the schedule of cost of the Edgar Thomson works is an item, under patent fees, "$5,000 for Holley's Improvements," a sum equal to that paid for the license to use the Bessemer patents. This represents the measure of their value.

The mechanical genius of Captain Jones, however, refused to be bound by precedent, and many innovations were made in the equipment of the Edgar Thomson works by his forceful insistence. An instance is here recalled:

Captain Jones had ordered a certain type of open-topped housing for the rail-mill which had been found unworkable in other plants. "But, Mr. Jones," remonstrated Mr. Holley in

"And why in Hades shouldn't I?"

his gentle way, "how can you justify the putting in of open-topped housings when you know that they tried them at the Lackawanna works and abandoned them?"

"Why," replied Jones in his positive way, "they put them

---

practically and commercially. Indeed it is to this country and to an American, Mr. A. L. Holley, that we are indebted for some of the most valuable inventions connected with the Bessemer plant, inventions that, taken in connection with those of the two Fritzes, have made it possible with an American plant of a given nominal capacity, to turn out two or three times as great a product as with the English. We have so often referred to the incredulous astonishment of the members of the British Iron and Steel Institute when Mr. Holley told them what we were doing in this country, that we need not repeat the statement here.

Notwithstanding this delay in taking up this process, Pittsburg can now congratulate herself that she has as fine a Bessemer plant as the world can boast, not so extensive as some, but as complete and perfect as any and much more so than others."

Plate V.

Captain **WM. R. JONES**
TO WHOSE GENIUS WAS PRINCIPALLY DUE THE FIRST SUCCESS OF THE
EDGAR THOMSON STEEL WORKS

down with three-inch round iron bolts. I'm putting mine in with four-inch square steel bolts."

"I grant you," answered Mr. Holley, "that if you put them in with four-inch square steel bolts you will be able to hold them."

"And why in Hades shouldn't I put 'em in with four-inch steel bolts if that will accomplish what I'm after?"

In this way Jones was constantly making little changes and improvements, too insignificant to patent or even to mention outside of the works; but they did much to ensure the perfect working of the machinery. The writer recalls one such improvement. It was only a couple of pieces of old rail, shaped to throw the half-rolled bloom onto a moving bed as it came through the rolls; but it saved the labor of a dozen men and did the work better.

But greater than all of Jones' inventions was his progressive policy. Familiar with all sorts of machinery, he saw to it that only the best and most modern appliances were installed; and thereafter he was quick to adopt improvements as fast as they were made. The young men whom he trained ably seconded him, as is shown in the remarkable achievements of Julian Kennedy and Gayley at the blast-furnaces, and by Schwab and Scott at Homestead. The famous scrap-heap for outgrown, not outworn, machinery was instituted by Jones, who never hesitated to throw away a tool that had cost half a million if a better one became available. And as his own inventions saved the company a fortune every year, he was given a free hand. Under this greatest of all the captains of the American steel industry a group of younger men grew up, trained in his broad views and habituated to his progressive methods; so that when, in 1889, he was removed from his sphere of activity in a horribly tragic way by the explosion of one of his furnaces, there were men ready trained to take up his work and continue it.*

* The following passages are from a beautiful obituary notice of Captain Jones, written and published by the late Joseph D. Weeks, who was so well qualified to appreciate his genius: "He was a Captain of Industry, unsurpassed

Nor can the important services of Mr. Shinn be overstated. As related in another place in a letter of Andrew Carnegie, his associates used his name as a prayer of thanksgiving every night before going to bed. An example of his contributions to the prosperity of the firm may be added to those given elsewhere in this history.

The moulds into which the molten steel was poured out of the converting-vessels were at first made out of a grade of cast-iron which soon fractured under the extremes of temperature to which they were subjected. The loss from this cause at one time added about sixty cents to the cost of making a ton of steel. In going over his cost sheets one day with Captain Jones, to try to find some detail capable of judicious pruning, Mr. Shinn's attention was arrested by the high cost of ingot-moulds. He thereupon worked out a metal mixture capable of

---

as an organizer, marvellous in his knowledge of detail, fertile in expedients and invention; always planning new victories and winning them. His success is written in the monster establishment at Bessemer, which will remain a monument to his energy, his skill, his achievements.

The position he filled was one that demanded a higher order of executive ability than that required of the President of the United States or any of his cabinet, and this fact was recognized by a salary equal to that of the President. As an executive officer alone he was great; but in addition to this executive ability his position demanded the possession of the inventive faculty in the highest degree, coupled with the power of analysis on the one hand and of generalization on the other that are rarely found combined in any one man. He not only knew what he wanted done but how to do it. Never trammelled by precedent he set all rules at defiance if he could more surely and quickly reach the object sought by so doing.

Many of the inventions of details that have made other inventions successes and have placed Bessemer steel-making where it is to-day are his.

And yet after all we doubt not that the fact that would give him the most sincere gratification is the knowledge that he preserved in such a high degree the respect, the love of the thousands that were under him, and he deserved all the love they bear him and all the respect they pay his memory. No one more honestly and with more singleness of purpose strove in every way to help and benefit those under him than Captain Jones. Himself from the ranks of labor, he never forgot the fact and looked at all questions affecting the relations of employer and employed in the works he managed from the standpoint of both of these relations; and both employer and employed have come to realize that his judgment was in the main wise as they have always believed it was honest."

—*American Manufacturer*, October 4th, 1889.

greater resistance to alternations of heat and cold, and had some moulds cast of this at the foundry of Macintosh & Hemphill. Instead of being destroyed after less than twenty heats, as heretofore, the new moulds withstood the strain of sixty heats or more; and the ingot-mould-cost per ton of steel dropped from sixty to fifteen cents. On a product of 10,000 tons a month, the saving was over $40,000 a year—a sum almost sufficient in itself to determine the financial success or non-success of the works under ordinary conditions of trade. Nor was this all. The new moulds were made of Bessemer iron; and when they broke they were simply passed into the converter and made into steel rails.

This metal mixture was kept a secret for some years, during which the Edgar Thomson Company had an important advantage over competitors. After a time the secret was given to Leander Morris, in whom Andrew Carnegie, his cousin, had an interest of a peculiarly close and confidential nature. This is a story in itself, full of romance and pathos. Mr. Morris was a member of the foundry firm of Morris & Marshall, and for years they had a practical monopoly of the business of casting ingot-moulds.

Another cause of success is to be found in the spirit of competition which animated every man about the place. A keen rivalry had existed from the first among the Bessemer steel men; and this was intensified by the building of the Edgar Thomson works, with all the improvements resulting from Mr. Holley's ten years of experiments. Captain Jones has graphically told the story of this rivalry in the paper already referred to, which was read at the meeting of the British Iron and Steel Institute in May, 1881. He says:

"Now as to the cause of the great output of American steel works.

On the introduction of the Bessemer process in America, quite a number of young men, who believed that the process would revolutionize the metallurgical world, became anxious to identify themselves with its development.   At the Troy works, which may be considered the pioneer Bessemer works of the country, Mr. A. L. Holley was applying his brilliant talents to the perfecting of American plants.   Forsythe, of the North Chicago works, was also assiduously studying the process.   A few years later the Pennsylvania Steel Works, the model of nearly all the subsequent American works, were constructed by Mr. Holley.   Some years later still the Cambria works were built.   At all these works there were ambitious young men closely studying and carefully watching all possible points of development.

From the Cambria graduated Mr. R. W. Hunt, general superintendent of the Albany and Rensselaer works; Jones and Fry, at present connected with the Cambria; Rinard, of the Edgar Thomson; Stanton, of the Vulcan; Williams, of the new Pittsburg Bessemer works; and myself.

Mr. Holley, as editor of Van Nostrand's *Eclectic Magazine*, a few years ago, records as follows : 'We have information from the (Penn.) steel works that on Tuesday of last week they had succeeded in making eight blows or conversions in ten hours.' I quote from memory.

Soon the Cambria Iron Works commenced to creep up to thirty-six heats or about one hundred and sixty tons in twenty-four hours.   After the dispersion at the Cambria works attendant on the death of Mr. George Fritz, one of the ablest of American metallurgists, Mr. Hunt assumed control of the Bessemer department of the Cambria works.   A strong rivalry immediately commenced between these two gentlemen; and great was my astonishment at this time on receiving from Mr. Hunt a telegram stating that 'in the last twenty-four hours we have made fifty heats, or about two hundred and fifty tons.'   This achievement caused great surprise in the Bessemer world.   In the meantime Forsythe, having concluded his studies at Troy, had assumed the reins at North Chicago; and reports soon circulated about what he was doing there.   This only stirred up Messrs. Fry and Hunt and Liebert, of Bethlehem, to greater achievements; and so the product kept on increasing, *while we of the Edgar Thomson were compelled (being engaged in erecting the works) to listen to their wonderful stories.*   In 1875 the Edgar Thomson began operations, followed soon afterwards by the Scranton and Vulcan works, while the Joliet works under an efficient organization had again entered the field.

In the latter year the output of American works began to assume those proportions which have caused so much surprise in England. The output soon reached 1,500 tons of ingots a week, then 1,800 tons, then 2,000 tons, and ultimately increasing to 3,000, 3,100, 3,200, and 3,300.

I am frequently asked by people, 'Where will you Bessemer men stop?' and 'What is the limit of your production?' I can only reply: 'Ask some one who knows more about it than I do.' But I really believe we are on the verge of the elastic limit of production, although it may yet reach a product of 14,500 to 15,000 tons for what I term a 'long month' of twenty-one days per pair of converters. [Julian Kennedy afterwards brought the record to over 19,500 tons.]

The output of American works is governed by the facilities for getting the ingots out of the road. This is the sticking-point just now. [This difficulty was met by casting the ingots on trucks and hauling them away by locomotives.] Therefore the works that cast their tonnage in the least number of moulds have a decided advantage in reaching the ultimate production of the present American or Holley plant. The race, so far as the Edgar Thomson works are concerned, will soon cease. A few months more and the Edgar Thomson will change from a two seven-ton converter plant to a three ten-ton plant, and then our efforts will be concentrated upon keeping pace with the Bethlehem four-vessel plant, and with the North Chicago and Pennsylvania Steel Company's three-vessel plants.*

Next to the strong but pleasant rivalry of the young men who have assumed control of the works, and who have worked hard and faithfully to excel, the development of American practice is due to the *esprit de corps* of the workmen after they get fairly warmed to the work. As long as the record made by the works stands the first, so long are they content to labor at a moderate rate; but let it be known that some rival establishment has beaten that record, and then there is no content until the rival's record is eclipsed.

Another marked advantage which the American works have is the diversity of nationality of the workmen. We have

---

* One day in November, 1891, the mill started out to beat the best day's record of the South Chicago mill of the Illinois Steel Company, which was 1,700 tons. The attempt was a remarkable success, as the following figures show:

Rails made in twenty-four hours................ 1,924 tons.
Ingots, same time .... 2,074 "
Best twelve hours (night turn) rails........... 981 "
"   "   "   "   " ingots............ 1,087 "
Best run two hours .... 201 "

representatives from England, Ireland, Scotland, Wales, and all parts of Germany, Swedes, Hungarians, and a few French and Italians, with a small percentage of colored workmen. This mixture of races and languages seems to give the best results, and is, I think, far better than a preponderance of one nationality.

In increasing the output of these works, I soon discovered it was entirely out of the question to expect human flesh and blood to labor incessantly for twelve hours, and therefore it was decided to put on three turns, reducing the hours of labor to eight. This proved to be of immense advantage to both the company and the workmen, the latter now earning more in eight hours than they formerly did in twelve hours, while the men can work harder constantly for eight hours, having sixteen hours for rest.

Another important matter connected with fast working is the maintenance of the machinery. As fast as the weak parts in the machinery are developed they are strengthened. In all new machinery the aim is to get an excess of strength; the usual factor of safety in new rolling machinery is not allowable. The machinery must be made extra heavy and strong, so that the inertia of the mass will swallow all strains thrown upon it." *

Following in importance the protective tariff, the mechanical excellence of the works, the inventive skill of its managers, and the rivalry of competing plants, as factors in the extraordinary success of the Edgar Thomson Steel Company, come certain personal influences. These were subtle and vague, and not easily traceable except in results which were rarely visible to outsiders. As a consequence, biographers and historians have been led into all sorts of fanciful conceits concerning the relative importance of some of the individuals connected with the concern.

One closely associated with the group, being asked to define the functions of the various partners in the Edgar Thomson Company, recently made the following trite comparison : " Shinn bossed the show; McCandless lent it dignity and standing;

---

* Which recalls Captain Jones' remark to Holley on the advantage of heavy steel bolts to hold the housings of the rail-mill.

Phipps took in the pennies at the gate and kept the pay-roll down; Tom Carnegie kept everybody in a good humor, with Dave Stewart as his understudy." "And Andrew Carnegie?" he was asked. "Oh, Andy looked after the advertising and drove the band wagon!" was the ready reply.

With due allowance for its humorous exaggeration, this blunt comparison fairly represents the facts. The high commercial and social standing of Mr. McCandless not only gave dignity to the enterprise, but won financial support for it in its days of need. Without him, the company would hardly have tided over the troublous times of 1873 and the lean years following the panic. The special capacity of Mr. Phipps has been abundantly illustrated in connection with preceding enterprises. Mr. T. M. Carnegie's abilities were too numerous and complex to be summed up in a sentence. He was a man of sterling integrity; and it was a common saying in Pittsburg that his

"Andy drove the band wagon."

word was better than some men's bond. He had remarkable judgment; and his opinion on commercial questions was valued above that of much older and more experienced men. Quick and keen in his perceptions, cautious but progressive in his ideas, faithful to his engagements, and just in all his dealings, he gave to his company that which corporations are habitually lacking, namely, a conscience. His death in 1886, at the early age of forty-three, was a loss not only to his associates, but to the whole business world of Pittsburg. To this day all who knew him, great and small, rich and poor, workman and master, revere his memory and regret his loss. Mr. Stewart never sought prominence, and was content to the day of his death, in 1889, to merge his own personality in the organization he worked for.   Devoted to Tom Carnegie, he allowed no personal injury to affect his loyalty to his friend; and more than once he stoically accepted the rough rebukes of the elder Carnegie because Tom wished for peace.   Once, indeed, exasperated at the gibes given at his own table, he rose in anger, saying that the bounds of all reason had been reached and the laws of hospitality outraged; but the apology which Tom arranged was at once accepted and peace was restored.

"An unconscious hostess."

The part at first selected by Andrew Carnegie for himself was the development of outside trade and the procurement of orders.   Here he displayed an originality so marked that it amounted to genius.   Endowed with a ready wit, an excellent memory for stories, and a natural gift for reciting them, he became a social favorite in New York and Washington, and never missed a chance to make a useful acquaintance.   His mental alertness, ready speech, and enthusiastic temperament made him a delightful addition to a dinner party; and many an unconscious hostess, opening her doors to the little Scotchman from Pittsburg, has also paved the way to a sale of railroad material. Carnegie early found that his power to promote sales grew in proportion to his own importance.   His natural love of prominence was thus fortified by its commercial value; and he lost no opportunity of adding to his interest in the firm.   As a result he was soon regarded as the sole founder and builder of the enterprise which bore his name, and his partners, if thought of at all, were ranked with the other machinery of the works.

At first Andrew Carnegie's attention was principally occupied in schemes of his own—construction companies for new railroads and bridges, and the marketing of bonds. But as the iron businesses in which he was financially interested grew in importance, he gave them more of his time and attention. Relieved of the routine of detail and the never-ending cares of management which were his partners' daily lot, he had a mind free to range over the industrial field, picking up scraps of information concerning the requirements of railroads, and bringing news of many a large contract. Supplied with daily reports of the product of every department of each of the works, he had leisure to make comparisons, and to prod with a sarcastic note any partner or superintendent whose work did not rank with the best. In time he became very expert at these postal proddings; and with half-a-dozen scathing words scribbled on the back of his address card, he could spur the best of his managers to still more heroic achievements. Captain Jones, who was too high-spirited a war-horse to brook such spurrings, sent in his resignation with almost rhythmical periodicity, and was then tempted back into harness by a handsome gift and still handsomer apology. As he put his head into the halter again, he would fling a gibe at the other managers who took their rowellings more tamely. "Puppy dog number three," he would say in sarcastic parody of the scribblings from New York, "you have been beaten by puppy dog number two on fuel. Puppy dog number two, you are higher on labor than puppy dog number one." And so on. This was the lighter side of the system of unfriendly competition which Andrew Carnegie originated and fostered. Some of these managers and partners did not speak to each other for years, so skilfully were their jealousies and rivalries played upon; and there was hardly a man at the head of

8

any department of the Carnegie concerns whose flanks were not ripped open in the fierce race for supremacy.   Some, like Coleman, Shinn, Scott, Griffin, Kennedy, Abbot, and Walker, revolted and flung back the taunts with interest.   Others let their anger be transmuted into fresh energy and a determination to win.   These are the ones who remained and became "young geniuses."

"You cannot imagine the abounding sense of freedom and relief I experience as soon as I get on board a steamer and sail past Sandy Hook," once said Andrew Carnegie to Captain

> " Carnegie did not roost in the tree. . . . He would sit afar off, on the rail-fence, apparently idly watching the spaders and waterers and trimmers and caterpillar-killers, all desperately at work, with the sweat streaming. Presently he would descend from his rail-perch, catch up a great club and lay frantically about him. Bruised skulls here; broken skulls there; corpses yonder; fellows with raw heads and aching bones, crawling rapidly into the cover of the tall grass; imprecations filling the air. A scene of peaceful industry transformed into a shambles. Grinning grimly at his club, Carnegie would stroll back to his rail-perch, usually Skibo."—"*The Men who Made the Steel Trust*," by *David Graham Phillips.*

Jones.   "My God, think of the relief to us!" exclaimed Jones with his usual bluntness.   The retort was not all in jest.

In his social campaign Andrew Carnegie did not neglect the quest for political influence.   The Government brooded lovingly over the industries which paid their owners fifty to a hundred per cent. per annum; and there is a law of political equivalents which Mr. Carnegie never ignored.   The leaders of both parties became his intimate friends; and liberal subscriptions to their respective campaign funds justified his reliance on their favor.   "How would you like to invest $10,000 in the senatorial fight in ——?" wrote James G. Blaine in 1886.   As the

Keystone Bridge Company had an uncollectable account of some $200,000 against one of the junior American republics for a steel building at the New Orleans Exposition, Mr. Carnegie was glad to make the investment; and the friendly offices of the State Department secured an early settlement of the claim. No one had more faith than Carnegie in the helpful effect of a congratulatory telegram to a president-elect or a new senator; nor did ever a Scotchman better gauge the trade possibilities of a dinner at which Western congressmen might meet the great ones of earth in literature and philosophy. Never was

> "My partners are not only partners, but a band of devoted friends, who never have a difference. I have never had to exercise my power, and of this I am very proud."
>
> "I never enjoyed anything more than to get a sound thrashing in an argument at the hands of these young geniuses."
>
> "When I could not bring my associates in business to my views by reason I have never wished to do so by force. As for instructing or compelling them under the law to do one thing or another, that is simply absurd. I could not if I would, and I would not if I could."—*Andrew Carnegie.*

band wagon driven with such skill. The box of Carnegie's chariot became the "seats of the mighty." Herbert Spencer's acquaintance was made on board a transatlantic liner, as was that of sundry British peers; and the visits of these personages to the Pittsburg works were reported in a thousand newspapers from Maine to California and from Land's End to John O'Groats.

And so a politico-social campaign went on hand in hand with the rail, bridge, armor-plate, and structural-steel business, through seasons of opera, concerts, lecturings, and book-publishings, until the name Carnegie was written in bright letters

across the sky of two hemispheres, and people forgot that there
were any other steel works in the world.

Meanwhile in Pittsburg the partners worked steadily on,
building dollar by dollar the great golden pyramid by which
their majority stockholder was to be immortalized.

Steel works by night.

CHAPTER VIII

QUARRELS AND EJECTURES

DESPITE this great and uninterrupted good fortune, the internal discord in which all the Carnegie enterprises were born and brought up continued without abatement, and wrought many changes in the personnel of the organization. Ranking with other evolutionary factors in the development of the business, and more influential than any in stamping it with the Carnegie personality, these disagreements are deserving of a more than passing reference.

At the organization of the steel company, Andrew Carnegie's interest was one-third of the whole; but it appears from a printed statement of Mr. Shinn that he early developed "a sentimental desire to have an even half." This he got, and more, as one by one the founders of the organization dropped away from it.

The first to go was Mr. Coleman; and his interest was bought by Mr. Carnegie "after a bitter quarrel between them," to quote from a letter addressed to the author by one of the old members of the corporation. Before its purchase, however, Andrew Carnegie repeatedly speaks of this Coleman interest as a desirable acquisition. In the letter of April 13th, 1876, now before me, immediately following the exclamation quoted, "Where is there such a business!" he goes on to say:

"I want to buy Mr. Coleman out & hope to do so. —Kloman will have to give up his interest. These divided between Tom, Harry You and I would make the Concern a close Corporation Mr. Scott's loan is no doubt in some Bankers hands & may also

be dealt with after a little   then we are right & have only
to watch the Bond conversions."

I note Pig at 25⁵⁰ 4 Mos. — equal 25 Cash
What do you really figure we can put rail
at Cost — running double. How Ems per Mo
on this bans — Cant we shade 50¢ ? If so
where is there such a bus'ness —
I want to buy Mr Coleman out & hope to do so.
— Kloman will have to fine up his interest
there divided between Tom, Harry, Jim & I
would make the Concern a close Corporation
Mr Scott's loan is no doubt in some Bankers
hands & may also be dealt with after a little
then we are right & have only to watch the
Bond conversions which will not be
great as our foreign friends will want &
stick to the same thing I think

Photographic reproduction of a letter written by Andrew Carnegie on April 13th,
1876, in which he outlines plans for the purchase of partners' interests.

In a letter written a little earlier he mentions the easy terms
on which he hoped to acquire the Coleman interest:

"Yesterday in talking with Mr Coleman . . . I said I
would be willing to take his 100.000$ stock 5 years at Par 6%
int pr ann payable semi annually principal payable after 5
years in 1 2 & 3 years say— He wanted much better bargain
but I would do no better finally he said to write Tom what I
offered & he would talk over it I suppose it will be arranged."

And so it was. At the same time disagreements arose
among the other members of the firm, growing out of the price

to be paid the Lucy Furnace Company for pig-iron; and Messrs. T. M. Carnegie and Phipps sold half of their stock in the Edgar Thomson to Andrew Carnegie, refusing to engage in the erection of a second Lucy stack unless he bought it. The dispute concerning pig-iron was finally settled by a sliding scale following the prices of rails; but before long fresh troubles arose through the inferior quality of the Lucy product. On April 27th, 1877, Mr. Shinn, general manager, in a letter marked " private and confidential," wrote to Andrew Carnegie as follows :

" Another matter comes up in this connection for most serious consideration. It is this. If the L. F. Co. is to furnish us the most, or all of, our metal, it is of the utmost consequence that we should have the fullest confidence in each other, and that we could feel assured at all times, that no material would be used to cheapen the metal, that would or could injure our product. That the cinder used last year did this I am very well satisfied; and when Mr. Phipps assured me in January last that no cinder was being used, and that no change would be made without consulting or advising us, I felt easy; but we have had some 'split ends' among our Lake Shore rails and now comes the (to me) painful rumor that cinder is being used. You are most interested in our getting and keeping a reputation for making *the best rails in America,* and to do that we must use the *best material.* My reputation, as well as my capital, is involved in the matter, and if I am to make it my life occupation, and cut loose from all RR. associations, it can only be, as you can readily see, upon a basis of full confidence between us, and between us all as associates, in all our relations."

The difficulties thus arising, joined no doubt to the ever-increasing output of the steel works, developed in the partners of the Edgar Thomson Company not interested in the Lucy furnaces a determination to make their own pig-iron. And thus it came about that the Edgar Thomson people erected their own blast-furnaces and inaugurated a new era in iron-making. But the cabal resulting from these disagreements precipitated the " ejecture " of those who were most strenuous in their opposition to the Lucy Company having any undue advantage through their connections with the Edgar Thomson.

The next one to go out was Andrew Kloman, under circum-stances already related. He had an interest of $50,000 in the Edgar Thomson, which Andrew Carnegie acquired.

Then came the little fellows who held the convertible bonds and wanted stock for them. To these Andrew Carnegie was frank enough to say that they were not wanted and that their most profitable course would be to quietly take back their money and get out. The privilege of conversion was highly valued when these bonds were sold, because it gave their holders a speculative chance of becoming permanently interested in the concern if it proved successful, and if not they still held a lien on a property that had cost three times the sum of their mort-gage. But the privilege was disputed; and in most cases the bondholders chose to accept their money rather than go into litigation with the now powerful corporation. Young Gardiner M. McCandless, however, insisted on his rights. He was reluc-tantly admitted to the firm, and became Carnegie's secretary.

Colonel Scott and Andrew Carnegie had a timely quarrel, and the former took back his money, declaring that nothing would induce him to become permanently interested in the Edgar Thomson. As for Mr. J. Edgar Thomson, he died be-fore the bonds matured, and his executors also waived their rights and accepted cash in discharge of the obligation.

The other partners included in the scheme of elimination were under a surveillance which they little suspected. Some of them had engaged in a disastrous stock speculation, which Andrew Carnegie, referring to Mr. McCandless' share in it, characterized in one of his letters as "miserable conduct," and hinted at certain changes he had long had in mind. But before this he wrote to Mr. Shinn (May 1st, 1877):

"There are possible Combinations in the future
It is n't likely McCandless Scott & Stewart will remain with us. I scarcely think they can—I know Harry & Tom have agreed with me that you out of the entire lot would be wanted as a future partner & I think we will one day make it a

partnership Lucy F Co U Mills, E T &c & go it on that basis
the largest and strongest Concern in the Country."

Mr. McCandless, however, was eliminated by the kindly
hand of death; and Andrew Carnegie's grief was intense and
profound.   Writing from Bombay on February 22d, 1879, where
he heard the sad news, he says:

" It does seem too hard to bear, but we must bite the lip &
go forward I suppose assuming indifference—but I am sure none

DAVID McCANDLESS,
First Chairman of the Edgar Thomson Steel Company.

of us can ever efface from our memories the image of our dear,
generous, gentle & unselfish friend—   To the day I die I know
I shall never be able to think of him without a stinging pain at
the heart— His death robs my life of one of its chief pleasures,
but it must be borne, only let us take from his loss one lesson
as the best tribute to his memory.   let us try to be as kind and

devoted to each other as he was to us.   He was a model for all
of us to follow   One thing more we can do—attend to his
affairs & get them right that Mrs. McCandless & Helen may be
provided for—I know you will all be looking after this & you
know how anxious I shall be to cooperate with you."

The partners accordingly carried Mr. McCandless' interest
undisturbed until Mr. Carnegie's return the following summer.
The great profits made during this period have been adverted to,
as well as Carnegie's joy on Mount Etna or some such elevation.
Despite this, he insisted on the purchase of Mr. McCandless'
interest at the book value shown by the appraisement made before Mr. McCandless' death.   The member of the old corporation previously quoted writes me:

"But this decision was not made until late in July following, after Mr. Andrew Carnegie's return from his trip around
the world, when large profits had been made and still larger
were shown by the orders entered on the books for delivery during the following nine months. . . . Legally the company acted
fairly."

No share of these profits was included in the price paid to
Mrs. McCandless, and she only received some $90,000 for her
husband's interest.   It had cost $65,000 in cash.

Mr. Shinn was the next to go out of the concern; and the
story of his leave-taking found its way into the courts.   When
Mr. McCandless died, Mr. Shinn expected to be made chairman
in his place.   He was the largest stockholder after the elder
Carnegie; and as he had done much to make the business a success, he felt that his services and interest entitled him to the
most honorable position in the company.   But Carnegie, who
controlled the board, had left orders before leaving on his trip,
that in the event of a vacancy in the chair his brother was to
be elected to fill it.   This was accordingly done, Shinn protesting by letter to Carnegie in Egypt, and plainly setting forth his
claims and disappointment.   Carnegie replied, urging Shinn to
"let the matter rest until my return, & we will meet as friends

desirous of pleasing each other, & I am sure our happy family will remain one."

Shinn's claim was a reasonable one, judged in the light of the letters he had received from Carnegie.

" Remember I can see no fault with your management as it is," Carnegie wrote him in August, 1876.

" On the contrary I assure you there are few nights in which before sleeping I dont congratulate myself at our good fortune in having you there—Tom and Harry ditto—but we dont think we can have too much of 'so good a thing' & want somehow or other to get you root & branch."

Photographic reproduction of part of a letter from Andrew Carnegie to William P. Shinn.

Again:

" I like the tone of your personal letter. Much— Have always known you would find it necessary—if E. T. proved what

we expected—to give it all your time and thought—   It is a
Grand Concern & sure to make us all a fortune.—   With you at
the helm, & my pulling an oar outside, we are bound to put it
at the head of rail making concerns—

My preference would be for you to double your interest &
manage it to the exclusion of everything else—we to carry the
second 50.000$ until you could pay it & allow you to draw on a/c
profits any sum required for expenses.   but this shall be as you
prefer.—We shall not quarrel about Your Compensation "—*

Accordingly Shinn had resigned his position on the railroads, had bought a part of the Coleman interest, and was now
giving his whole time to the management of the Edgar Thomson works.

On the elder Carnegie's return, however, the chairmanship
was permanently vested in his brother Tom.

Meanwhile other matters of dispute had arisen between
Shinn and his colleagues which had become the subject of outside gossip and comment; so that the slight was doubly felt by
him, and he sent in his resignation.   In his letter of withdrawal
from the management of the company, dated September 13th,
1879, he says:

" I have full confidence in the pecuniary success of the E. T.
S. Co. Limited and purpose to remain your business associate;
and it will be my desire, as it will be my interest, to advance
its success by any and all means in my power."

This, however, did not accord with Carnegie's plans, nor
with the policy, now first inaugurated, that no officer of the
company should retain his interest after he had resigned his
office; and a committee was appointed by the Board of Managers
to confer with Mr. Shinn about the purchase of his interest.
This committee consisted of John Scott and Andrew Carnegie.
The former has reduced his statement of the transaction to
writing.   It is as follows:

---

* In this and other Carnegie letters the spelling and punctuation of the
originals are preserved.

Plate VI.

WILLIAM P. SHINN
FIRST MANAGER OF THE EDGAR THOMSON STEEL WORKS

"In the month of September 1879, the latter part of the month, the E. T. Board met and accepted the resignation of Mr. Shinn. At the meeting the board appointed Mr. Carnegie and myself to confer with Mr. Shinn about the purchase of his interest in the Company. After the board adjourned Messrs. Carnegie, Shinn and myself remained, the others having retired. Mr. Shinn then proposed to sell his whole interest for a certain sum, the amount I have forgotten. Mr. Carnegie refused to recognize that the stock in dispute had any value to him. Mr. Carnegie offered Mr. Shinn on behalf of the E. T. Co. one hundred and five thousand dollars for his interest standing in his name on the books of the Company, which offer Mr. Shinn declined. Some time during the interview Mr. Carnegie made the remark that he would rather have given one hundred thousand dollars than have Mr. Shinn leave.

The next day when the board were about ready to meet, knowing Mr. Shinn was at the office of F. Wayne Co. I went up to see Mr. Shinn and urged him to accept the offer of $105,-000 which had been made him the day previous by Mr. Carnegie. At my earnest solicitation Mr. Shinn finally gave his consent to accept the offer. Mr. Shinn shortly after came down to the Edgar Thomson office and asked Mr. Carnegie and myself to come out into the hall. Mr. Shinn then stated to Mr. Carnegie and myself, that he was willing to accept the offer of $105,000 whenever they could agree on a satisfactory agreement to refer the question of the stock in dispute to arbitrate. This being reported to the board, they authorized the officers to close the purchase. The board did not make the condition for the agreement to arbitrate, that having been done by Mr. Shinn."

The agreement to arbitrate here referred to concerned the right and title of Mr. Shinn to the stock which Andrew Carnegie had sold him out of that which he had bought from Messrs. Coleman, Phipps, and T. M. Carnegie. It was a full share of $50,000. Mr. Carnegie denied Shinn's right to this stock and the premium to which it had advanced, on the ground that part of the consideration Shinn had agreed to pay for it was that he would remain general manager of the works as long as Mr. Carnegie wanted him. Shinn indignantly repudiated such an understanding, which he characterized as "slavery;" and the matter was submitted by agreement to the arbitrament of Messrs.

B. F. Jones, John W. Chalfant, and William Thaw, prominent business men of Pittsburg.

The documents in the case assumed voluminous proportions, as the disputants brought charge and countercharge against each other; and some of them became almost virulent in character. Andrew Carnegie injected into his statement of the case charges against Shinn and his friends amounting to conspiracy to defraud; but unfortunately he entered into irrelevant details and tripped up on his facts. The most singular of the lapses of memory by which his case was injured was contained in the following statement to the arbitrators:

"When in India I was rendered anxious by receiving a telegram from him [Shinn] asking me to get an important letter at Aden, and reply by telegraph. You can imagine what thoughts arose. The most probable emergency that suggested itself to my mind was that some important financial question had arisen, and that it was necessary parties should receive my personal guarantee in some way, and at once. It was several weeks before I could obtain the expected letter, and judge my surprise, nay rather indignation, when the document proved to be five closely written pages in Mr. Shinn's own handwriting, setting forth his personal disappointment and dissatisfaction at the board of managers not having seen fit to promote him to the chairmanship, in place of our late lamented friend Mr. McCandless, I was requested to telegraph a reply, instructing the board to undo its action. Instead of this, I wrote an indignant answer, but as there were many days before the mail left, I had time to reflect, and finally destroyed the letter, and sent instead a short note asking him to await my return."

Shinn's answer, for a few pages, was a clever piece of judicial reasoning; but having been accused in no equivocal terms of dishonorable and contemptible practices, he later allowed himself the free use of his somewhat caustic pen, and marred his otherwise able presentation of the case by charging his opponent with "wilful and malicious mendacity."

"In regard to his [A. C.'s] statements," he says, "it may well be said as has been said of a much more prominent person,

'Where most people remember, his lordship fancies, and in his case what is most convenient naturally offers itself. This has very much increased his brilliancy, for the process leaves its practicer utterly unhampered. But nobody should ask for both strict accuracy and Lord B.'s quick free wit. It is demanding an unreasonable combination.' So much on the 'go-as-you-please' style is Mr. Carnegie's historical account of our transactions, that the above quotation is unavoidably suggested. . . .

Mr. Carnegie refers to a telegram which he received in India, asking him to get an important letter at Aden, and reply by telegraph, and tells you of his emotions when he received it.

I sent no such telegram to Mr. Carnegie while he was in India, nor indeed was any such telegram sent him at any time. The letter he refers to was written to him Feb. 22nd, 1879, addressed to him at Aden, which was the address he gave for letters to be sent at that date. The author of 'Around the World' says : 'Bombay, Monday, Feb. 24th, We sailed at six in the evening by the splendid P. and O. steamer, Pekin,' that being the date he left India. On March 12th we received a telegram from him dated Cairo, Egypt, and on that date I telegraphed him as follows :—

Carnegie, Cairo. Bison, Cling, Black, Cloak, Angel, Feb. 22nd, Aden, Bacon, telegraph and mail. Shinn.

The first four words related to our profits in Jan. and Feb., the balance is translated thus : Angel. Have you received our letter of Feb. 22nd, Aden? Bacon. Where shall we address you, telegraph and mail?

Not one word, as you will see, about answering by telegraph, or about letter being important, and sent sixteen days after he left India.

But you would expect a matter which caused him so much anxiety as he alleges to be mentioned in his letters, and what does he say?

In his letter dated Bombay, Feb. 22nd, he does not mention it, for the good reason that he knew nothing of it. In his letter dated Sorrento, March 23rd, the first received after he got the telegram, he writes,

'I expected your Aden letter to-day, but next mail will undoubtedly bring it, reaching me at Naples, Wednesday evening on our arrival.'

In his next, dated Rome, March 29th, he says :—

'Yours from Aden not yet received although I ordered it here. May come Tuesday, when I will telegraph.'

You find no trace of anxiety or other deep emotion in these letters. . . .

To complete the record I inclose my pressed copy of the Aden letter which instead of 'five closely written pages,' consists of *two* closely written and *one-half* page, not very close. In it you will look in vain for any request to telegraph a reply. In fact the whole of these emotions over the Aden letter seem to be a case of 'reflex action' excited by the claim in controversy.

You will note in his reply to the Aden letter that he says: 'Let the matter rest until my return and we will meet as friends desirous of pleasing each other, and I am sure our happy family will remain one.' This was his 'indignation' referred to.

He has told you how we 'met as friends' in the first conversation we had on the subject, when he says: 'And upon my return and before any question of this claim arose, I told him I had twice already bought his life work,' etc.; he also insulted me still further by telling me, in reference to the increase of salary voted me unanimously by the Board, 'You might as well have put your hand in my pocket and taken out $750' (his half of it).

On the same day he told another person who subsequently informed me that he 'hoped most sincerely he (I) would resign his (my) connection with the E. T. Steel Co., Limited, as he was determined to get rid of him' (me), and later on, in the same conversation, he said I had better resign now, as he would make it *so warm for me* that he would have my resignation before Christmas. (Sworn evidence of this statement can be had if desired by the arbitrators.)

Without further conversation with, or notice to me, at a meeting of the Board of Managers held late in July, at which he had no official standing or right (not being a member), he insultingly demanded my resignation as Treasurer, under the false pretence that I had myself suggested it in my Aden letter, which pretence he repeats in his statement to you. . . .

He thus took from me, as by violence, the responsible and honorable office of Treasurer, which I had held since the formation of the company and now comes before you asking 'equity,' alleging that I left the company without his consent.

I myself saw a letter in his handwriting, in which he said, referring to me by name:—'Thank God his name is off our paper,' and 'Mr. Shinn is on trial,' etc.

Under these circumstances you will not wonder that I left

Mr. Carnegie's company, and I do not therefore feel called upon to reply to his history of my departure."

To all this Carnegie retorted in kind, becoming if possible more offensive than before in his charges of conspiracy.

"In a very short time," he says, "the Edgar Thomson Company would have been fleeced upon most of its supplies. With the railway manager bribed and the purchaser of our supplies interested, the combination seemed complete, and does credit to the genius of our late general manager."

This ended for the time being the effort at a "peaceful" settlement, for Shinn angrily revoked his agreement to arbitrate and withdrew all the papers. On the same day he tendered the purchase-money of the stock in dispute, and brought suit in the Allegheny County Court. Carnegie then petitioned for removal of the case to the United States Circuit Court, which was granted; and Shinn in his turn secured an order of court for the production of the Edgar Thomson books. For obvious reasons this was a measure distasteful in the highest degree to the Carnegies; and when the case was called for trial on June 16th, 1881, an adjournment was asked for an hour. The lawyers then got together in an adjoining room and patched up another agreement to arbitrate. The case was thereupon submitted to the same arbitrators as before on the old pleadings, subject, however, to a re-statement of Shinn's claim on the question of value, and leaving that question wholly to the arbitrators free from the restrictions of the original submission, which limited the premium to fifty per cent. This was an important gain for Shinn, since it left to arbitration the question of Shinn's right to participate in the enormous increase in value which the stock had undergone during the previous two years.

The exact terms of the award were long kept secret; but it is betraying no confidence to state now that Shinn won on the main issue and received his full claim with a substantial premium representing the increased value of his stock. It was just under $200,000. But he lost his contention that he could re-

9

main a member of the corporation after he had accepted service with a competing concern.

The pleadings and answers in the civil suit were withdrawn from the court files, so that to-day there is nothing in the official archives but the most meagre record of the case.

The next "ejecture" was that of John Scott, in 1882. Like so many others before and since, it was the outgrowth of personal difficulties with Andrew Carnegie. Mr. Scott obtained, however, a very high premium for the $50,000 which he had originally invested in the company; as did also Gardiner McCandless, who was induced to sell out the same year. Mr. McCandless received $183,000 for his original investment of something like $42,000 in the convertible bonds.

Thus did events justify the amazing foresight displayed by Andrew Carnegie when, only eight months after the opening of the Edgar Thomson works, he outlined, in his letter of April 13th, 1876, the principal changes in the personnel of the organization which have just been described. It is an astonishing, almost an uncanny, exhibition of that clairvoyant faculty for which he has always been noted. In one aspect, too, it illustrates the practical working of the Carnegie motto: "Concentration! First honesty, then industry, then concentration."

A further change was hinted at in Carnegie's letters for which the way was thus being gradually prepared. This was the combination of the Union Iron Mills, the Lucy Furnaces, and the Edgar Thomson Steel Works.

The causes which brought about this consolidation are not very complex. On the one hand was the elder Carnegie's ambition to make the works, which were now to bear his name, as impressive as possible. On the other hand, was the wish of his brother and Mr. Phipps to have a larger share in such a good thing as the Edgar Thomson Company. Forty odd per cent. in dividends is very attractive; and no doubt both Mr. Phipps and young Carnegie were by this time thoroughly sorry that they had sacrificed any part of their shares in the Edgar Thomson Company. Accordingly a scheme of consolidation was made, and the manner in which it was carried out is told, with much interesting detail, in the following letters :

PITTSBURGH, PA., Mch. 31st. 1881.

Wm. P. Shinn, Esq., Pittsburgh, Pa.

DEAR SIR : In 1879, the subject was broached, I do not remember by whom, to consolidate the Lucy Furnace Co. and the Union Iron Mills with The Edgar Thomson Steel Co. Limited.

We had so many disagreements and much trouble in fixing the price of pig-iron furnished by the Lucy Furnace Co. that I at once concluded that it was a good thing to do, and expressed myself in favor of the scheme provided it could be carried out on a fair basis. I was governed entirely to vote on your recommendation that the proposition of 55 for the E. T. S. Co. Limd. and 45 for the other property.

Now that I have become familiar with the subject, and our experience of working the past year under the consolidation, I do not think the property put in should have [been] taken at over 30%.

Having had the utmost confidence in your judgment, in such matters, I have a curiosity in learning what governed you in giving the advice you did, and thought it due you to give you an opportunity to explain how you made such a mistake.

Yours truly

JOHN SCOTT.

PITTSBURGH, April 4th. 1881

John Scott Esq. Pittsburgh, Pa.

DR. SIR : I have your letter of March 31st, in which you refer to the basis of consolidation of interests of the Edgar Thomson Steel Co. Limited with the Lucy Furnace Co., Carnegie Brothers & Co and Carnegie & Co. on the basis of 55 per cent to the former and 45 per cent to the latter, and ask how I came to recommend what you characterize as "such a mistake."

In reply, I will state the circumstances under which the proposed consolidation was first discussed, and what led me to assent to the basis named.

In August 1879 I was invited to Mr. T. M. Carnegie's one evening, where I found Messrs. A. Carnegie, T. M. Carnegie and H. Phipps.

The subject of the consolidation was broached, and they

produced statements of cost and earnings of their properties as
follows:

	Cost to July 1st.	Earnings, 1878.	Six mos. 1879.
Union Iron Mills........	$813,000.00	153,000.00	98,000.00
Lucy Furnaces	662,000.00	120,000.00	70,000.00
Coke Works, 4/5ths......	100,000.00	20,000.00	16,000.00
Total.............	1,575,000.00	293,000.00	184,000.00

The cost of E. T. works, exclusive of the amount expended
on furnaces and the earnings for the same period had been as
follows:

Cost of E. T. works July 1, '79.........................$1,522,159.16
Profits, 1878.............................$401,800
"   6 mo. 1879...................... . 252,845
                                                   654,645.00

The costs and earnings of the two properties compared then
as follows:

	Cost.	Earnings 18 mo.
E. T. S. Works........................	$1,522,000	654,645
Carnegies' Works......................	1,575,000	477,000

But the E. T. S. Co. had furnaces A and B well under way, and
expected to complete them by Jan. 1st, 1880; and I claimed
there should be added to the cost and earnings of E. T. S. Co.
an amount equal to four-fifths the cost and earnings of Lucy
Furnaces, or to cost say $528,000
and to earnings   200,000

This made them compare as follows:

	Cost.	Earnings 18 mo.
E. T. S. Works......................	$2,050,000	$854,645
Carnegies' Works	1,575,000	477,000

the proportions of which were relatively

	Cost.	Earnings 18 mos.
E. T. S. Works of cost	$56\frac{5}{10}$	of earnings 64 per cent.
Carnegies' Works " "	$43\frac{5}{10}$	" " 36 " "

the average of which gave

E. T. S. Works....................... 60
Carnegies'............................ 40

and I therefore proposed to accept 60 per cent for E. T. S.
works.

T. M. Carnegie demurred to this, alleging that the E. T. S.
Works had been unusually profitable in past 18 months, while

Plate VII.

ANDREW CARNEGIE
IN 1884

the furnace property had been very unusually depressed, pig-iron having sold at very low prices; and he insisted on 50 per cent for the Carnegie Works.

A. Carnegie then pointed out that the E. T. S. Works had a debt of $186,000 on its land, which would have to be assumed by the joint interest, which if deducted would allow only $1,864,-000 as cost of E. T. S. Works, or 54 per cent of the whole.

Upon these considerations, and for the reason named by you, viz. to destroy the unceasing strife and bad feeling in the fixing of prices for metal bought of Lucy Furnace Co. in which I had been annoyed almost beyond endurance, I suggested 55 per cent as a compromise which was agreed to.

It was not mentioned, nor was I aware, that the land on which the Lucy Furnaces and Union Iron Mills were built was not owned by them; and when Mr. Carnegie urged the mortgage on the E. T. S. property in reduction of its value, he knew that a similar and much more important incumbrance was on the Union Iron Mills property, which I now understand was only leased, at a rental of $4,855 annually and liable to be greatly increased when present leases expire.

This is equal to a mortgage of	$ 80,900
Mortgage on Lucy Furnace property	160,000
Making a total incumbrance of .	$240,900

of which no mention was made at the time, of which I had not the slightest knowledge or suspicion, and which good faith required should have been set forth.

Had I known of these incumbrances I never would have agreed to consolidating on the basis of 55 and 45 per cent, nor would I have agreed to it at all, except to harmonize our interests on the point which had caused so much difficulty and hard feeling.

I see that in the new firm of C. B. & Co. Limd. they put in the respective properties

E. T. S. property	$2,500,000	62½ per ct.
Carnegies' "	1,500,000	37½ " "
	4,000,000	

which is much nearer what the real proportionate value was a year ago. Yours truly

Wm. P. Shinn

The following interesting data appeared in a foot-note to Mr. Shinn's letter :

```
1880
Profits—E. T. S. Works.....................................$1,625,000.00
        Lucy........................$294,524.97
        Coke ........................  96,295.97
        Union Mills.................  55,836.71
                                     ───────────
                                                   446,657.65
                                                 ─────────────
                                                 2,071,657.65
Chgd. Impts.                                     ─────────────
Lucy Fur. Co ........................ 131,259.57
Union Mills..........................  55,200.62
                                     ───────────
                                                   186,460.19
                                                 ─────────────
    Leaves actual profits.. ............          260,197.46
```

The new firm referred to by Mr. Shinn was Carnegie Brothers & Co., Limited, which was organized on April 1st, 1881, with a capital of $5,000,000.   Of this, $4,000,000 was represented by the Union Iron Mills, the Lucy Furnaces, certain unimportant coke interests of Andrew Carnegie, and the Edgar Thomson works.   The rest was to be paid in cash.   In this consolidation the interests were apportioned as follows :

```
Andrew Carnegie...........................$2,737,977.95
Thos. M. Carnegie...........................  878,096.58
Henry Phipps................................  878,096.58
David A. Stewart ..........................  175,318.78
John Scott ................................  175,318.78
Gardiner McCandless........................  105,191.00
John W. Vandervort.........................   50,000.00
```

The last named was Carnegie's companion on his trip around the world.   He soon fell sick and withdrew from active business to California, where he died in 1897.

The earning powers of the several properties are given in the foot-note to Mr. Shinn's letter quoted above.   Their estimated values are given in the articles of incorporation as follows :

		Mortgage.
Edgar Thomson works....................	$2,385,000	594,000
Coal mines and Coke ovens at Unity.........	80,000	
Ore lands at Patton.......................	35,000	
Lucy Furnaces	750,000	160,000
Union Iron Mills.........................	630,000	
Four-fifths interest in Larimer Coke works......	120,000	
	─────────	
	$4,000,000	

The advantages of industrial consolidation had not, at this date, received any general recognition; and, as we have seen, it was other considerations than increased efficiency and economy that prompted the first imperfect combination of the Carnegie properties.

As illustrating how vague and incoherent were the plans of the group of men controlling the property at this time, it may be mentioned that two months after the consolidation described, the Lucy Furnaces were taken out of it and turned over to Wilson, Walker & Co. During these eight weeks, however, their value was supposed to have increased from $750,000 to $1,000,000; and Messrs. John T. Wilson, James R. Wilson, and John Walker each subscribed for $142,857 of stock in the Lucy Furnace Company, Limited, with its million-dollar capital. Andrew Carnegie's share in it amounted to $420,627; the rest of the group holding interests from $58,539 in the cases of Thomas M. Carnegie and Henry Phipps, to $3,333 in the case of John Vandevort.

CHAPTER IX

A GLANCE AT PROCESSES

Blowing engines for blast-furnace.

AT this point a brief description of the processes of iron and steel making is necessary in order that readers unfamiliar with these arts may intelligently follow the course of this narrative. While it is not possible that such a rough outline can convey more than a hint of the wonderful transformations involved in modern methods of iron and steel manufacture, it may nevertheless help the reader to appreciate the nature of the great industrial evolution we are tracing.

There is not a State in the American Union in which iron-stone is not found. Indeed, one may say there is no considerable area of the earth's surface where it does not exist. The ancients undoubtedly knew how to mine and smelt it; but, unlike other metals found in the tombs and habitations of vanished races, iron, unless protected from air and moisture, rapidly perishes through oxidation. In other words it rusts away. The oldest known piece of wrought-iron of any great size is found in the pillar of a temple at Delhi, India. It is sixteen inches in diameter and weighs about seventeen tons. No one knows when or how it was made.

Many tribes of savages existing in our own time have been found in possession of primitive means of smelting. Speke and Livingstone describe the miniature blast-furnaces of the natives

136

of Central Africa; and it is not improbable that these simple operations were learned from the Egyptians, whose routes of trade are now known to have penetrated into what had become in our own time " Darkest Africa."

It is not, however, with ancient practices that we are now concerned. It is rather with those mammoth operations which have given a special character to modern civilization and made it different from anything that has preceded it.

The first operation is to mine the ore. This needs no description for the present. The separation of the metal from the earthy substances usually associated with it is effected in the blast-furnace, where it is converted into pig-iron, the crudest form of manufactured iron.

A modern blast-furnace is a giant structure shaped somewhat like the chimney of a kerosene-oil lamp. The point of greatest diameter—where the lamp chimney swells out to make room for the flame—is called the bosh, frequently mentioned in this work. This furnace is filled with a mixture of iron ore, fuel, and lime; and a blast of air is forced through it from below. This draft at first was cold air; but an ingenious Englishman discovered, sixty or seventy years ago, that the ore was reduced more quickly, and with a smaller consumption of fuel, if the blast was heated before being forced into the furnace. To the bewilderment of the scientists of that day this simple change resulted in doubling the iron product of a given quantity of fuel. Before that happy discovery the output of a blast-furnace had ranged from fifteen and a half tons a week, in 1788, to thirty-five tons in 1827; and at the former date the yearly product of the whole of England did not amount to as much as was recently produced in four months by a single American furnace. In these forty years the total annual iron production of England rose from 70,000 to 700,000 tons. In the forty years following the introduction of the hot blast the furnace product rose from thirty-five tons weekly to four hundred tons. This shows a wonderful development of the art of iron production; but the latter figure was multiplied seven times by the Lucy furnace in the succeeding twelve years, and almost fifteen times by one of the furnaces built since at Duquesne.

In the early blast-furnaces the gases freed in the process of reduction were allowed to escape in flames at the top of the stack, illuminating the country for miles around; but towards the middle of the nineteenth century means were devised for utilizing this vast volume of flame for the purpose of raising steam and heating the blast.   For the latter purpose it was led from the throat of the furnace into ovens containing iron pipes through which the blast was blown.   These iron pipes limited the tem-

Lucy furnaces, showing hot-blast stoves.

perature of the blast to that of their own melting-point. Presently the pipes were displaced by enormous stoves containing fire-brick, against which the flames are now directed. After the fire - brick has been brought to a great heat, the gas is turned into a second stove, to perform the same service there; while the air-blast is admitted to the first stove, where it is raised to a very high temperature—1200° to 1600° Fahrenheit. So in alternation the stoves are thus heated, and the blast passed through them one after the other, on the regenerative principle invented by Dr. Siemens. To the higher degree of temperature thus secured is due a large part of the increased output of the Lucy and Isabella furnaces during their long contest. In the first photograph of the former made in 1873 the stack seems to stand alone, because the hot-blast stoves were small at this date. In the second illustration the stack can hardly be seen for the stoves,

which, indeed, to the untrained onlooker, seem the most important part of the plant.

At the time the Lucy furnace was built the lines of blast-
furnaces were not the graceful curves of the lamp chimney that

Drawing the finished coke. The method of charging the raw coal is also seen. It is
dropped from the donkey-car through an opening in the top of the oven.

has been used to illustrate them. They were almost straight
lines; and the bosh formed an angle. A few months after the
Lucy had been started, the mass inside got chilled, so that the
metal stopped running down. The furnace was therefore emp-

tied; and to the surprise of everybody connected with it, the wooden lining that had been built to protect the inside from the first loads of ore, etc., which were poured into it, was found in some places almost intact.   Of course it ought to have been

burnt up; but instead of that large parts remained and were hardly charred. This set some men thinking; and the outcome of their cogitations was the idea that the shape of the furnace was all wrong.   It was evident that in this furnace the zone of fusion did not extend beyond the narrow range of the central funnel, and that, consequently, the benefit of its large interior capacity was mainly lost.   Builders therefore gradually changed the shape of furnaces, cutting out all angles, lengthening the curves, and increasing the size of the hearth.   In 1872 the Lucy furnace was 75 feet high, 20 feet in diameter at the bosh, and 9 feet wide at the hearth.   The product was fifty to sixty tons a day.   In 1902 the same furnace was 90 feet high with the same diameter of bosh as formerly, and 12½ feet wide at the hearth.   The product has been as high as 500 tons a day and 12,000 tons a month; and for every man employed the average product of pig-iron is now two tons a day, as against one ton thirty years ago.

Casting-pit of blast-furnace, where the metal is made into "pigs."

The fuel first used in blast-furnaces was charcoal; but the threatened depletion of the forests of Britain caused the substitution of pit-coal.   As early as 1773 charred coal or coke was tried in England; but its use did not become general until well into the last century. In America charcoal was largely used long after it was found that anthracite, which is a natural coke, was suitable for smelting. As related elsewhere in this work the use of coke—or "cake" coal—did not become general until the early seventies. It was the proximity of the Connellsville beds of bituminous coal—which is singularly free from sulphur and other impurities—that gave Pittsburg its leadership in the iron industry of America.

The purpose of changing this coal into coke is to rid it of the sulphur and phosphorus which is found in greater or less quantities in all soft coals. There is a saying among iron-workers that these elements are to iron what the devil is to religion. As a matter of fact they are worse; for there are some good workable religions that could not get along without the devil, but there is no good workable iron with sulphur and phosphorus in it. The process of coking consists of baking the coal in hot ovens, so that, to continue the theological simile, the diabolic parts are driven off as flaming gas from the top of the oven. These flaming ovens give a wild and picturesque aspect to the coking country as one passes through it by night. Presently the coal fuses into a cake, which is cooked for forty to sixty hours, until hardly anything but carbon remains. This cake is then drenched with water, and pulled out of the oven by a door which up to this time has been sealed. The sudden cooling of the mass splinters it into the form so familiar to all who travel on the railroads. In the best furnace practice seventeen or eighteen hundred pounds of coke are now used to smelt one ton of pig-iron. In the Lucy furnace the amount first used was about double that amount.

The lime which accompanies the ore and coke into the blast-furnace produces certain chemical changes which are too complicated for description here. It also serves as a flux to carry away the earthy matters with which the iron is associated in its mineral form. These residues constitute the slag, or scum of the liquid iron.

The furnace is tapped about every four hours; and the molten iron runs, a limpid, glowing stream, into channels and moulds that have been prepared for it, where it cools and hardens into shapes which have suggested the name "pig." Hence pig-iron. The channel leading to the pigs is called the "sow," and as they are seen lying together the simile is obvious. In modern practice the iron is usually poured into enormous ladles, which are drawn by locomotives to the converters, where it is made into Bessemer steel.

Train of ladles.

Before following a train of these ladles to the converting house, it is worth while to see what becomes of the pigs of iron as soon as they are cold enough to be taken out of their moulds. In former days they were usually converted into wrought-iron in such places as the Union mills. Placed in a puddling-furnace—an oven with a concave floor—with a certain amount of ore for "fettling," they were reduced to liquid form and boiled and stirred about until most of the impurities were driven off. When the bubbling mass thickened and assumed a pasty consistency, the puddler passed a long bar through a small opening in the furnace door, and rolled the paste into a ball. This ball was then withdrawn and carried, dripping with liquid fire, to a queer arrangement of big wheels which crushed and rolled the ball over and over, squeezing out all sorts of useless stuff and further solidifying the mass. This machine has been mentioned in another chapter as the squeezer. The ball was then re-heated, and passed under hammers and through rollers; and the kneading it thus repeatedly underwent gave it

the fibrous quality of wrought-iron. When it had been finished
into bars it was ready for the market. This was the material of
which Kloman made his famous axles.

The Bessemer process of steel-making has displaced the art
of puddling, except for a few special purposes. Steel rusts more
readily than iron; and for this reason chains for cables are still
made of puddled-iron.

Cast-iron is pig-iron mixed with ore and scrap, melted in a
cupola and then cast into moulds of the shapes required. When
cold it is drilled, planed, and finished into the heavy parts of
machinery where great resistance is called for. When fractured,
cast-iron is seen to have a granulated form, like dirty sugar;
whereas wrought-iron has a fibrous quality that makes it ductile
and tough.

And now it is necessary to return to the train of ladles before the contents cool. Covered with coke dust to retain the
heat, the liquid pig metal can be transported a dozen miles to a
converter; and this is sometimes done. At every curve and
bump of the locomotive, some of the metal slops over the edge
of the ladle, and breaks into a galaxy of shooting stars. Presently the train arrives alongside the Jones mixer, a huge iron
chest lined with refractory bricks, and capable of holding fifty
to two hundred and fifty tons of liquid pig metal. It is hung
on trunnions, so that it may be swung to and fro like a cradle;
for here the contents of many ladles are mixed to equalize the
variations of both chemical composition and temperature of the
furnace product. Before the invention of the mixer, the pig-
iron had to be re-melted in a cupola before it could be converted
into steel. One by one the ladles are emptied into the mixer,
the liquid flowing clean and creamy, with fairy lights dancing
over its surface. Whenever a few drops spill to the ground
they rebound in thousands of tiny points of fire, exploding with
the noise of a miniature fusillade. A boy of thirteen or fourteen, his imp-like face black with soot, stands near the flaming
funnel of the mixer, shouting shrill directions to his fellow

demon, who, somewhere concealed among the dark shadows of the wheels and chains aloft, reverses the five-ton ladles with the ease of a society woman emptying her cup of tea.   At night the scene is indescribably wild and beautiful.   The flashing fireworks, the terrific gusts of heat, the gaping, glowing mouth of the giant chest, the quivering light from the liquid iron, the roar of a near-by converter, the weird figure of the child and the pipings of his shrill voice, the smoke and fumes and confusion, combine to produce an effect on the mind that no words can translate.   Dante in his most hellish conception never approached such a reality.   The most eloquent preacher that ever described the condition of the damned was as a babbling brook in a soft summer landscape compared with this.   And who shall tell of what goes on in the giant chest where two hundred and fifty tons of liquid iron have just been poured, to be rocked to and fro, a seething, swirling, bubbling mass?

In one aspect this is the cradle of civilization.   Here, in the Jones mixer, goes on the first of the processes by which is made the steel of locomotives, rails, and ships that link race to race throughout the world; of the engines of mines and factories; of the machines of thousands of mills; of the reapers and harvesters of farms; of the beams and angles and bars of which modern cities are largely built.   Here rocking in this huge box are the springs of chronometers that keep pace with the progress of the stars; the needles that point the mariner's way; the tubes through which the astronomer watches the birth of worlds; the disks that talk through a thousand miles of space; and most of the other miracles that make the sum of modern civilization.   To the intelligent onlooker there is as much poetry in Jones' box as there was in Pandora's; and even this does not contain all the wonders of the beautiful transformations which have given Pittsburg a yellow crown of light.

From the mixer the molten iron, now uniform in composition, is transferred to the converter.   Samples have been quickly cooled and analyzed, so as to afford a guide to future operations, that the final product may have just the qualities of resistance or ductility required of it. With the same spluttering and scintillations as before, the liquid is poured through the lower opening of the mixer into fresh ladles, which in turn are emptied into an egg-shaped vessel. This is the Bessemer converter, the most beautiful and perfect piece of mechanism ever devised by the human mind. Itself of enormous proportions and weight, it is so delicately poised that when filled with ten or fifteen tons of liquid iron, it can be moved at the touch of a finger. The metal is poured into the vessel while suspended in a horizontal position. A blast of cold air is then forced through a number of holes in its lower end, and simultaneously the great oval mass becomes erect. Sir Henry Bessemer has himself eloquently depicted the beauty of the transformation which now takes place:

" The powerful jets of air spring upward through the fluid mass of metal. The air expanding in volume divides itself into globules, or bursts violently upward, carrying with it some hundredweight of fluid metal which again falls into the boiling mass below. Every part of the apparatus trembles under the violent agitation thus produced; a roaring flame rushes from the mouth of the vessel, and as the process advances it changes its violet color to orange, and finally to a voluminous pure white flame. The sparks, which at first were large like those of ordinary foundry iron, change into small hissing points, and these gradually give way to soft floating specks of bluish light, as the state of malleable iron is approached. During the process the heat has rapidly risen from the comparatively low temperature of melted pig-iron to one vastly greater than the highest known welding heats; the iron becomes perfectly fluid, and even rises so much above the melting-point as to admit of its being poured from the converter into a founder's ladle, and from thence to be transferred to several successive moulds."

The chemical changes accompanying this gorgeous display are equally beautiful. The liquid pig metal contains a percentage of manganese, silicon, and carbon. If we could conceive of these elements as endowed with human emotion, we might

10

say that every particle is in love with some atom of oxygen. The converting-vessel is the meeting place of the lovers and the scene of their marriage. With noisy celebration the union of the little globules of air and the tiny atoms takes place, and

emerging from the lip of the converter in sparkling radiance the happy pairs soar away to spend their short lives together. Scientists stolidly call this marriage "chemical affinity." Goethe named the similar union of human souls "elective affinity."

Filling ingot-moulds with molten steel.

The comparison suggested is not so fanciful as it seems. Every atom of every element in the twelve-ton charge now roaring and flaming before us will eventually find and unite with the atom of oxygen for which it has an affinity—chemical or elective it matters not. It may be this moment or the next, in the violent ebullition of the Bessemer converter; it may be thousands of years hence in the beam of a sky-scraper; but sooner or later, every atom of iron as well as every atom of silicon and carbon will find its mate in the oxygen of the air, and so separate itself from its fellows. This is a predestination of matter not found in theologies.

When the flame at the lip of the converter becomes white it is a sign that the manganese, silicon, and carbon have united with the oxygen blown through the mass and escaped into the air. Now the iron itself is following the same course, and that means waste. So the youth, who has been watching the conflagration through colored goggles from a distant platform, touches a lever; and the huge vessel slowly bends forward so

Plate VIII.

BESSEMER CONVERTER IN OPERATION

as to let the metal flow into the body of the converter, and un-
cover the air-holes beneath.   With a mighty rush the blast now
sweeps along the surface of the metal, detaching a million minor
particles of glowing matter and sending a shower of sparks
across the converting-pit.   It is the brilliant finale of the gorgeous display.   To replace a part of the lost carbon, a few
shovelfuls of spiegeleisen or ferro-manganese are thrown into
the mass, which is then poured into moulds, to solidify into
ingots of steel.   When taken out of the moulds the steel is
passed under heavy rollers to give it the shapes needed for its
intended use as rails, beams, or plates, as well as to knead it into
that fibrous texture which we saw resulted from similar action
in the making of wrought-iron.   The first rolling thus makes
blooms; and these cut into lengths make billets, which again
are shaped into a hundred and one things as needed.   Such in
brief, and in rough outline, is the process of Bessemer steel
manufacture.

Henry Bessemer, who was knighted in recognition of his
beautiful invention,
took out his first
patent in 1856. Ten
years l a t e r the
world's output of
B e s s e m e r steel
amounted to about
100,000 tons.   By
1870 it r e a c h e d
300,000 tons.   In
the first year of the
present century it
had attained a total

Steel ingot about to enter the rolls.

of 19,000,000 tons, of which nearly 9,000,000 tons were produced in the United States.

Since 1886, however, a newer method of steel-making has
grown with even greater rapidity.   This is known as the open-

hearth basic process.   It is probable that this will soon displace
the beautiful and simple invention of Sir Henry Bessemer, just
as the latter displaced puddling.

Huge ingot being forged for armor-plate under the 12,000-ton hydraulic press at
Homestead.

The advantage which the basic open-hearth possesses over
the Bessemer converter is that it enables the steel-maker to use
ores high in phosphorus.   It also permits the easy working-
over of scrap, spoiled ends of billets and rails, and old stuff of

all kinds. At Homestead are two large basic furnaces from which the entire top can be removed; and parts of old machines weighing many tons are lifted bodily into them for re-conversion. Moreover, the capacity of the largest Bessemer converter is about fifteen tons. In the basic furnace fifty tons are often made at once; and the product of several hearths can be drawn at the same moment to make an ingot of a hundred and fifty tons if desired. This has been done at Homestead.

The basic open-hearth is simply a huge and improved puddling-furnace. A bath of pig metal is used in which to dissolve scrap of all kinds with a mixture of ore. The charge and lining of the furnace are alkaline, so as to convert the acids of phosphorus into a neutral base, which, with other so-called impurities, floats on the metal as slag as it is drawn off. The process has none of the picturesque aspects of the Bessemer converter. The most interesting thing about it to a layman is to see, through colored glasses, how the steel boils and bubbles as if it were so much milk. The bigness of it—its fifty-ton ladles swinging in space, its hundred-ton ingots under a twelve-thousand-ton press as seen at Homestead—makes it impressive; but the gentle boiling of steel for hours without any fireworks or poetry, in a huge shed as empty of workmen as a church on week-days, is not a very interesting sight. Indeed, it would seem as if all that is spectacular will have been lost in the manufacture of steel with the passing of the Jones mixer and the Bessemer converter. To the chemist, however, the basic process is full of interest; but this short description is not designed for him. In 1886 the product of this process was 218,973 tons in America and in England, 694,150 tons. In 1902 it approximated five and a half million tons in America, and in England three and a half million tons. The present rate of increase in the United States is over a hundred thousand tons a month.

CHAPTER X

THE RISE AND GROWTH OF HOMESTEAD

 AMITY HOMESTEAD was the name given by John Mc-Clure four generations ago to a quaint country seat which he built in the bend of the Monongahela a mile or so below Braddock's crossing, and ten miles from Pittsburg. He is said to have been a fox-hunting Presbyterian, with all the rigorous rectitude, blunt virtues, and frank hospitality which this implies. Thus planting the traditions of the old home in a new environment, he passed the picturesque place on to his son John, and through him to his grandson Aldiel. In 1872 the latter sold one hundred and thirteen acres to a banking and insurance company; and a town was forthwith laid out and called Homestead. The first sale of lots was made to all the old-time accompaniments of a brass band and free junketing; and the Pittsburg, Virginia and Charleston Railroad building across the empty lots the following year, the town took a good start and bade fair soon to grow as big as the older places in the region. But the panic of 1873 came and gave it a set-back from which it was long in recovering. In 1879 there were less than six hundred inhabitants in the place.

On October 21st of that year, however, an event occurred of first importance in the history of Homestead. This was the incorporation of the Pittsburg Bessemer Steel Company, Limited, with a capital of $250,000. The founders of this company were all connected with the firms which had been supplied with merchant steel for a time by the Edgar Thomson Company and, as already related, had been suddenly cut off from supplies through the refusal of that firm to fill orders for billets. Their subscriptions were as follows:

Wm. G. Park, of Park Bros. & Co....	5	shares,	$50,000
Curtis G. & C. Curtis Hussey, of Hussey, Wells & Co.	5	"	50,000
Wm. H. Singer, of Singer, Nimick & Co...........	5	"	50,000
Reuben Miller, of the Crescent Steel Works.........	4	"	40,000
Wm. Clark, of the Solar Iron and Steel Works	4	"	40,000
Andrew Kloman, of the Superior Mill, Allegheny....	2	"	20,000

The Singer concern made a specialty of tool cast-steel, patent rolled saw-plates, spring and plow steel, axles, tires, etc. The Hussey firm made refined cast-steel for edge tools, homogeneous plates for locomotives, boilers, and fire-boxes, and cast-steel forgings for crank-pins, car-axles, etc. Park Brothers were the owners of the Black Diamond Steel Works, and were in a somewhat similar line; while Kloman had leased the Superior Mill in Allegheny and had recommenced the manufacture of eye-bars and structural material. He was also rolling light rails.

Kloman's lease ran out in 1879; and he decided to build a mill of his own. He bought a small tract of land adjoining the City Farm at Homestead, and commenced the erection of a building 684 feet long by 85 wide; to contain a twenty-one inch rail-mill, two Universal mills, a sixteen-inch bar-train, and a muck-train. At the same time the Pittsburg Bessemer Steel Company bought some forty or fifty acres of land adjoining Kloman's, and commenced the erection of a converting works and blooming-mill. The two concerns were designed to work together, Kloman taking the surplus product of the Bessemer Steel Company and working it up into structural shapes. One Universal mill and four steam-hammers were to be constantly run on the Kloman patent solid eye-bars; and he gauged the capacity of his plant at 50,000 tons of steel rails and 30,000 tons of structural material annually.

While building his own mill Kloman supervised the erec-

tion of the adjoining converting works; and his skill and experience, joined to those of Macintosh & Hemphill, who had the
contract for the engines, and later became stockholders in the
enterprise, proved of inestimable value to his associates.

The result was unsurpassed not only in the completeness and
efficiency of the works, but in the rapidity of their construction.
While the Edgar Thomson plant was over three years in building—a delay not entirely due to the panic—the Homestead
works were put in operation fifteen months after the land was
bought. The first steel was made on March 19th, 1881, and
the first rail on August 9th of the same year.

Before the mill was quite completed, however, Kloman died.
After a life of patient and fruitful endeavor, of numberless victories in the realm of invention, of successes ever ripening into
fortune but always falling at the feet of others, the pathos of
his career reached its culmination when hope was brightest.
From the very conception of the great industry whose growth
we are tracing, until the moment of his death, Andrew Kloman's influence persisted without a break. He founded the
business; built the Twenty-ninth Street mill; rebuilt and made
successful the Thirty-third Street mill. He was prominent in
the Lucy Furnace enterprise; and he worked hard for the Edgar
Thomson works. Finally the great Homestead plant was of
his founding; and even to-day some of the machines he built
there are running in testimony to his thoroughness.*

The Pittsburg Bessemer Company at once purchased Kloman's unfinished mill, and carried out the contracts for rails
that he had made. By September, 1881, they were turning out
200 tons of rails a day and had orders booked for 15,000 tons
at profitable prices. The Carnegies looked on with surprise

---

* "In broad charity, in great patience, *in uncomplaining endurance of
wrongs*, in conscientious veracity and uprightness of integrity, in calmness and
serenity of manner, we recognize the higher type of Christian manhood."—*From
the resolutions of the Board of Directors of the Pittsburg Bessemer Steel Company, on the death of Andrew Kloman.*

and alarm.   Up to this time they had been the only makers
of rails in the Pittsburg district.   Here was competition at
their very door.   Councils of war were held once more on Braddock's Field; for it looked as if the prosperity which had hung
so lovingly over the Edgar Thomson works had now crossed the
river and alighted upon the rival enterprise at Homestead.

Had the wisdom which governed the designing and construction of the works been maintained in their management, it is
likely that their initial prosperity would have continued until
they had surpassed their great rivals at Braddock.   That the possibilities of a phenomenal success were there was brilliantly

An assessment notice.

demonstrated a few years later under other leaders.   But, unfortunately, there was no Captain Jones to weld into unity the
conflicting racial elements with which the new works were filled.
The rail-mill was controlled by the Welsh; and if a desirable
post became vacant, it was not filled by the next man, but by
some newly imported friend of the Welsh foreman.   The Irish
were supreme in the converting works; and in the blooming-
mill yet a third nationality was in power.   Over all was an unreasonable and arbitrary management ever tending to open conflict with the workmen.   In a few months this conflict came,
and set up dissensions which ultimately destroyed the corporation.

William Clark, who was put in charge of the works, was a
bitter opponent of labor-unions; and before going to Homestead
he had incurred the dislike of the men for his prowess as a
"strike-breaker," of which he was rather proud.   It was not
long before the trouble he was ever looking for came.   One day

after the furnaces had all been charged with ingots, the men came to him in a body and made some demand which he had previously refused. As a stoppage would have involved the firm in a great loss, the workmen's requirements were met, but with mental reservations on the part of Clark. At the end of the year he issued an order requiring employees to sign an agreement renouncing their right to join labor-unions, and requiring union men to leave their organizations at once. The alternative presented was dismissal from the company's service. Most of the men were members of the Amalgamated Association of Iron and Steel Workers; and on the 1st of January, 1882, these refused to sign the agreement, and were locked out. After the works had been idle a week, the company gave notice that the men could not return to work, even if they signed the agreement, unless they would accept a reduction of wages. This intensified the bitterness of the workmen; and the Amalgamated Association took cognizance of the dispute.

At this time the Amalgamated Association was the most powerful labor organization in existence, having a membership of 70,000, and controlling every department of the iron and steel industry. Except in a few small works, there was not a wheel turning nor a fire burning from Maine to Texas that was not cared for by an Association man. From the newly established furnaces in Colorado to the oldest rolling-mill in the Keystone State the authority of the Amalgamated Association was almost supreme; and, generally speaking, its power at this date was beneficently and properly exercised. Its origin may be briefly outlined.

In 1858 some men in the Pittsburg iron-mills attempted the formation of a society for the protection of working men against unreasonable exactions of employers, and for the discussion and reform of long-standing grievances. Inasmuch as the new movement was regarded by employers with suspicion, the workmen were obliged to conduct their deliberations with secrecy; and thus disadvantaged the movement failed. A couple of years later the effort was renewed, and the United Sons of Vulcan was established by the puddlers, heaters, rollers, and roughers. The new organization won recognition from employers; and in February, 1865, it justified itself by securing the first sliding scale of wages. Following the example of the Sons of Vulcan came other labor organizations, until every department of iron and steel working was included in the movement. After the long strike of 1874 the obvious advantages of consolidating these different bodies led to the formation, in August, 1876, of the Amalgamated Association of Iron and Steel Workers of the United States, with Mr. Joseph Bishop as president. In January, 1880, Mr. John Jarrett took Mr. Bishop's place; and the contest at Homestead now came under his direction.

Mr. Jarrett at once sought an interview with the managers of the company; and while his right to meddle in the dispute was not questioned, he was put off from day to day with various excuses, and was admitted to a conference only after the gravity of the situation had been increased by mutual charges and recriminations in the newspapers. Nothing came of the conference; and the labor leaders, seeing in the attitude of the owners of the Homestead mill a disposition to attack the Amalgamated Association throughout the Pittsburg district, threatened to call out the men from every other mill in which these owners were interested. " If this condition of affairs continues at Homestead," said Mr. Jarrett, "the stockholders in the Homestead works who have mills in Pittsburg may have to fight the association in their own mills. We shall not much longer permit several firms to conveniently fight us in this concentrated shape." Response was promptly made to this threat by the eviction of the striking workmen from the homes they had rented from the company. The labor leaders thereupon embodied their threat in a formal resolution, and a date was fixed for the sympathetic strike.

Thoroughly alarmed the company now offered to withdraw

the objectionable agreement; substituting one requiring the men to give three days' notice of an intention to stop work, and not more than three men to give such notice at one time. This might have been satisfactory to the men; but they refused to accept the reduced scale of wages. In vain the company urged that the improved machinery at their command made the work easier and the output greater than at similar works. The men had won one concession and were determined not to yield a point so important as that which remained. So both sides made ready—in the newspapers—for a general strike in all the works belonging to the owners of Homestead, to begin on the 11th of March; and the labor leaders took the opportunity of including in their resolution three other Pittsburg mills in which disputes of various kinds had long been pending. This meant the calling out of about 6,000 men, with dangerous possibilities of extensions; and the manufacturers of Pittsburg were not unnaturally alarmed at the prospect.

It is interesting in the light afforded by a hundred sympathetic strikes since, to read the naïve expressions of opinion published at that time by the Homestead managers. Mr. Singer "could not see how the Amalgamated Association could order a strike in mills where there was no trouble existing between employers and employees;" and similar views were voiced by others who took the employers' side of the dispute. So the thing went on, each side daily publishing columns of protests, accusations, and threatenings, until it seemed as though all the iron works in Pittsburg would be involved in the struggle.

The days of grace accorded to the Homestead people thus passed by, the dispute ever waxing fiercer—in the newspapers —until the very eve of the threatened sympathetic strike, when the company capitulated. On the 11th of March the first Homestead strike was reported settled; and men of all classes throughout the Pittsburg district read their papers that morning with relief and thanksgiving. It had lasted ten weeks.

The joy was short-lived, however. The next day misunderstandings arose between Mr. Clark and the Amalgamated Association concerning the force and scope of a verbal agreement made at the time of the supposed settlement; and the strike was resumed with greater bitterness than ever. At Homestead there was great excitement, resulting in a pitched battle between deputy sheriffs and strikers, in outrages on "scabs," and even in murder. Demands were made for the state militia by the company, and requests for fresh conferences by the labor leaders. The newspaper war was renewed; and Clark threatened to close the works indefinitely. Appeal was made by outside interests to the other owners, who, publicly vowing they were powerless, nevertheless stepped between Clark and the strikers and insisted upon a settlement. For a time the contest was transferred to the council-chambers of the owners and there waged with hardly less bitterness than before. Indeed, the differences which now arose were mainly responsible for the final disruption of the company.

Some degree of harmony was at length reached; and on March 20th the newspapers announced that the strike was "settled once more." The terms of the peace were so worded as to give it the aspect of a compromise. Practically it was a victory for the men. Clark promptly sent in his resignation, and it was as promptly accepted.

Encouraged by its success, the Amalgamated Association a few weeks later demanded a general advance of five to fifteen per cent. in the wages of all iron and steel workers throughout the country. A thunderbolt out of a clear sky, to which this demand was compared, could not have excited greater surprise and consternation. Anathematizing the Homestead works and all its managers, the iron manufacturers of the country prepared for the greatest contest with labor that had ever been seen. June 1st, 1882, was the day fixed by the association for the beginning of this struggle; and on that day the Carnegies and two of the firms connected with the Homestead works, who by this time had come to hold the Amalgamated Association in awe, agreed to the latter's demands. In all other mills where union labor was employed, work was suspended—in Pittsburg, Wheeling, Cleveland, Cincinnati, St. Louis, Springfield, Chicago, and other places. The iron industry of the country was paralyzed in a day; and for nearly four months the struggle thus inaugurated continued, marked with wonderful endurance on the part of the men and great determination on the part of the manufacturers.

For a while the works at Homestead managed to struggle along, under the terms of the settlement, with a force composed partly of union and partly of non-union men; but the disorganization of the iron and steel trade was more than it could cope with, and, on August 21st, the works were shut down for lack of orders, as the management frankly stated.

"Shot one of them in self-defence."

On September 21st the general strike ended in the complete discomfiture of the men, who for over a month had been dropping from the Amalgamated Association, starved into submission. The struggle had cost millions and benefited nobody.

On the very next day a fresh strike occurred at Homestead, where an effort had been made, a couple of weeks before, to start up again. The cause was a trifling incident growing out of the previous dispute. The men objected to the presence of a "scab" who, during the troubles, had shot one of them in self-defence; and to even things up the management also expelled the workman who had been thus wounded.

The new trouble did not last long; but it served to increase the discontent of the stockholders of the concern, whose greater interests in their respective mills were thus repeatedly jeopardized; and their dissensions became acute. About this time, too, the price of steel was rapidly falling; and, alarmed by the imminent call for more capital, some of the Homestead stockholders hastened to get out of the company. One of them having secured an option on the shares of some of his associates, went to the Carnegies and offered them the control thus acquired.

The offer was promptly accepted. Although trade was now very bad and daily growing worse, the Edgar Thomson works in the past had been inconveniently drawn upon for supplies of steel by the Hartman Steel Company at Beaver Falls, and for billets by the Union Iron Mills. The Keystone Bridge Works were also using increasingly large quantities of steel; and the Carnegie people were prompt to embrace the opportunity offered them of acquiring possession on easy terms of a plant which would at once relieve the pressure from the Edgar Thomson works and remove from their immediate neighborhood a dangerous rival.

Accordingly in October, 1883, the Homestead mills became the property of the Carnegie group. The price paid was the cost of the plant, with a reasonable allowance for increased land values. Little cash was paid; and the notes given in payment were subsequently liquidated out of the profits of the mills.

The Carnegies, with a view of holding for themselves the markets created by the old stockholders, offered the latter the privilege of remaining in the enterprise; but with one unimportant exception they declined the offer, and, taking their little checks and notes, went out of the enterprise with grateful hearts. The interest of the one who remained was eventually sold for about eight millions.

It is illustrative of the unfailing luck of the Carnegies that the Homestead works, thus acquired when the steel trade was

suffering an unparalleled depression, should pay their cost
within two years.   Few of the steel works of the country were
working up to their full capacity at the end of 1883, and many
of them were closed.   At $35 a ton, none but the best-equipped
mills could make rails without loss.   Even at this price there
were few orders to be had; and six of the nine Western mills
were shut down.   At the beginning of December the Edgar
Thomson had only
enough w o r k in
sight to last a few
days and one con-
tingent o r d e r of
8,000 tons of rails,
not to be rolled until
the order had been
c o n f i r m e d.   The
Homestead works
had been put on bil-
lets for the Union
Iron Mills, and had
only enough work in
sight to keep running
till the middle of Janu-
ary.   Wilson, Walker &
Co. stopped work on December 5th for lack of orders.
The Joliet mill had just shut
down; and the old Chicago mill
had long before stopped running
for like reasons.

"Went out of the enterprise with
grateful hearts."

But the Carnegie partners had faith in the future, and still
greater confidence in the genius of the men who had made their
other enterprises successful; and so, utilizing these dull times
for repairs and changes, and profiting by low prices of labor and
material for extensions, they struggled through the period of

depression and were ready for the harvest of prosperity when it came.

The conversion of the Homestead works to the production of steel specialties is a very striking indication of the new uses to which steel was then being put. As we have seen, the works —apart from Kloman's—were projected for the manufacture of steel ingots and billets to be used by the crucible steel-makers of Pittsburg. They were not now used for their original purpose, but for the manufacture of steel specialties which were fast taking the place of iron. Steel bridges were now used to replace those of wood; and the low price of Bessemer beams and other structural shapes gave an impulse to their use in architecture which, in a few years, wrought the revolution culminating in the sky-scraper. There were thus developed new markets which soon brought back prosperity to the trade; and the temporary depression had but served to benefit the far-sighted manufacturer who knew enough to utilize the period of low prices to add to the capacity of his works.

At the time of its purchase the Homestead mill was already one of the best-equipped plants of its size in the country; but during the next few years important additions were made to it which put it at the head of the steel works of the world. On October, 1885, a new bar and angle mill was constructed, giving employment to four hundred men; and by the middle of July, 1886, the converting works, under the skilful management of Mr. Julian Kennedy, were turning out six hundred tons of Bessemer steel a day. In the month of March, 1887, the two four-ton converters produced the unexampled total of 19,572 tons of ingots, and further broke the record with an output of 915 tons in one day.

During their most active period of growth Mr. Julian Kennedy was superintendent of the works; and their success was in no small degree due to his exceptional engineering skill. Just as a new era in blast-furnace construction and product was inaugurated under his management at the Edgar Thomson works

11

THE HOMESTEAD STEEL WORKS IN 1886.

in the early '80s, so now was initiated a revolution in rolling-mill practice.   The slabbing-mill, already mentioned as the giant descendant of the little Zimmer mill at Kloman's, was erected by him, as was also the 119-inch plate-mill, the largest machine of its kind that up to that time had been built.   A slight modification in the arrangement of the slabbing-mill—a machine that cost nearly a million—fitted it for the rolling of armor-plate and doubled its usefulness.   Mr. Kennedy invented

Ninety-ton steel ingot at Homestead.

ingenious labor-saving devices by which massive shapes of red-hot steel were tossed lightly about at the will of a single oper-ator, and excited the wonder, not only of chance visitors, but of trained engineers who travelled half round the world to see them.

By the insistent progressiveness of Mr. Phipps the first basic open-hearth furnace in America was erected by Mr. Kennedy at Homestead, and was so successful that others followed in quick succession.   To this early entry into a new field and to persistent cultivation of it is due the supremacy which the Homestead plant has won over the steel works of the world. This broad statement is verified by a comparison.   In 1886, when the first open-hearth plant was built at Homestead, the production of steel by this process was only a little over 200,000 tons in the whole of the United States.   Last year (1902) the Homestead works alone produced over 1,500,000 tons of open-hearth steel.   This is about twenty-five per cent. of the total output of the country, although there are seventy-seven other works in America making open-hearth steel.   Added to the product of the Bessemer process this gives a total of 1,889,000 tons of steel made at Homestead last year.

These results are in a large measure due to the use of natural gas in the open-hearth furnaces.   The chance which placed the Carnegie enterprises in the natural-gas region is to be credited with much of their exceptional success; and in the manufacture of open-hearth steel this fortuitous factor has been of first importance.   The heating power of natural gas is far greater than that of the ordinary "converter gas" used elsewhere, thus making the operation of fifty-ton furnaces an easy matter; while its cost to the Carnegies does not exceed five cents a thousand feet, thanks to the enlightened policy of Mr. Frick, who, in spite of much opposition, secured large areas of gas territory for his firm.   It is to this single fact that much of the astonishing growth of the business, described later, is due.

It is at Homestead that wonders are performed as amazing as those of the Arabian Nights.   Here machines endowed with the strength of a hundred giants move obedient to a touch, opening furnace doors and lifting out of the glowing flames enormous slabs of white-hot steel, much as a child would pick up a match-box from the table.   Two of these monsters, appro-priately named by the men " Leviathan and Behemoth," seem gifted with intelligence.   Each is attended by a little trolley-car that runs busily to and fro, its movements controlled by the more sluggish monster.   This little attendant may be at one end of the long shed and the Leviathan at the other; but no sooner does it seem to see its giant master open a furnace door and put in his great hand for a fresh lump of hot steel, than it runs back like a terrier to its owner and arrives just as the huge fist is withdrawn with a glowing slab. This the Leviathan gently places on its attendant's back; and, to the admiration of all beholders, the little thing trots gayly off with it to the end of the building. Even then the wonder is not ended; for the little fellow gives a shake to his back, and the glittering mass,

The Leviathan and its attendant.

twice as big as a Saratoga trunk, slides onto a platform of rollers which carry it to the mill. And no human hand is seen in the operation.

In another place lady-like machines seem to dance lightly in front of the furnaces, occasionally stretching out a hand, seizing a red-hot billet, and waltzing with it to the rolling-mill. These marvels of mechanical skill have swelling skirts that make the idea of the ball-room irresistible. Being suspended from above so that their mechanism is not visible by night, they move backwards and forwards, from one side to the other, tripping along a row of furnaces and pirouetting diagonally back with a swift, graceful, and noiseless sweep in a fashion that suggests nothing but play and Virginia reels. And the beautiful lumps of steel, white-hot and dripping with fire, are carried as lightly as a girl's bouquet, and deposited just as lightly in the lap of a chaperone, when their owner glides with easy turnings out into another dance.

In yet another place is a comical being that runs busily about carrying hot things round corners. When this grotesque machine gets to the end of his track he makes a quick half-turn to the right and runs on again. And all the while he holds in one hand a long rubber tube, like a boy at a May-pole. This contains the electric wires that give him life and intelligence.

The wizard who has endowed these machines with their amazing power is a quiet, modest young fellow, Alva C. Dinkey, the present superintendent of the great works. If any of the junior partners merit the title of "young geniuses," Mr. Dinkey is certainly one of the first.

Mr. Dinkey has also charge of the four Carrie blast-furnaces just across the river at Rankin, which supply a part of the pig-iron used at Homestead. One of these was removed from Ohio by the Carrie Furnace Company, rebuilt here in 1883 and blown in on February 29th, 1884. Another was built by the same company in 1888–90. The Carnegie Steel Company built the others. They are each 100 feet high, with 23-foot bosh and 15-foot hearth. Their total annual capacity is 672,000 tons of metal, which is hauled, in a molten state, by locomotives across the river bridge to Homestead. The last built of these furnaces produced 206,650 tons of pig-iron in 1902. This is believed to be the world's record.

CHAPTER XI

THE INCOMING OF HENRY CLAY FRICK

Coke-ovens.

IN 1882, the iron and steel business whose growth we are tracing may be said to have attained its majority. Just twenty-one years had elapsed since the building of the Kloman mill at Twenty-ninth Street, when the infant industry emerged from the embryonic state of Girty's Run. Thanks to skilful nursing, it had passed easily through the dangers and diseases of childhood; and under the stimulating pabulum of a high tariff it had waxed big and lusty beyond all precedent. Like most overgrown things, however, it was ill-proportioned and awkward. There was an uncertainty about its movements which showed that its physical growth had outstripped its mental development. There was none of that harmonious working of parts and effective unity of interests which bespeak the well-balanced organism.

This was now to be changed—not suddenly and by a conscious effort, but, as is the nature of all growth, quietly, gradually, and by unnoticed movements.

The most conspicuous step in the mental evolution of this industrial organism was the simple and prosaic incident which brought Henry Clay Frick into contact with it. At the time this seemed a very commonplace occurrence. Similar things had happened in the history of the enterprise a dozen times without attracting more than a passing attention. The present

one produced a revolution.   A simile from the science of biol-
ogy suggests itself.   One of the lowest forms of life exists as a
little floating globe of jelly, which surrounds and absorbs into
itself every smaller thing that bumps against it.   Sometimes,
however, a more highly developed creature comes along and
reverses the process.   Something akin to this happened now.

Up to the time of the incoming of Mr. Frick the group of
men with whom he now allied himself had had no definite policy.   The several industrial establishments had all been started
by some outer accident, and each had developed along its own
line as the needs of the day required, and as the fostering hand
of the Government was laid more or less kindly upon it.   The
Kloman germ grew under the stimulus of the war; and the
Twenty-ninth Street mill was built to meet the increased demand for Kloman axles.   The Cyclops or Thirty-third Street
mill was but an accidental offshoot of the Kloman stem; and
the business of both grew with the country's growth and the
general development of the iron trade.   The Keystone Bridge
Company was simply the incorporation of an existing business.
The suggestion of the Lucy furnaces came from outside; as
did also that which resulted in the steel business at Braddock.
The Homestead works were built by outsiders ; and their absorption by the Carnegie group was a mere accident.   And yet, in
conformity with those laws underlying all growth, the line of
progress was one which ever tended to round out and complete
the series of operations in the conversion of crude iron ore into
finished materials.   But this was a natural and unconscious
development growing out of trade conditions.   There was at no
time a well-defined plan or policy of expansion.

With the incoming of Mr. Frick, however, this vague pro-
gression at once assumed a definite character.   It was the
marshalling of hosts into a coherent unit, with one mind ruling
all for the good of each.

To give a just idea of the revolutionary character of the
changes inspired by Mr. Frick, it is necessary to anticipate

Plate IX.

HENRY CLAY FRICK

events a little, and give a rough outline of the perfected organization which he built up out of the scattered units which he found. These units were the Upper and Lower Union Mills, the Lucy Furnaces, the Edgar Thomson Steel Works, the Keystone Bridge Works, the Pittsburg Bessemer plant at Homestead, and the little interests in coke and coal at Larimer and Unity, and in ore at Scotia. There was also, at Beaver Falls, the Hartman Steel Works, an unqualified failure and source of uninterrupted vexation to its owners. Apart from the Edgar Thomson works and the Upper Union Mill, which had been consolidated, each of these plants had its separate organization. Such exchange of benefits as was possible among them was offset by the petty factions and jealousies which the Carnegie system of unfriendly rivalry had established.

While there was a feeble attempt at consolidation made in 1886, before Mr. Frick assumed supreme power, it did little more than modify the disunion described. Once in control, Mr. Frick assembled these disorganized units into a solid, compact, harmonious whole, whose every part worked with the ease and silent motion of the perfectly balanced machine. This mammoth body owned its own mines, dug its ore with machines of amazing power, loaded it into its own steamers, landed it at its own ports, transported it on its own railroads, distributed it among its many blast-furnaces, and smelted it with coke similarly brought from its own coal-mines and ovens, and with limestone brought from its own quarries. From the moment these crude stuffs were dug out of the earth until they flowed in a stream of liquid steel into the ladles, there was never a price, profit, or royalty paid to an outsider. Without any cessation of motion and with hardly any loss of heat, this product passed with automatic precision into the multitudinous machines which pressed it into billets, rails, armor-plate, bridge structures, beams, and the endless variety of shapes required in modern architecture. Finally these highly finished materials were often conveyed to consumers over the same transportation systems as before; and the profit of every movement, as of every process and change of form, passed without deduction into the exchequer of what was now the Carnegie Steel Company, Limited—a single organization with one mind, one purpose, one interest. The annual earning power of this great institution increased under Mr. Frick's direction from $1,941,555 to $40,000,000 in a dozen years; while its annual product of steel increased during the same period from 332,111 tons to 3,000,000 tons. The change thus baldly and inadequately expressed in terms of dollars and tons makes the most impressive record, for such a short period, of any manufacturing organization in this or any other country.

"Small farm chores."

Henry Clay Frick, to whose remarkable executive and administrative ability this miracle of industrialism is due, was only thirty-three years of age when he joined the Carnegies; and already he had achieved the most noteworthy success in the coke industry of Pennsylvania. Born at West Overton in 1849, young Frick is found at the age of ten gathering sheaves in the wheat-fields, carrying wood and water, and doing such small farm chores as came within his child's strength. This was his way of spending the summer holidays. It afforded him the best of exercise, and probably gave him that vigor and recuperative power which, later, astonished the surgeons who were probing to find the assassin's bullets in his sadly wounded body. In undertaking this farm work the child acted on his own impulse. He did it to earn enough money to buy his clothes. Then he went back to school, where he displayed the same earnestness of purpose. At the age of fourteen he not only bought his own clothes but entirely maintained himself, working behind the counter of a country store. At nineteen he became bookkeeper in his grandfather's flouring-mill and distillery at Broad Ford, in the centre of what is now the Connellsville coke region. At the threshold of manhood he thus found himself fortuitously placed in the field of his future activities, where he was destined to find both wealth and honor.

The history of the development of the Connellsville region is necessarily a sketch of the personal career of Henry Clay Frick. He was one of the first, even at this youthful age, to recognize the importance to the expanding iron industries of Western Pennsylvania of this wonderfully rich deposit of coking coal. He has been the leading spirit in its development; so that to-day, in some of the iron-producing centres of the United States, Connellsville coke is known only as Frick coke. He built railroads for transporting it; and he alone effected the consolidation of the industry as it now stands.

Every great industry has its romance. That of Connellsville coke began in 1842, when a couple of small barges loaded with it were floated down the Ohio to Cincinnati. There the furnace men looked on it with suspicion and called it " cinders." It was sold in small lots at eight cents a bushel; and a large quantity remained after three weeks' effort to dispose of it. This remainder was finally traded for a small patent grist-mill, which was brought to Connellsville, and turning out to be a failure, was there sold for $30.

But the foundryman who got the coke afterwards thought well enough of it to make a trip to Connellsville to get more. In this he was disappointed. No one was willing to repeat the experiment, for a time at least. In 1850 there were only four establishments making coke in the whole of the United States. In 1860 the census shows that there were twenty-one such establishments, all in Pennsylvania; and ten years later, when Frick had already appeared on the scene and had become interested, there were but twenty-five coking plants in the country.

In 1871 young Frick organized the firm of Frick & Co. with Abraham O. Tintsman, one of his grandfather's partners, and Joseph Rist. They had three hundred acres of coal lands and a plant of fifty coke-ovens. At this time there were not four

Coke-ovens under construction.

hundred ovens in the whole Connellsville region, which included an area of one hundred square miles. The Mount Pleasant and Broad Ford Railroad, of which Frick was one of the projectors, was opened about the same time. The next year Frick & Co. erected one hundred and fifty more ovens. Then the panic of 1873 came, and everybody but Frick thought the business had come to an end. But he had gauged its possibilities; and, with a confidence in the country's growth rare in one of his years, he realized that the depression was of that tidal character which would eventually carry the business to higher levels than before. Timid competitors anxious to sell out at any price found a ready purchaser in the firm of Frick & Co.; and in the lean years following the panic he acquired the interests of his partners, who, burdened with unpaid-for purchases, staggered and finally fell in the storm. By a singular paradox the panic which ruined his partners made Henry C. Frick's fortune. When the trouble had passed, the price of coke rose from ninety cents to $4 and $5 a ton; and the boom put young Frick at the head of the coke industry. By 1882, when Frick admitted the Carnegies into his business, he had acquired 1,026 ovens and 3,000 acres of coal land.

The business was now reorganized with a capital of $2,000,-000; and a year later this was increased to $3,000,000 to keep pace with the expansion of the trade. By 1889, when its capital was increased to $5,000,000, the H. C. Frick Coke Company owned and controlled 35,000 acres of coal land and nearly two-thirds of the 15,000 ovens in the Connellsville region, three water plants with a pumping capacity of 5,000,000 gallons daily, thirty-five miles of railroad track, and 1,200 coke-cars. The company employed 11,000 men. The volume of shipments amounted to 1,100 car-loads a day, or 330,000 cars a year. This is equivalent to 10,000 train-loads, which, strung together, would extend from New York to San Francisco, or from London across the continent of Europe, through Persia, and well on the road to India.

In 1895 the capital of the H. C. Frick Company was further increased to $10,000,000. It now owned 11,786 ovens: 40,000 acres of Connellsville coal lands, out of a total of sixty to sixty-five thousand acres, and its capacity was 25,000 tons of coke a day, or eighty per cent. of the entire production of the Connellsville region. A little later its monthly output amounted to an even million tons!

Such, baldly stated, are

Coke-ovens under construction.

the achievements of the man who from now on becomes the most conspicuous and imposing figure in this history.

CHAPTER XII

THE CAPTURE OF THE DUQUESNE STEEL WORKS

Kloman's successor forging an axle.

MR. FRICK'S first great achievement after assuming the leadership of Carnegie Brothers & Co. was the capture of the rival steel works at Duquesne, on the Monongahela River, a short distance above Homestead and Braddock. This masterly move eliminated a dangerous competitor from the rail market, and gave the Carnegies one of the most modern and best-equipped steel works in the country without the outlay of a single dollar. Even the unparalleled record of Carnegie successes contains no greater industrial victory than this; and business men in Pittsburg still regard it as the greatest example of skilful financiering and management in the history of the American steel trade.

The building and early history of the Duquesne steel works recall those of Homestead. In a sense, indeed, the former may be considered a continuation of the latter; for they were planned for similar reasons, completed by the same men, failed for kindred causes, and were eventually sold to the same purchasers.

The Duquesne Steel Company was organized on June 4th,

1886, with a capital of $350,000. Before the plant was completed, disagreements arose among the promoters, and these, joined to a call for more money, resulted in the suspension of construction work. The enterprise was subsequently reorganized; and the Allegheny Bessemer Steel Company was formed, in March, 1888, with a capital of $700,000, to take over the unfinished plant and carry it through to success. Among the incorporators were E. L. Clark of the Solar Iron Works and William G. and D. E. Park of the Black Diamond Steel Works. These gentlemen subscribed for nearly six-sevenths of the total capital. The other members of the corporation were also practical men. Mr. C. Ansler, consulting engineer of Macintosh & Hemphill, superintended the building of the works; and neither money nor pains were spared to equip them with the most improved machinery. The buildings were of an unusually substantial and enduring character. They comprised converting and blooming house, 75 feet by 200; a rail-mill 68 feet by 380; a building covering the hotbeds 80 feet by 200; while the wings inclosing the finishing machinery were 48 feet by 64. There were two Bessemer converters, each with a capacity of seven tons.

Operations were commenced in the blooming-mill on February 9th, 1889, and a month later in the rail-mill. The long-threatened competition with the Carnegie rail monopoly in the Pittsburg district had begun. It was met by Andrew Carnegie in a distinctly original fashion.

The Duquesne people, in their search for improved methods, had planned to run their ingots from the soaking-pits, without further heating, through the various rolls that pressed them into billets and rails. This was an unheard-of innovation in America, although something of the kind had been done in England; and Sir Henry Bessemer had long ago predicted that the practice would become general. The ingots, having passed through the 32-inch blooming-mill, went at once through the 26-inch roughing-train. After shearing, the piece went straight

on to the two finishing-trains, which were equipped with especially powerful engines.   Thus the re-heating of ingots was
dispensed with; and from the mould to the finished rail the
steel passed only once through the furnace, instead of twice
or thrice, as in other works.

On learning of the adoption of this economy by a competitor, Andrew Carnegie drafted a circular to the railroads, warn-

Ingots going from the Duquesne soaking-pits to the rolls. The mechanical
perfection is shown by the small number of workmen visible.

ing them against using the rails thus made, which he represented as defective through lack of homogeneity.   Although
this was not believed by the Carnegie officials, the circular,
having been sent to Pittsburg for that purpose, was printed
and mailed to the purchasing agents of the railroads throughout
the country.   When asked if he considered this a legitimate
form of competition, one of the Carnegie partners of that time
replied that "under ordinary circumstances he would not have

thought it legitimate; but the competition set up by the Duquesne people was also not legitimate, because of their use of this direct rolling process." In further self-justification he added: "They were a thorn in our flesh and they reduced the price of rails. If they had made rails by our method, we would have recognized them as legitimate competitors; but when we were attacking their method of rolling we could not recognize them by letting them take a contract."

Pressed to explain the last sentence, Mr. Carnegie's partner said: "We could not divide business with them as we otherwise would have done."

It is worthy of remark that this method of direct rolling was not abandoned when the Carnegies acquired the Duquesne mills. On the contrary it was adopted in all their other works, and is now general throughout the country. Presumably steel-makers have learned to overcome the lack of homogeneity against which Mr. Carnegie warned the railroads.

The mechanical superiority which the Duquesne works showed over every similar plant in the country was not enough in itself to offset the deficiencies of

The offensive placards.

management which soon became manifest. There were also contentions with labor. The old antagonism to trades-unions that brought trouble to the first owners of Homestead, cropped out at Duquesne. Signs were put up all over the yards and shops announcing that "no union men are allowed on these works." When Mr. William G. Park saw them he gave orders that such signs as were accidentally destroyed should not be renewed. The directors dared not discredit their manager by removing the offensive placards; but they let it be quietly known that a driver who knocked one of them down and destroyed it would not be punished for carelessness. Some of these signs were still in existence when Mr. Frick bought the works.

There were also defects in the operating department; so that large quantities of second- and third-rate rails accumulated in the yards. The dissatisfaction of the owners with the management was augmented by several serious losses growing out of undesirable contracts. In fairness to the managers, however, it should be confessed that they were really obliged to take these contracts in order to keep running; for the rail pool, at the instigation of the Carnegies, constantly headed them off from all desirable business, and obliged them to take such orders as no mill in the pool wanted. As a result the stockholders were soon called upon for additional capital. First $100,000 was called for; then twice as much. This the stockholders refused; and Mr. William G. Park had to pay it all. So that a suggestion from Mr. Frick that the Carnegie Company might buy the property at a bargain found Mr. Park in a particularly receptive mood.

The price first talked about by Mr. Frick—$600,000—was considered too low by Mr. Park, as no doubt it was. The works had cost nearly twice that sum. They had made as much as five hundred tons of rails and billets in twenty-four hours; and while their cost from pig-iron to rails was high—$8.14 in October, 1889—the stockholders were loath to accept any very great loss. On the other hand, Mr. Frick showed no disposition to increase the bid which he had thrown out in a tentative way; and so the thing dragged on for nearly a year. During this time Mr. Park obtained options on his partners' holdings; and when the negotiations were resumed he was able to offer the entire stock of his company. During the month of August preceding the final sale the output of the rail-mill was the largest in its history—16,814 tons. The output of raw steel was over 20,000 tons; and 17,000 tons of blooms were made.

On this showing Mr. Frick, in October, 1890, raised his bid for the plant to $1,000,000 in bonds, material on hand to be appraised and paid for in cash. On the 30th of the month this offer was accepted; and a couple of weeks later the plant was turned over to the Carnegies. Once more they were without a rival rail-mill in their own territory.

At this time the works consisted of two seven-ton converters, six cupolas—four for iron and two for spiegel—seven soaking-

Pouring steel from converter into ladle.

pits, four trains of rolls, and the necessary boilers, engines, and other equipment to successfully operate a blooming and rail mill of that size.

It is commonly believed in Pittsburg that the plant thus bought with nothing but an issue of bonds, paid the new owners $1,000,000 in the first sixty days. This is not true; but the works did pay for themselves within a year, for, with his habitual foresight, Mr. Frick had provided a market for their product before he bought them. The rail-train was changed to make billets; and these were promptly marketed at good prices.

Before the bonds became due the plant had paid for itself six times over; and the surplus earnings had gone into the construction of four large blast-furnaces.

Mr. Frick always had an instinct for picking out the right man for every place; and his intuition did not fail him when he selected Thomas Morrison for Duquesne's first superintendent under the new régime. This young man was a distant connection of Andrew Carnegie; but he made no attempt to trade the fact for favors. He took a humble place in the machine-shops at Homestead, and caught the notice of his superintendent, Mr. Potter. Mr. Frick's attention having been drawn to the youth, he watched him for a while, and decided that he was capable of better things than he was doing. Greatly to the young man's surprise he was selected for the responsible position of superintendent at Duquesne. Here the men tried to take advantage of his youth; but he met the attempt with dignity, and, being supported by the firm, had no further trouble of that kind. In one of Mr. Frick's weekly reports in June, 1891, he says: "Matters have been looking threatening at Duquesne. Morrison has handled the matter very well. He is not much of a talker." In that he was a man after Mr. Frick's own heart.

Early in 1892 Morrison was instructed to get up plans for two blast-furnaces at Duquesne, which he did; and the same month he was given a small interest in the Carnegie Company. During this time the plant was being operated as the Allegheny Bessemer Steel Company, the former owners not having yet closed all the old transactions. By July this had been done; and the plant was taken into the consolidation of all the Carnegie works that formed the Carnegie Steel Company.

Owing to the disturbing effects of the Homestead strike the two Duquesne furnaces, planned early in 1892, were not commenced until November 5th, 1894. By August of the following year, 1,700 men were at work on them; and the first one was blown in on June 8th, 1896. On October 7th the second furnace went into blast. In May, 1897, a third furnace was lighted; and a fourth followed in June.

Three of these stacks are 100 feet high by 22 feet at the bosh. The fourth is the same height and a foot narrower. For nearly four years they held the world's record; as much as 18,809 tons of metal being produced by a single furnace in a month.* Then the broom of supremacy, previously flaunted by

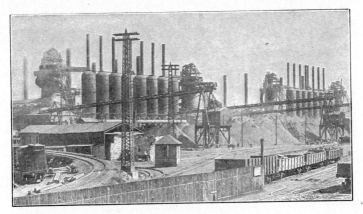

Duquesne furnaces.

the Lucy, and then by the Edgar Thomson furnaces, passed to another Carnegie stack, that known as Carrie No. 3.

It is worthy of remark that when the Duquesne furnaces were put in operation, with all their labor-saving appliances, they cut the cost of labor per ton of iron produced to one-half that prevailing elsewhere.

The rivalry started thirty years ago by the Lucy and Isabella furnaces still persists. Late in 1901 Carrie No. 3 made 790 tons in twenty-four hours. A month or so later furnace No. 2 of the National Steel Company at Youngstown, Ohio, produced

---

* In October, 1898, the output of these four furnaces was as follows:

No. 1 .... 18,672 tons.
2 .... 17,717 "
3 .... 18,809 "
4 .... 18,060 "

806 tons.   This furnace is 106½ feet high and 23 feet in
diameter.   Later, furnace E at the Edgar Thomson works made
901 gross tons.   It is probable that before these pages are in
type some more modern furnace will make a thousand tons in a
day.   If so, the difference between the 50 tons that the Lucy
first made, and 1,000 tons, will mark, in a way easy to understand, the progress in blast-furnace construction and practice of
the period covered by this story and the one group of workers
to which it relates.*

To describe the further growth of these works in detail
would take more space than is possible here.   They were Mr.
Frick's pride; and he lavished his best thought upon them.
Hardly a month passed that did not see some important change
and addition; until for economy of operation they stood unri-
valled among the steel works of the world.   Here are the most
important items in this record of growth and improvement :

1896—June 11—Purchase of 57 acres of Hays estate adjoining.
  "   Oct.   9—Purchase of 65 acres from Oliver estate, including plats
                        between railroad and river ; price about $200,000.
  "   Nov. 10—Purchase of 50 acres from Dr. W. S. Huselton for
                        $150,000.
  "   Dec. 19—Jones mixer, 200 tons,. put in operation ; largest in the
                        country.

1897—Feb.   2—Work commenced at Duquesne on Union Railroad.
  "   May   6—No. 3 furnace blown in.
  "   June 10—No. 4 furnace goes in blast.
  "   Dec. 19—Work started on new billet-mill.

1898—June 1—Union Railroad completed and first run of hot metal
                        from Duquesne to Homestead.
  "   July   8—New 16-inch continuous mill put in operation.
  "   July 19—Union Railroad bridge finished, connecting Duquesne,
                        with Edgar Thomson works.
  "   Aug.   1—Duquesne tube works sold by sheriff for $141,500 to
                        Carnegie Steel Company.

---

* At the Lucy furnaces at this date, 1903, the present superintendent, James
Scott, was employed at the same plant soon after its construction, thirty years ago.
No man in the Carnegie Steel Company, or indeed anywhere else, has been closer
to the great changes described than Mr. Scott, and few men have contributed
more to produce these changes.

1899—Feb. 7—Howard Glass House and 27 acres purchased for
$300,000.
"   Apr. 10—Coal dock on Monongahela River contracted for.
"   Oct. 6—New blooming and billet mills and open-hearth plant to
cost $2,500,000 first publicly announced.
"   Nov. 20—Excavations for open-hearth plant started.

1900—Feb. 16—Plans for new 14-inch continuous billet-mill announced.
"   Apr. 5—Plans for new 10- and 13-inch double-storage mill an-
nounced.
"   Oct. 1—Two new open-hearth furnaces started.
"   Nov. 27—40-inch mill began operations.
"   Dec. 13—Two more open-hearth furnaces started.

1901—Jan. 2—Excavations started for new 14-inch mill.
"   Feb. 7—Excavations for foundations of two new merchant mills.
"   Mar. 1—Date of merger with United States Steel Corporation.

The present capacity of the works is 750,000 tons of pig-iron a year, and 600,000 tons of raw steel. The whole of this material can be made into finished products on the place. These totals are twenty times as great as the first year's output of the Edgar Thomson works. In view of the short time in which these results have been attained, the enthusiasm of the local editor is pardonable, even when—after comparing Duquesne to "the meteor that has darted out of space and cut a brilliant path across the sky" yet "remains in the horizon, more lustrous than ever,"—he calls it "the acknowledged young giant and the mastodon of the unconquered and the unconquerable Monongahela valley." There is certainly much in Duquesne to arouse local pride.

CHAPTER XIII

LABOR CONTESTS IN THEORY AND PRACTICE

Personification of "a principle."

THE great Homestead strike, which forms the most dramatic episode in the history of all the Carnegie enterprises, grew out of conditions without parallel in the industrial history of this or any other country. Superficially, this contest was a commonplace struggle between capital and labor concerning the equitable division of the results of their joint efforts. But behind this were certain moral causes, growing out of the conflict between the idealistic platform-theories of Andrew Carnegie and the unsentimental exigencies of business. A brief glance at the attitude towards labor of Carnegie the manufacturer, as contrasted with the academic utterances of Carnegie the philanthropist, is necessary to an understanding of the remoter and more obscure causes of this titanic struggle, which, marked as it was with all the ferocity of civil war, caused a shudder to run through the civilized world. Incidentally such a retrospect will also show that no successful business can be built on philanthropic aphorisms. Nor can Utopianism be grafted upon an industrial system still rudimentary in its development, without producing fruit of an unexpected and injurious variety.

The first strike in the history of the Carnegie iron business was that of 1867, when, as has been related, the puddlers resisted a reduction of wages. This was ended by a sudden boom in the iron trade which called all idlers back into the shops at better wages than before. The Carnegies, however, in common with other manufacturers, had attempted to break the strike by the wholesale importation of foreign labor.   While at this time there was no open hostility on the part of the manufacturers to labor-unions *per se*, there was also no public glorification of them.   As for Carnegie himself, his influence was too unimportant to have much effect on his partners; but so far as is known, the business man was still dominant in the dual personality which later puzzled partners and workmen alike by an altruism never before professed by any employer.

At the end of 1875, just after the starting of the Edgar Thomson works, mutterings of discontent were heard amongst the men, and a strike became imminent.   During the few weeks that the plant had been in operation some minor weaknesses and defects had shown themselves in the machinery; and, to remedy these, the excuse offered by the discontent of the men was seized upon to shut down the works.   Stunned into submission by the swiftness of the blow, the men readily signed the agreement presented to them by the company before they were allowed to return to work; and the lesson thus learned lasted long.   Many years of peace supervened at the Edgar Thomson works.   There was still no philanthropic posturing. It was all business, and very properly so.

In July, 1884, the Carnegies had a strike at their Beaver Falls mill.   This plant, known as the Hartman Steel Works, was an unimportant but costly side-issue growing out of an effort to find new markets for raw steel.   Designed to lead the world in nails and wire rods, the enterprise was an unqualified failure from the start; and, except for a brief period under the management of Mr. P. R. Dillon, it remained so to the end, when it was cleverly sold by Mr. Frick to the Wire Trust, and closed and dismantled.   The strike referred to was a frank trial of strength between the Carnegies and the Amalgamated Association.   Andrew Carnegie entered upon it with many misgivings, telling Hartman, his partner, that no one could successfully fight the Amalgamated Association " within the smoke of

Pittsburg." Hartman thought otherwise; and, being empowered to carry the fight to a finish, did so in excellent style and
won a complete victory over the labor organization. The contest had all the usual features—the importation of workmen
from other districts, followed by rioting among the strikers, attacks on the "black sheep," and the arrest, trial, and conviction
of the rioters. There was no display of sentimentality among
the owners; and the labor-union was temporarily crushed out
of the mill.

The folly of thus crippling a labor organization that gave
the Carnegies an advantage in their iron works over competitors
whose plants were less favorably located, was not yet recognized.
With the possible exception of Mr. Walker, none of the Carnegie partners seemed aware of the economic principle underlying
the Amalgamated Association's requirement of uniform wages
for the same class of work regardless of other conditions—a
principle that inured to the advantage of the best-equipped and
most favorably located plants. Given a uniform price of labor
throughout the country, the Pittsburg iron-mills, by reason of
their proximity to coal and ore, and their unequalled transportation facilities, possessed enormous advantages over competitors
in other districts; and an enlightened business policy would
have encouraged any organization that, without unduly interfer-
ing with the management, kept the cost of labor down to the
level of that possible in the worst-equipped and least favorably
situated works in the country. Recognition of this principle
came later; and brought a change in the company's treatment
of labor organizations. But unfortunately the change was
credited to humanitarian motives, instead of being frankly stated
as a business principle; and there inevitably arose conflicts
between the ideal and the real—between Andrew Carnegie's
philanthropy and his material interests.

In 1885 Andrew Carnegie made his first public address,
and began that series of lectures and essays on the natural
rights of labor with which his name has since been identified.

A year later *Triumphant Democracy* was published. Ostensibly a record of the material progress of the United States during the preceding fifty years, this book was made a vehicle for the advanced views of Carnegie on the political and social equality of all men. It was also a glorification of the toiler. The book attained a large circulation, especially among workingmen, who were enabled to buy it at a nominal cost through their labor organizations.

In the same year he also published, in the *Forum*, an essay on the relations of capital and labor, in which appeared the following paragraph:

"While public sentiment has rightly and unmistakably condemned violence even in the form for which there is the most excuse, I would have the public give due consideration to the terrible temptation to which the workingman on a strike is sometimes subjected. To expect that one dependent upon his daily wage for the necessaries of life will stand by peaceably and see a new man employed in his stead is to expect much. This poor man may have a wife and children dependent upon his labor. Whether medicine for a sick child, or even nourishing food for a delicate wife, is procurable, depends upon his steady employment. In all but a very few departments of labor it is unnecessary and I think improper to subject men to such an ordeal. In the case of railways and a few other employments it is, of course, essential for the public wants that no interruption occur, and in such case substitutes must be employed; but the employer of labor will find it much more to his interest, wherever possible, to allow his works to remain idle and await the result of a dispute than to employ a class of men that can be induced to take the place of other men who have stopped work. Neither the best men as men, nor the best men as workers, are thus to be obtained. There is an unwritten law among the best workmen: 'Thou shalt not take thy neighbor's job.'"

Lofty in spirit and purpose as this essay was, its humanitarian intent was grossly perverted by the labor agitator; and its broad and liberal principles were garbled so as to seem an authoritative excuse for violence. Unfortunately for the work-

men of Braddock and Homestead, they mistook these high philanthropic views for the serious designs of their employer towards
themselves; and this misunderstanding was intensified by Carnegie's method of ending the coke strike, mentioned later, and
also by an incident which happened about this time at Braddock.
This was somewhat as follows:

On account of some grievance the women employed in the
Pittsburg laundries refused to work, and enlisted the aid of the
Knights of Labor to keep other women from taking their places.
The Knights of Labor went to Captain Jones and demanded
the discharge of an old Carnegie employee, whose two daughters were working in one of the proscribed laundries. Jones
refused in that sonorous language with which he was so highly
gifted.   The matter was thereupon taken direct to Mr. Carnegie, who ordered the man's dismissal, with the remark, "We
cannot afford a strike for a principle."   At the same time he
ordered the old man's wages to be continued for a couple of
months.   Strange to say, the sturdy old fellow refused them.

No one was more surprised at this compliance with their
demand than the Knights of Labor themselves; and its effect
on this dictatorial organization was most disastrous for the Carnegies.   Within a little while they had a strike of their own as
a result of the meddling of the leaders of this most offensive of
all labor-unions.

In Captain Jones' statement of the causes of the great output of the Edgar Thomson works, quoted in a previous chapter,
he says:

"I soon discovered it was entirely out of the question to
expect human flesh and blood to labor incessantly for twelve
hours, and therefore it was decided to put on three turns, reducing the hours of labor to eight."

He adds that

"this proved to be of immense advantage to both the company
and the workmen, the latter now earning more in eight hours

than they formerly did in twelve hours, while the men can work harder constantly for eight hours, having sixteen hours for rest."

Jones' praiseworthy effort to amend the lot of the laborer was afterwards found to put the Edgar Thomson works at a disadvantage with competing establishments where two twelve-hour turns were the rule; and an effort was made in 1887 to induce the Edgar Thomson men to return to the old system. At the same time a sliding scale of wages was proposed, similar to that which had been found successful in the North Chicago rolling-mill and in the Crescent Steel Works at Pittsburg. The men were willing to accept the sliding scale; but they were unwilling to return to the twelve-hour system. The usual strike resulted; but before it had gone far a committee of the strikers went to see Mr. Carnegie at the Windsor Hotel, New York. There he reasoned with them, and talked them into a conciliatory frame of mind; and they agreed to sign the contract he put before them. The affair seemed to have reached a happy conclusion; and the labor leaders left for Pittsburg in the best of spirits. As Mr. Carnegie bade them good-bye, he pressed into the hands of each a copy of his *Forum* essay. This the men read on the train; and on their arrival at Braddock they promptly repudiated the agreement they had signed and continued the strike.

Mr. Carnegie made no effort to conceal his disappointment and chagrin. Summoning Captain Jones to New York, a brief conference was held at the Windsor; and from there Jones went over to Philadelphia and engaged a little army of Pinkerton guards for service at Braddock. Then Mr. Carnegie retired to Atlantic City, where he was kept posted as to the current of events by his cousin, George Lauder.

Under the protection of Pinkerton guards the works were now put in operation by non-union men. The usual disorders took place, resulting in a slight loss of life; but eventually the contest was won by the company. The struggle lasted from

December, 1887, till May, 1888. Thus ended the eight-hour day in a night of sorrow and suffering.

Unfortunately the effect of this incident did not end with the strike. It is being used in 1903 as an argument against the compulsory eight-hour day which Congress is now considering; so that this great step in the elevation of the laborer will probably be delayed by Jones' unlucky experiment.

Andrew Carnegie's later opinion of the Knights of Labor, whom he blamed for the untoward result of his efforts at conciliation, was not very high. When asked by an English reporter if we have not such an organization in America as the Knights of Labor, he replied with emphasis:

" Say rather we had. It was one of those ephemeral organizations that go up like a rocket and come down like a stick. It was founded upon false principles, viz., that they could combine common or unskilled labor with skilled."

The coke strike, to which reference has been made, also took place in 1887. This at first was a matter of wages pure and simple; but, as in so many contests between master and workmen, higher considerations were soon involved.

As has been related, the Carnegies bought a large interest in the H. C. Frick Coke Company in 1882. In 1886, by the withdrawal of two of Mr. Frick's earlier associates, this interest was largely increased; and the Carnegies acquired a majority of the coke company's stock. For the regulation of output and to control competition, the coke operators of the Connellsville region had some sort of a gentlemen's agreement; and when, in 1887, trouble concerning wages arose, these owners acted in unison, and all conferences with the workmen's unions were conducted by a joint committee. By agreement with the trades-unions—the Knights of Labor and the Miners' and Mine Laborers' Amalgamated Association—the matters in dispute were submitted to arbitration. The Board of Arbitration consisted of two members appointed by the manufacturers, two by the labor-unions, and these four elected a fifth, who was to serve as umpire in case of a failure of the whole board to reach an understanding. This contingency arising, the decision was left to the umpire; and his award, when issued, was unfavorable to the men. Thereupon a strange condition arose. The main bodies of the labor-unions accepted the umpire's judgment, as in good faith they were required to do; but the local lodges denounced it as "unjust and unwarranted," and refused to be bound by it. A strike ensued, which the Knights of Labor called illegal; and, as if to further justify the characterization, the men resorted to all the old-time acts of violence. Men who were willing to work were maltreated and shot; dynamite was used to blow up the mines; machinery was destroyed, and thousands of tons of coke were allowed to spoil in the ovens.

It was at this stage that Carnegie cabled from Scotland a positive order to accede to the strikers' demands; and, as he and his partners controlled the Frick Coke Company, the order was carried out regardless of outstanding obligations to the other manufacturers. Naturally the defection of the most important member of the group excited in the rest the bitterest of feelings; and Mr. Frick promptly resigned the presidency of the company which bore his name but which he no longer controlled. The rest of the manufacturers set their teeth and continued the struggle; and, to the surprise of everybody, finally gained a complete victory over their men.

The apparent act of bad faith on the part of the Carnegies received universal condemnation. It was ranked above that of the strikers who had repudiated the decision of their umpire. The breaking up of the combination was also deplored because it involved demoralization of prices on which the wages ultimately depended; so that in the long run the workmen would suffer by the act. But those who made these criticisms did not consider the risk which the Carnegies ran in banking up their blast-furnaces. The best furnace will not stand banking for more than three months; and during this time there is always

a danger of its becoming chilled.   When this happens it has to
be blown out, and partially if not wholly relined at a cost of at
least $35,000.   At this date the Carnegies had seven furnaces
banked; so that there was almost a quarter of a million dollars
in hourly peril.   In addition, there was a positive loss amounting to many thousands of dollars daily through the stoppage of
iron production, and further losses in the steel-mill through lack
of material.   On the other hand, the advantage which the Carnegies would have over competing iron manufacturers by getting a regular supply of coke and continuing work while all
others were idle, was one almost beyond compute.   While this
alone might not tempt the average manufacturer to a breach of
faith, it would do much to console him for it if other conditions
produced it.

Of course the workmen were not informed as to all the
reasons which prompted the Carnegies to yield to their demands; and they not unnaturally supposed that their victory was
due, in some mysterious way, to the inalienable rights of labor
and all the other pretty texts with which they had become
familiar.   There is no doubt that this misunderstanding gave
rise to the frightful disorders that ensued, three or four years
later, in the same region.

The settlement just narrated was made in July, 1887.   From
that time until early in 1890 the H. C. Frick Coke Company
paid twelve and one-half per cent. more for labor than did other
operators.   In February, 1890, however, a general scale was
agreed upon covering wages in the Connellsville region under
which all operators paid the same rate.   This scale expired a
year later; and the men refused to sign the new one designed
in continuation of it.   After repeated conferences, at which no
agreement was reached, an effort was made to start the mines
and ovens with new workmen.   For three months the whole
region was given over to rioting, arson, and murder.   Armed
mobs attacked the mines and coking plants, killing and maim-
ing the workers, destroying the machinery, and defying the

county officials who sought to bring order out of the industrial chaos. Gangs of men marched through the night terrorizing the peaceful members of the community; and when deputy sheriffs attempted to arrest them, the strikers assumed military formations and shot their pursuers at sight. One such body marched across a large extent of the country, occasionally brought to bay, when battle was given and taken with all the tactics of irregular warfare. In this guerilla-like march and pursuit eight of the strikers were killed and many more were seriously wounded. As the Carnegies had a fair supply of coke on hand at the outbreak of hostilities, and as the prices of steel and rails were low, the war was fought to the bitter end. Eventually the rioters were caught or driven out of the region, and others willing to accept the wages they refused received adequate protection.

A year after the establishment of peace came the Homestead strike. In the mean time, however, Mr. Carnegie's *Forum* essay, in the hands of undiscriminating workmen, had become a veritable manual of etiquette for strikers. The last quoted sentence, the Carnegie contribution to the decalogue, became in its terse and picturesque vigor, the most understandable of all the tenets of "the little boss;" and there was no Slav nor Hungarian at Connellsville and Homestead so mean of intellect as not to realize its full purport. As for the Knights of Labor, over whom Mr. Carnegie had pronounced so slighting a funeral oration, they sprang to a joyful resurrection with this text as their watchword: "Thou shalt not take thy neighbor's job."

Before proceeding to a review of the immediate causes of the greatest of all the Carnegie struggles with labor, it is fitting that a glance should be given at the material conditions surrounding the workmen at Homestead. To this end may be quoted the sympathetic summary of a description of the men at work which is published in Bernard Alderson's biography of Mr. Carnegie under the latter's own supervision:

13

"Thus far," says Mr. Alderson, "we have studied Mr. Carnegie in theory. Now let us see how he has put all these admirable sentiments and unimpeachable principles into practice. The best test that can be applied is the condition of labor surrounding his own workmen. Mr. Hamlin Garland, a well-known writer, though having no technical experience, describes the impressions he received from a visit to the Homestead works. His training as a novelist naturally impelled him to look at things from the descriptive writer's point of view, and not become interested in the picturesque, both horrible and attractive. In his approach to Homestead Mr. Garland was struck by the desolate appearance of the district, and the wretchedness of the town itself, he says, was deplorable. 'The streets were horrible; the buildings were poor; the sidewalks were sunken and full of holes; and the crossings were formed of sharp-edged stones like rocks in a river-bed. Everywhere the yellow mud of the streets lay kneaded into sticky masses, through which groups of pale, lean men slouched in faded garments, grimy with the soot and dirt of the mills. The town was as squalid as could well be imagined, and the people were mainly of the discouraged and sullen type to be found everywhere where labor passes into the brutalizing stage of severity.'

Copyright by S. S. McClure Co.

"Looks like hard work."

These depressing conditions are apparently inseparable from a newly established iron or steel mill in any locality, and this is especially true where soft coal is used. Grime, heat, hard, exhausting labor, these are conditions that are to be found in every steel-mill, and the works of the Carnegie Company differed little from other manufactories of the same kind except in extent, but it may be truly said that the larger the mill the more depressing the conditions.

After commenting on the muggy, smoke-laden atmosphere, he [Garland] proceeds to describe the conditions inside the mills, and the men engaged at their tasks, and tells us that they worked with a sort of desperate attention and alertness.

'That looks like hard work,' I said to one of them to whom my companion introduced me. He was breathing hard from his labor.

'Hard! I guess it's hard. I lost forty pounds the first three months I came into the business. It sweats the life out of a man. I often drink two buckets of water in twelve hours; the sweat drips through my sleeves and runs down my legs and fills my shoes.'

'But that isn't the worst of it, said my guide, a former employee. 'It's a dog's life. Now those men work twelve hours, and sleep and eat out ten more. You can see a man don't have much time for anything else. You can't see your friends or do anything but work. That's why I got out of it. I used to come home so exhausted, staggering like a man with a jag!'"

With this picture in mind it is worth while to quote from Mr. Alderson's preceding page a characteristic phrase from Andrew Carnegie:

"The lot of a skilled workman," he says, "is far better than that of the heir to an hereditary title, who is very likely to lead an unhappy, wicked life."

Little wonder that the skilled workman, with the sweat dripping through his sleeves and running down his legs and filling his shoes, failed to understand the man in whose interest he was making such terrific exertions. "Kind master," he cabled during the strike, "tell us what you want us to do and we will do it!"

"Again and again he [Hamlin Garland] is impressed," continues Mr. Alderson, "with the general appearance of exhaustion that is shown in the haggard faces of the toilers, and he says 'their work is of the sort that hardens and coarsens.'

Everywhere in the enormous sheds were pits gaping like the mouth of hell, and ovens emitting a terrible degree of heat, with grimy men filling and lining them. One man jumps down, works desperately for a few minutes, and is then pulled up, exhausted. Another immediately takes his place; there is no hesitation. When he spoke to the men they laughed. It was winter when he made his visit. They told him to come in the summer, during July, when one could scarcely breathe. An old workman, relating the experience of his first day's toil, says he applied for work, and the superintendent, saying he looked strong and tough, set him on the pit work. For the first time in his life he fainted repeatedly, and when he left at night he could scarcely drag himself home.

Preferable to a peerage.

They take great risks, too; and the injuries sustained are of a most frightful character. An explosion in the pouring of the molten metal, and half-a-dozen men are terribly mangled and one or two killed. Such incidents are not infrequent. The continuous dread of an accident, combined with the intense drive of the work, constitute a fearful strain. This is a fearful picture, painted in the darkest, most repulsive colors, but this is but one side of it. Nothing is said of the comfortable homes which steady employment at from four to ten dollars a day enable the steady, sober workman to maintain—the self-confidence that continuous employment begets. The environments of the mills were improved as rapidly as possible, streets were paved, schools were established, and public institutions of various kinds were initiated. Several free educational institutions were founded by Mr. Carnegie in an attempt to help his workmen help themselves. The other side of the picture is full of light and hope, though there are many exceptions.

Many of the men have happy families, and those of the better class are very well off. The company houses are very good, and have all modern conveniences, and the men who are sober and care for their families, besides being prosperous live comfortably.

The effect of the work on these men was brought out in a conversation which Mr. Garland had the morning after his visit to the mills. 'The worst part of the whole business,' said the workman, 'is, it brutalizes a man. You can't help it. You start to be a man, but you become more and more a machine, and pleasures are few and far between. It's like any severe labor; it drags you down mentally and morally just as it does physically. I wouldn't mind it so much but for the long hours. Twelve hours is too long.'"

Allowing for a certain journalistic exaggeration this lurid picture is a fairly truthful one. But in the glare of furnace fires shadows loom big and black; and these have caught the journalist's attention. The fierce heat, the ruddy light, the tense, stripped figures of the workers, inevitably suggest Dante's Inferno; and thoughts of bodily suffering and mental anguish come to the onlooker in the natural sequence of associated ideas. Greater familiarity with the processes of open-hearth steel-making would have given Mr.

Copyright by S. S. McClure Co.

"More and more a machine."

Garland the means of distinguishing subjective impressions from outside facts. If a furnace man drinks two buckets of water in twelve hours, the sweat will run down his legs and into his shoes; and while his condition may not be preferable to that of an heir to a peerage, it may yet be free from bodily suffering.

It is, however, this peerage idea and others akin to it which, coming with all the glamour of the Carnegie name into such works as those just described, wrought trouble for the managers, and did more than any one thing to make the men obstinate and unreasonable. The man who climbs down into the pit to break up the red-hot slag is not himself an idealist, nor has he the mental equipment to make necessary allowances for the

"Not an idealist."

enthusiastic idealism of another. In his hands *Triumphant Democracy* became not the gospel of a universal emancipation it was intended to be, but a special message of independence from his master to himself. The exaltation of labor turned the laborer's head; and he gravely accepted the tributes to his superiority with which the mere capitalist endowed him. This was shown a hundred times during the strike, when the men thought that all they had to do was to let Andrew Carnegie in Scotland know what his wicked managers at Homestead were doing, for him to order its discontinuance by cable.

Concerning the difficulties under which the Board of Managers constantly labored through this tendency of their chief to talk for publication, Mr. Lauder, his cousin, relates how he once told the following parable to Mr. Carnegie. It is more grewsome than funny, but it has a moral.

Once upon a time a man collided with a street car. The remains were collected and built up into some human semblance, and placed on view in the undertaker's for identification. After a while a lady drove up and claimed the corpse as that of her husband; and she ordered the handsomest funeral that money could buy, with flowers, plumes, and every costly accessory to mourning. As she was about to leave the establishment, the undertaker's assistant, in hastening to open the door for her to pass, gave a jar to the slab on which the deceased reposed; and the dead man's jaw fell open, revealing a golden tooth. At sight of this the lady hurriedly countermanded the orders she had given for the imposing obsequies, saying that she saw by the golden tooth that she had made a mistake and that it was not her husband after all. As she passed out of the door, the disappointed undertaker turned and apostrophized the deceased. "What kind of an idiot are you anyway? If you'd only known enough to keep your mouth shut—!"

Mr. Carnegie, who tells so many stories on others, laughed heartily and promised to moderate his speech-making.

Coming now to the more immediate causes of the great strike of 1892, mention should be made of the difficulties which preceded it in 1889, when the sliding scale of wages first went into effect at Homestead.

Up to the summer of 1889, the wages of workers making merchant steel, or steel to take the place of merchant iron, had not been put upon a settled basis. At first the work was done in iron-mills; and after some discussion the same wages were paid as were given for working iron. With the building of mills especially to work Bessemer and open-hearth steel into merchant sizes and shapes, and with their improved machinery and appliances, the output per worker was very largely increased; and as the wages were based on tonnage, earnings had grown beyond all reason. Rollers and heaters, for instance, were earning from five to ten times as much as the skilled mechanics who had erected the machinery on which the former worked. A general reduction amounting to about twenty-five per cent. was therefore proposed by the firm; and a suggestion was made for the automatic regulation of future wages by a scale which should follow, from month to month, the movements of the prices received by the firm for raw steel. This was naturally resisted by the tonnage men; and both sides prepared for the struggle which seemed unavoidable.

On the Carnegies' side these preparations took on somewhat of an opera-bouffe character. Detectives in greasy caps and smutty clothes were sent into the local stores and saloons,

A detective.

where they sat on barrels or stood at bars listening to the workmen's talk. They sought lodgings in the town, and talked with wives and mothers; and the gossip thus picked up was sent to New York, where Andrew Carnegie read it surrounded by the humanitarian texts and quaint heraldic devices in honor of the toiler with which he had covered his library walls. Then he planned a strenuous campaign for his partners, and went to Scotland.

The result was very much as if Napoleon had attempted the conquest of the Rhine provinces from Josephine's bower in the Tuileries. A hundred or more deputy sheriffs, picked off the streets of Pittsburg, went up to Homestead, where they were met by the strikers, relieved of their maces, caps, and coats, and sent back home. And this was the comedy out of which grew the tragedy of Homestead.

Henry Clay Frick was not yet in full control; and the workmen interpreted the weakness and vacillation of the company as fresh expressions of the benevolent theories of " the little boss." The discomfiture of the deputy sheriffs was followed by a conference with the leaders of the strikers' union, the Amalgamated Association of Iron and Steel Workers of the United States, and again the firm received a defeat. Mr. Abbot, who conducted the negotiations for the Carnegies, proclaimed that "both sides are victors, and both sides are probably vanquished in minute details." The principle of the sliding scale was accepted by the men; but instead of a monthly adjustment of prices, as the Carnegies first demanded, the rate was fixed for six months, and "the average price of said six months shall be the basis upon which wages shall be paid for the next three months, the rate to change every three months thereafter based upon the average price of the preceding three months." This excellent rule was nullified by numerous exceptions, which led to constant bickerings and disputes for the next three years. In many departments the rate of payment was left unchanged —with more exceptions. These exceptions, in the form of foot-notes, were more numerous in the agreement than the rules they were designed to elucidate. The old force of men was retained; but where places could be found for any of the newcomers no objection was to be made to them.

The organ of the labor-unions, commenting on this settlement, remarked that the Amalgamated Association now "stands head and shoulders higher than ever before, for it comes out of one of the most difficult crises in its history intact, with honor and with the renewed confidence of the public. It is a victory to the association, for thoroughly prepared as that body was to pursue the contention to the bitter end, yet in the midst of hours when minds were naturally inflamed conciliation prevailed, and the strength and usefulness of organization were demonstrated. It is a victory for the firm in that the management displayed reason, substituting as they did concession for the 'ultimatum.' "

And verily the "concession" thus substituted was far-reaching beyond anything ever dreamed of by the management. Every department and sub-department had its workmen's "committee," with a "chairman" and full corps of officers, who, fearing that their authority might decay through disuse, were ever on the alert to exercise it. During the ensuing three years hardly a day passed that a "committee" did not come forward with some demand or grievance. If a man with a desirable job died or left the works, his position could not be filled without the consent and approval of an Amalgamated committee. Usually this committee had a man in waiting for it; and the firm dared not give it to any one else. The method of apportioning the work, of regulating the turns, of altering the machinery, in short, every detail of working the great plant, was subject to the interference of some busybody representing the Amalgamated Association. Some of this meddling was special under the agreement that had been signed by the Carnegies, but much of it was not; it was only in line with the general policy of the union. This is shown by the constitution of the Amalgamated Association, in which, to take an instance from its rules for puddling-mills, it was provided that "when a vacancy occurs in the boiling department the oldest boiler, if he so desires, shall have the preference of the furnace so vacated." The heats of a turn were designated, as were the weights of the various charges constituting a heat. The product per worker was limited; the proportion of scrap that might be used in running a furnace was fixed; the quality of pig-iron was stated; the puddlers' use of brick and fire clay was forbidden, with exceptions; the labor of assistants was defined; the teaching of other workmen was prohibited; nor might one man lend his tools to another except as provided for. And under similar irksome regulations the Carnegie managers conducted their business for three years, losing money on almost every ton of ingots, blooms, and billets turned out. During this time some of the men earned from $12 to $15 a day; and Homestead became familiar with the sight of steel-workers being driven to the mill in their carriages. Thus did their lot become comparable to that of an heir to the peerage.

CHAPTER XIV

THE HOMESTEAD BATTLE

Strikers arresting a newspaper correspondent.
—*From Harper's Weekly.*

THE chagrin experienced by Andrew Carnegie at the unsatisfactory outcome of his plans in 1889 was forcibly expressed in many of his characteristic letters to Pittsburg during the three-year term of the agreement with the Amalgamated Association ; and as the time approached for its revision measures were taken to avoid a repetition of the former fiasco. What these were may now be frankly stated.

The injudicious attempts of Mr. Carnegie's literary friends to deprive him of his proper share of the honor or responsibility of planning the discomfiture of the Amalgamated Association, joined to his own modest disclaimers, have led to much mystification in the public mind concerning his real position in the matter. It is time to let in the light on this much-debated question.

On April 4th, 1892, nearly three months before the expiration of the agreement with the Amalgamated Association, Andrew Carnegie sent to Pittsburg the draft of a notice to the Homestead employees. Mr. Frick, who was to be chairman of the consolidated Carnegie Steel Company, then in process of formation, disapproved of this notice, so that, despite Mr. Carnegie's wishes, it was never issued, and has never before been published. It is as follows :

ANDREW CARNEGIE,

5 West 51st St.

New York, April 4, 1892.

NOTICE

TO EMPLOYEES AT HOMESTEAD WORKS.

These Works having been consolidated with the Edgar Thomson and Duquesne, and other mills, there has been forced upon this Firm the question Whether its Works are to be run 'Union' or 'Non-Union.' As the vast majority of our employees are Non-Union, the Firm has decided that the minority must give place to the majority. These works therefore, will be necessarily Non-Union after the expiration of the present agreement.

This does not imply that the men will make lower wages. On the contrary, most of the men at Edgar Thomson and Duquesne Works, both Non-Union, have made and are making higher wages than those at Homestead, which has hitherto been Union.

The facilities and modes of working at Homestead Works differ so much from those of steel mills generally in Pittsburgh that a scale suitable for these is inapplicable to Homestead.

A scale will be arranged which will compare favorably with that at the other works named; that is to say, the Firm intends that the men of Homestead shall make as much as the men at either Duquesne or Edgar Thomson. Owing to the great changes and improvements made in the Converting Works, Beam Mills, Open Hearth Furnaces, etc., and the intended running of hot metal in the latter, the products of the works will be greatly increased, so that at the rates per ton paid at Braddock and Duquesne, the monthly earnings of the men may be greater than hitherto. While the number of men required will, of course, be reduced, the extensions at Duquesne and Edgar Thomson as well as at Homestead will, it is hoped, enable the firm to give profitable employment to such of its desirable employees as may temporarily be displaced. The firm will in all cases give the preferences to such satisfactory employees.

This action is not taken in any spirit of hostility to labor organizations, but every man will see that the firm cannot run Union and Non-Union. It must be either one or the other.

On his original draft of this notice Mr. Carnegie adds:
"Should this be determined upon, Mr. Potter [the superintendent] *should roll a large lot of plates ahead*, which can be finished, should the works be stopped for a time."

At this time an exchange of views had taken place between the Amalgamated Association and the firm; and the workmen had been given till June 24th to definitely decide whether they would accept a new agreement embodying certain reductions in the wage-scale. Before any word had been received from the workmen's organization Mr. Carnegie went abroad; and on June 10th he sent a long letter setting forth his views as to the conduct and possible outcome of the negotiations. The part relating to these is as follows:

> COWORTH PARK,
> SUNNINGDALE,
> BERKS.
> June 10, 1892.

"As I understand matters at Homestead, it is not only the wages paid, but the number of men required by Amalgamated rules which makes our labor rates so much higher than those in the East.

Of course, you will be asked to confer, and I know you will decline all conferences, as you have taken your stand and have nothing more to say.

It is fortunate that only a part of the Works are concerned. Provided you have plenty of plates rolled, I suppose you can keep on with armor. Potter will, no doubt, intimate to the men that refusal of scale means running only as Non-Union. This may cause acceptance, but I do not think so. The chances are, you will have to prepare for a struggle, in which case the notice [*i.e.* that the works are henceforth to be non-union] should go up promptly on the morning of the 25th. Of course you will win, and win easier than you suppose, owing to the present condition of markets." . . . . . .

. . . .

> ANDREW CARNEGIE.

Notwithstanding Mr. Carnegie's desire, thus expressed on June 10th, that no further conference should be held with the workmen, Mr. Frick, in his anxiety to avoid open conflict, met

Mr. Weihe, the president of the Amalgamated Association, and a committee of about twenty-five men from Homestead on June 23d. The conference lasted from ten o'clock in the morning until late in the afternoon; and resulted in Mr. Frick's making an important concession on one of the three points of difference between the firm and the men. Neither side being willing to yield on other points, the conference broke up and preparations were made for the struggle.

In the mean time other letters had been received from Mr. Carnegie, showing his uncompromising attitude towards the labor-union. Writing from Coworth Park, Sunningdale, Berks, on June 17th, 1892, he underlined a passage as follows:

"Perhaps if Homestead men understand that *non-acceptance means Non-Union forever*, they will accept."

Again on June 28th, he wrote, also from Coworth Park, Sunningdale, Berks:

"Cables do not seem favorable to a settlement at Homestead. If these be correct, this is your chance to reorganize the whole affair, and some one over Potter should exact good reasons for *employing every man*. Far too many men required by Amalgamated rules.

From indications, I cannot resist the conclusion that the 'Force Report' has not received necessary attention at Homestead, but I see you are pegging away on the right track."

The outstanding differences between the firm and its workmen at this time were truly insignificant; and there is no doubt they would have been promptly settled but for the fact that the general rolling-mill scales were also under discussion; and the Amalgamated Association feared that any concessions at Homestead would weaken them in their contest with the iron-mills throughout the country. The questions involved were these:

First, a reduction in the minimum of the wage-scale. This was based upon the price of 4 by 4 Bessemer billets; the reduction proposed being from $25 to $22.

Second, a change in the date of the operation of the scale from June 30th to December 31st.

Third, a reduction of tonnage rates at those open-hearth furnaces and mills where important improvements had been made and new machinery added, whereby the output had been largely increased.

As to the justice of the company's demands there is no question. The price of all the products of the Homestead mills had fallen, during the term of the last agreement, from sixteen to thirty-nine per cent.; and billets had dropped from $27 a ton to $22. Under the old agreement there was no decline in wages after billets had got below $25 a ton, no matter how low prices went; and the steel company not unreasonably claimed that as they were willing to pay proportionate wages when prices rose, the men ought to accept reductions to a reasonable point when prices declined. So they fixed upon $22 as a minimum; and Mr. Frick, at the conference of June 23d, raised this to $23. The men contended for $24, and there the matter ended.

Concerning the second point, the company claimed that as contracts for material were generally made at the beginning of the year, the price of labor ought to be fixed at the same time. This was resisted by the men on the ground that if a contest arose between themselves and their employers it was better that it should come in summer than in winter. No doubt past experience of the horrors of mid-winter strikes justified their opposition to the change; but unfortunately for the consistency of the men, the steel company was able to point out that in some competing establishments the Amalgamated Association permitted their scale to expire on December 31st. The company's demand was therefore strengthened by precedents.

As to the third point, which involved the most important matter of all, the reasonableness of the Carnegie demand was beyond question. The proposed reduction in tonnage rates applied to only three departments in the works: namely, the

32-inch slabbing-mill, the 119-inch plate-mill, and the open-hearth furnaces.   An illustration will best serve to make clear the point at issue.

When the scale for 1889 was signed for the 119-inch plate-mill, it was based on rolling plates direct from ingots, and the output was about 2,500 tons a month.   But when the ingots were first passed through the 32-inch slabbing-mill—the great

Copyright by S. S. McClure Co.

The 119-inch plate-mill.

machine that had developed out of Zimmer's little Universal mill —and then through the 119-inch plate-mill, the tonnage of the latter was more than doubled.   With the sweet unreason of the toiler, the men who operated the 119-inch plate-mill refused to share with their employers the cost of running the slabbing-mill, and demanded just as much for rolling plates from slabs as they had been getting for rolling plates from ingots; insisting, moreover, upon receiving all the benefit of the investment that had gone into this million-dollar machine.   Similarly in the open-hearth department. When the 1889 scale was signed, this was a comparatively new business; and in three years it had been vastly improved. Tonnages had increased; labor had been made easier by the substitution of machines; but the benefits had mainly gone to the workmen.

Most striking of all, however, is the fact that out of over 3,800 men employed at Homestead, the wages of only 325 were affected by the new scale. Over 3,500 men stood exactly as they did before, and were satisfied. During the previous week most of them had signed agreements with the company for the ensuing three years; and although 3,000 of them belonged in no way to the Amalgamated Association, and, indeed, were for the most part ineligible for membership in it, they broke their contracts and joined the dissatisfied clique that controlled the local lodges of the labor-union. It should be said, however, in justice to them, that ninety-nine men in a hundred believed the Carnegie Company was simply " bluffing " as it had done in 1889; and even the hundredth man was convinced that "the little boss " would never enter into a serious conflict with workmen for whom he had expressed such affection. So they hanged Chairman Frick and Superintendent Potter in effigy; and when an assistant was sent to remove the figures he was drenched with streams of water from hose pipes and jeered out of the shops. One man who ventured to express his intention of continuing at work was badly beaten, then conducted to the train, and banished from the town.

A few days after the fruitless conference of June 23d the eight lodges of the Amalgamated Association at Homestead created an Advisory Committee, consisting of five delegates from each lodge, with Hugh O'Donnell as chairman. The purpose of this Advisory Committee was to take charge of the strike. Its first active measure was to pass a resolution ordering the mechanics, laborers, and other employees of the mill, who had made new contracts with the company, to refuse to work until the Amalgamated Association was recognized and its

14

terms agreed to. It being evident that the order would be obeyed, the company gradually closed the several departments of the works, until on the 1st of July there was not a wheel turning nor a furnace burning in the entire plant.

At the same time the Advisory Committee proceeded to organize an army and navy for offensive and defensive operations, and a local government to supplant the municipal authorities. In speaking of these proceedings the chairman of the Advisory Committee used the following language:

"The Committee has, after mature deliberation, decided to organize their forces on a truly military basis. The force of four thousand men has been divided into three divisions or watches, each of these divisions is to devote eight hours of the twenty-four to the task of watching the plant. The Commanders of these divisions are to have as assistants eight captains composed of one trusted man from each of the eight local lodges. These Captains will report to the Division Commanders, who in turn will receive the orders from the Advisory Committee. During their hours of duty these Captains will have personal charge of the most important posts, i.e., the river front, the water gates and pumps, the railway stations, and the main gates of the plant. The girdle of pickets will file reports to the main headquarters every half hour, and so complete and detailed is the plan of campaign that in ten minutes' time the Committee can communicate with the men at any given point within a radius of five miles. In addition to all this, there will be held in reserve a force of 800 Slavs and Hungarians. The brigade of foreigners will be under the command of two Hungarians and two interpreters."

Details of pickets were sent out upon every highway leading to Homestead, or towards the steel works, instructed to permit no person who could not give a satisfactory account of himself to enter Homestead. A steamboat was chartered to patrol the Monongahela River with an accompanying fleet of some fifty rowboats, located where they would be available for an armed body of men on the shortest possible notice. A system of signals was adopted, flags being used in daylight, and lights and Roman candles at night. A large steam-whistle was pro-

cured and placed upon the Electric Light Works in the borough
of Homestead; and a code of signals arranged so that the number of blasts from this whistle would be understood to indicate
the point at which the commanders desired their men to assem-
ble for battle.

The efficiency of this organization was quickly put to a test.
On the very first evening of the lockout intelligence was received at headquarters that two hundred "black sheep" were
on their way to the works.   In less than two minutes shrill
blasts from the steam-whistle conveyed the false news to the
waiting scouts; and before another ten minutes had elapsed a
thousand men had been marshalled at the point of the expected
landing.   Such alarms becoming inconveniently frequent, camp-
fires were lighted along the river-banks and more pickets established; and all night long the stream was patrolled by the
strikers' steamer *Edna*, which had been furnished with special
steam-whistles for signalling.

On the second day a slight indication of smoke was observed at one of the chimneys of the works; and the Advisory
Committee sent a written notice to the company that the fact
"caused considerable excitement among our men," and that "if
the gas is not turned off we cannot be responsible for any act
that may be committed."   At the same time placards were
printed and posted in the hotel and places of business in Homestead, saying:

**All Discussion of the Wage Question
in This Place is Positively Forbidden.
By order of the
ADVISORY COMMITTEE.**

In the same arbitrary manner the strikers refused to admit
men to the works whose presence and attention was necessary
to prevent deterioration and destruction of machinery.

On July 4th the Carnegie Company served a written notice
upon the sheriff of Allegheny County, calling upon him to protect the property, and holding the county responsible for its
injury or destruction.   The next ·day the sheriff accompanied
by deputies went to Homestead, and was escorted round the
works by the Advisory Committee, who pointed out their
"guards," and asked the sheriff to give them an official status
by making them his deputies.   The astonished official declined
the request and returned to Pittsburg.   The same day he sent
up a dozen deputies, who were met by the strikers and promptly
hustled out of town.   The Advisory Committee aided their
departure by conveying them across the river in their steamer
and putting them in the trolley-cars for Pittsburg.   A sheriff's
proclamation against unlawful. acts was torn down and the bill-
poster escorted out of town.   Such were the results of the attempts of the county officials to safeguard the works.

The same night two barges, containing some three hundred
watchmen hired by the Carnegie Steel Company through Pinkerton's Detective Agency and destined for Homestead, were
towed up the river from a point a few miles below Pittsburg.
The men were accompanied by a deputy sheriff; and arrangements had been made to deputize them, if circumstances arose
to require it.   The barges were fitted up with sleeping bunks
and cooking arrangements; and, besides a store of provisions,
they carried several cases of firearms and ammunition.   In
other respects they were just like any of the other barges used
on the river.   In spite of all precautions to keep the character
and destination of the boats secret, they were observed by a spy
of the Advisory Committee as they passed under the Smithfield
Street bridge, Pittsburg, soon after midnight; and a warning
was promptly telegraphed to Hugh O'Donnell.   Similar notice
was sent from Lock No. 1, some three miles below Homestead.
At once the preconcerted signal was given; and the sleeping
town was roused by the shrieks of the committee's steam-
whistle.   Men, women, and children tumbled into the streets

in wild disorder and hurried towards the river-bank. Many openly carried guns, rifles, and revolvers; and others armed themselves with staves torn from the garden fences as they ran along.

At the river all was dark and silent. A mist hung over the water and dimmed the glare of the electric lamps and fires of the Carrie furnaces across the stream. In a little while the lights of the barges were sighted; and the strikers' steamer *Edna* gave the alarm by blowing her whistle. Pistols were also fired from numerous little boats and by dozens of pickets along the bank. Every steam-whistle in town joined in the shrill demonstration; and the slumbering Pinkertons turned out of their bunks at the sound and started to break open the cases of rifles to defend themselves. Only a dozen were at first allowed to have the rifles. Thus the barges, pelted by the strikers' bullets, passed the town of Homestead; while the shouting crowds ran along the banks, keeping pace with them and firing as often as they could reload their arms. One bullet passed through the pilot-house of the *Little Bill*, the towing steamer, and others rattled against the sides of the barges.

When the people on the banks reached the steel works they were stopped for a moment by the wooden fence which surrounded the place; but a section of this was soon torn down, and the crowd swept through the gap, arriving at the pumping station in time to see the barges thrust against the shore.

By this time the dawning light of a new day was breaking upon the scene. As the gangplank was shoved ashore from the barges, the crowd rushed down the slope to the water's edge with loud cries and threatening gestures. One of them, a young fellow, who, curiously enough, was a religious leader in the community, threw himself flat upon the gangplank, as if daring the Pinkertons to march over his prostrate body. During the struggle to push the fellow aside a shot was fired, followed first by a scattering volley from the crowd, then by the return fire of a dozen of Pinkertons. The fusillade lasted for a couple of minutes, during which most of the crowd on shore scrambled up the bank in terror and confusion, and took refuge behind the piles of steel in the yards. During this exchange of shots two of the strikers were killed and several wounded. A number of the Pinkerton men were also injured, one of them fatally.

After the people on shore had retreated behind the piles of metal and the Pinkerton men had taken refuge inside the barges,

The Homestead Battle.
— *From Frank Leslie's Illustrated Weekly.*

the firing ceased; and a short conference was held between the leaders on shore and the chief of the watchmen. The latter explained that he and his men had been sent there to take possession of the works to guard them for the company, and that they would certainly enter the place, using force if need be. The strikers defied the leader of the watchmen, saying that before he entered those mills he would "trample over the dead bodies of 3,000 honest workingmen."

A couple of hours later a number of watchmen stepped ashore from the barges, and were met by a rattling volley from the strikers, who had erected barricades of steel billets and beams in the mill yard.   The Pinkertons rapidly sought shelter in the boats again; and then returned the fire through windows and port-holes.

Soon after nine o'clock the mill workers secured a small cannon; and with this they opened fire from the opposite side of the river.   During the second skirmish the tugboat *Little Bill*, which was the only means of moving the barges, went up the river with the dead and wounded; and when she returned an hour or two later to haul away the two barges, she was subjected to a merciless fusillade.   One of her crew was killed and several wounded; and the pilot was obliged to lie down to avoid being shot, as the boat drifted through the gauntlet of fire and so escaped to Pittsburg.   Thus, left helpless in their stranded barges, the wretched watchmen spent the long sultry day—a day in which American workmen seemed inspired with the spirit of the French Reign of Terror.   There was no horror conceived in that barbaric time that had not its counterfeit presentment at Homestead.   Oil was pumped onto the boats and spread upon the river, to burn up the imprisoned Pinkertons.   Burning rafts were floated down to them.   Dynamite was hurled upon the barges to break them open that sharpshooters might more readily pick off some crouching figure.   A car, loaded with oil, was set on fire and run down an inclined track towards the barges, in the hope that some of the burning stuff would reach them.   Natural gas was directed from a main near by so as to envelop the boats, and rockets were fired into it to explode it.   The cannon on the opposite bank, soon re-enforced by a second one, played upon the barges and their helpless occupants; and riflemen from a hundred points of vantage potted any unwary sufferer who ventured near a window or other opening for a gasp of fresh air.   But as if to keep the name of the American workman from everlasting infamy, every diabolical effort failed.

The dynamite exploded harmlessly; the oil-covered waters flowed away from the barges; the burning car stopped short in its course; the fire of the cannon was wild, and it was stopped after a shot had taken off the head of a striker. But the horrors that were achieved were enough to give this 6th of July a place of its own in the history of Western Pennsylvania. A white flag was shown on the barges, and greeted with shouts of

Shooting at the Pinkerton guards from behind barricades of steel.
—*From the London Daily Graphic.*

"No quarter," and a volley of bullets. A man was seen to fall near the flag; and the shouts of anger changed to cheers. Every eminence about the works, the long trestle and the new station in the mill, were black with vociferous crowds. The adjoining hills were lined with watchers; and everywhere the thirst of human blood was manifest. No voice was raised in pity; no word was spoken for peace. From Pittsburg, and even from the Edgar Thomson works at Braddock, armed re-enforcements marched to help the strikers, who were already fifteen to one, and sheltered by fortifications of solid steel. The wretched watchmen, cooped up in stranded boats, had neither the power to advance nor to retreat.

The events of this dreadful day have been told by Myron R. Stowell, an eye-witness, in a little book full of sympathy for the workmen. For this reason his story cannot be impugned on the ground of prejudice against the strikers. He says:

" Many a battle has gone down in history where less shooting was done and fewer people were killed. There were hundreds of men, well armed, thirsting for the lives of others in the boat, while thousands of men and women stood just out of range and cheered them on. Each crack of a rifle made them more blood-thirsty and each boom of the cannon more eager for the blood of the officers. One of the strikers remarked:
'There are but two weeks between civilization and barbarism, and I believe it will take only two days of this work to make the change.'
Indeed, it looked as if the veneering of gentility had already been cracked.
Then another shot and another cheer told that somebody had been hit. The Pinkertons were too badly scared to make any effort to shoot, and were crowded like sheep into the barge which lay farthest from shore. Fresh ammunition and arms had arrived from Pittsburg for the strikers and the men bent harder to their tasks. They worked nearer the river that their fire might be more deadly. The workers could be seen dragging their bodies like snakes along the ground to where they could get a better shot. The cannon would again roar, but the shot would land in the water above the boat. Once a piece of one of the doors fell with the shot. Several of the imported officers were revealed, and a score of shots were fired in quick succession. Some one must have fallen, for cheer on cheer of triumph went up from thousands of throats. At every shot of the cannon thereafter a volley of shots was heard from the sharpshooters, who had seen some one on the boat. They only shot when they saw something, and every crack of a rifle meant an attempt on a human life.
At one o'clock there was a wild commotion at the new station. A tall, brawny workman waved two sticks of dynamite high above his head. By his side was a basket full of the deadly explosive. The excited gathering, that a moment before had been wild, was silent, and listened. His voice was loud and distinct. He said:

'Men of Homestead and Fellow Strikers: Our friends have been murdered—our brothers have been shot down before our eyes by hired thugs! The blood of honest workmen has been spilled. Yonder in those boats are hundreds of men who have murdered our friends and would ravish our homes! Men of Homestead, we must kill them! Not one must escape alive!'

'Aye, aye, aye!' shouted a half thousand voices. Then the Herculean workman continued:

'The cannon has failed to sink the boats—the oil has failed to burn them. Who will follow me? These bombs will do the work!'

As he spoke he flourished the dynamite. A score of men raised their clubs, and regardless of the fact that they were within the range of the Pinkerton rifles, followed him. They ran in their haste to take human life. They were not savages, but men of families, who, perhaps a few hours before, had held infants on their knees or kissed their wives farewell. They were good, strong men, wrought up by the sight of blood, and ready to take the lives of those who threatened them and theirs.

With their penknives they scooped up holes for the cartridges and fuse. The latter was very short—it would burn quickly. The crowds could see them light the matches and hold the messengers of death until they burned closely. Then, with strong right arms drawn until every muscle showed like a whipcord, they let fly, and the explosions were cheered by the excited men and women. The distance was long, and the bombs had to be thrown from behind some shelter, and many of the missiles fell short of the mark, but when one landed on the roof cheer upon cheer went up. One man had crawled down on the structural iron, and then, by making a throw of nearly a hundred feet, struck the boat. The front end heaved and a few boards flew. He lighted another fuse and another stick of dynamite. It described a semi-circle in the air, leaving a trail of smoke behind. It was going to land squarely on top of the Monongahela, but instead of striking the roof it splashed into a bucket of water. It sizzled for a moment and then went out without exploding. It had hardly died, however, when another from the pump-house fell on the roof. It lay there smoking a moment while the strikers prayed it might wreck the craft. There was an explosion, and a hole was torn in the roof. It was not then known whether it killed anybody inside, but when the boards flew up a gondola hat went flying into the air. Another bomb was thrown into the bow of the boat. The clearing smoke showed a door was gone. Human forms were seen within, which was a sign for the sharpshooters to do some execution. At 1:35 o'clock several men went out on the bow of the boat to pick up their dead and wounded companions. There were a half-dozen shots and two more men fell. Then came more curses for the firm and additional cheers of victory.

Another stick of dynamite fell five minutes later, and in three minutes more another tore off a part of the planks. Then the men drew closer and their work became more deadly.

Then it was decided to throw oil again and burn the boat. At 12:10 o'clock the hose carriage belonging to the city, and half a dozen barrels of lubricating oil were brought to the water tanks, together with a fire engine, but there was great difficulty in getting it to work. In the meantime a new supply of dynamite had arrived. The boxes were knocked open and the men drew out the explosives as unconcernedly as they would have handled their dinners. Then they made another rush for the barges and there was more sharp firing.

About this time a coal steamer's whistle was heard and the sharpshooters stampeded to the rear for an instant, thinking another corps of deputies had arrived. The alarm was false, and they soon resumed operations. Then they got the oil to flowing, but, as in the morning, it circled around the boats and refused to burn.

The fight still continued and more attempts were made to burn the boats and the three hundred Pinkertons within. It was four o'clock when the giant form of President William Weihe, of the Amalgamated Association, appeared. Hundreds followed him into one of the mills. He tried to address the men but they refused to listen to him. President-elect Garland was there also, but the cries of 'Burn the boats, kill the Pinkertons, no quarter for the murderers,' drowned his voice."

Towards five o'clock a fresh attempt at surrender was made by the men in the barges. Again a white flag was displayed. Fortunately at this moment the leaders of the strikers were conferring as to what measures should next be taken; and the Pinkertons' signal suggested a way of ending a desperate situation. O'Donnell, chairman of the Advisory Committee, stepped down the embankment to receive the message of peace. The spokesman of the imprisoned wretches offered to surrender on condition of protection from mob violence. This being agreed to, the doors were flung open, and the victorious strikers crowded into the barges. The reporters who followed them found one dead and eleven wounded watchmen. The rest were disarmed and marched out, while the crowd swarmed over the boats for loot. Cases of provisions were broken open and the contents distributed among the women and children; bedding and every portable thing was taken away. Then the barges were set on fire; and the strikers turned to escort their prisoners to a public hall in town. One by one, with bared heads, the latter de-

The burning barges, the evening of the surrender.

scended the gangplank, climbed up the incline to the mill yard, and across it to the public road; and never did captives suffer more in running a gauntlet of redskins. For nearly a mile the watchmen walked, ran, or crawled through a lane of infuriated men, women, and children; and at every step they were struck with fists, clubs, and stones. Their hats, satchels, and coats were snatched away from them; and in many cases they were robbed of their watches and money. Not a man escaped injury. One of them, Connors, unable to move and defend himself, was deliberately shot by one of the strikers and then clubbed,

Another, named Edwards, also wounded and helpless, was clubbed by another striker with the butt end of a musket. Both of these men died; and another became insane and committed

The attack on the surrendered guards.
—*From Leslie's Weekly.*

suicide as a result of the fearful beating received after surrender. About thirty others were afterwards taken to the hospital with broken arms and disjointed ankles, shattered noses, gouged eyes, bruised heads, and injured backs.

At midnight a special train went to Homestead in charge of the sheriff of Allegheny County, and took the Pinkerton men to Pittsburg for safety. The day's casualties were ten men killed and over sixty wounded. Several died later.

Flushed with victory the strikers now put the borough of Homestead into a state of siege. All strangers were excluded, including a party of prominent railway and state officials who chanced to be passing through Pittsburg. Many citizens were arrested and taken before the strikers' committee, just as in the early days of the French revolution. Hotel keepers were notified not to lodge or accommodate newspaper reporters whose accounts were not favorable to the insurrectionist government. Telegraph operators were compelled to exhibit to the self-constituted authorities private messages that were left for transmission over the wires of the public companies, so that it might be ascertained if anything detrimental to the dignity or the interests of the Advisory Committee was being sent out. Several journalists were arrested and held until satisfactory evidence could be obtained as to their identity; and all reporters were required to have credentials and passports from the Advisory Committee, and to wear a conspicuous badge of the Amalgamated Association to insure their personal safety. Some reporters who had incurred the strikers' ill will by publishing reports unfavorable to the workmen were arrested, and compelled, hatless and coatless, to leave the town at midnight afoot, the privilege of securing even a private conveyance being denied them. And while these conditions obtained, a delegation of strikers was at Harrisburg, assuring the governor of Pennsylvania that perfect peace and tranquillity prevailed in the borough of Homestead; that the civil authorities were respected and obeyed; and that the sheriff's call for troops should be disregarded.

It chanced, however, that the governor's own representative, sent to Homestead for the purpose of reporting on the condition of affairs, was arrested by the strikers and roughly escorted out of town. He returned, and again he was hustled away. This happened three times. Such a practical illustration of the negation of the rights of citizens sufficed to convince the governor of the need for state troops; and on July 10th he issued an order to Major-General Snowden to call out the entire division of the National Guard, numbering some 8,000 men, and mass them at Homestead to aid the sheriff of Allegheny County. Two days later the troops arrived; the open reign of terror at Homestead came to an end; and the Carnegie officials were put in possession of their property.

CHAPTER XV

ATTEMPTED ASSASSINATION OF MR. FRICK

BEFORE the country had recovered from the thrill of horror which succeeded the Homestead battle, an attempt was made to murder Mr. Frick; and the bloody details of the assault were cabled to the ends of the earth, bringing fresh disgrace upon the unhappy town of Homestead. On Saturday, July 23d, a Russian anarchist shot and stabbed Mr. Frick while he was seated in conversation with his associate, Mr. Leishman. This man had made several previous visits to the Carnegie offices, where he represented himself as the agent of a New York employment bureau. Once he had a brief interview with Mr. Frick, who told him he thought there would be no need for the services of any agency, as the managers were making arrangements by which they hoped to get their old employees back.

On the day mentioned this man called again and sent in his card to Mr. Frick, who had just returned from lunch and had dropped into a chair at the end of the flat-topped desk at which he usually worked. It was not his usual seat; and he had moved into it to be nearer Mr. Leishman, who sat diagonally opposite. Mr. Frick had swung round in his chair so that his side was turned to the door through which the boy brought the card. Before the boy could regain the front office with Mr. Frick's message, the man stepped through the swinging door and glanced quickly around. Mr. Frick looked up in surprise at the sudden entry of a stranger, and saw the man make a quick movement towards his hip pocket. Realizing the meaning of the movement, Mr. Frick sprang to his feet. At the same moment the fellow had drawn and fired a revolver with lightning rapidity, and the bullet, after passing through the lobe of the left ear, struck Mr. Frick in the neck. The shock sent him to the floor; and as he lay on the carpet the assassin fired a second time, and again the bullet struck Mr. Frick in the neck.

While this was happening Mr. Leishman had jumped from his seat and was running round the long desk to get at the fellow. He reached him just as he fired a third time, and either seized or knocked up his hand, so that the shot went wild, the bullet striking the wall near the ceiling. Mr. Leishman courageously grappled with the fellow, and while he was wrestling with him for the revolver, Mr. Frick struggled to his feet and grasped his assailant from behind. In this way the three men swayed violently to and fro for a few thrilling moments, and then all three fell with a crash against the low wall just under the window overlooking Fifth Avenue, the Russian underneath. A crowd, attracted by the shots, stood on the opposite side of the street; and seeing Mr. Frick struggling near the window, thought he was trying to raise it to give an alarm, or to escape from some enemy invisible from the sidewalk. This occasioned one of the many erroneous reports sent out to the newspapers.

The fall had loosened Mr. Frick's grasp of the fellow's left arm; and while Mr. Leishman still held on to the right hand and the revolver, the Russian drew a dagger made from an old file and plunged it again and again into Mr. Frick, who, bending over him and weak from his exertions and wounds, was unable to avoid the blows. First the dagger was thrust into his hip, just behind the head of the femur; then it struck him in the right side and glanced along one of the ribs; and a third blow tore open the left leg just below the knee. Despite his terrible injuries Mr. Frick again threw himself on the ruffian, and finally pinioned his arm to the floor. Then the clerks, who had watched the struggle from the door as if spellbound, rushed in and

15

secured the anarchist.   The revolver and dagger were torn from his grasp and he was dragged to his feet.   Covered with the blood that had flowed from Mr. Frick's wounds, he was a sorry looking object; and Mr. Leishman looked almost as bad.   The latter, who had so bravely seized the smoking revolver a few moments before, and heard the trigger snap even a fourth time, now collapsed utterly, and had to be carried from the room. Mr. Frick, the only calm person present, leaned against the desk and watched the last ineffectual struggles of the wretch who had tried to kill him.

Thrown at last into a chair and held there, the Russian appeared to be mumbling something, and all but Mr. Frick were too excited to notice it.   At this moment a deputy sheriff rushed in with a drawn revolver and made as if he would shoot the man.   Mr. Frick interposed.   "No, don't kill him," he said; "raise his head and let me see his face."   As they did so it was seen that the man's apparent mumbling was caused by his chewing something; and on his mouth being forced open, a cap containing fulminite of mercury, such as anarchists had previously used to commit suicide, was found between the desperate fellow's teeth.   Even when overcome by numbers, he still sought to carry out his devilish purpose by an explosion which would involve Mr. Frick and a dozen innocent men in his own destruction.

By this time the office was filled with an excited crowd.   A German carpenter, who had been at work in the building, broke through the throng and aimed a blow at the Russian's head with his hammer.   It missed him.   Then arose cries of "Shoot him!" "Lynch him!" and amid all the excitement no one seemed to give a thought to Mr. Frick, who still stood leaning against the desk, with the blood streaming from his many wounds.   A number of policemen who had been attracted by the noise quickly surrounded the assassin to protect him, and led him from the room.   Then the others turned to Mr. Frick. A score of hands hastened to his support; and he was gently placed on a lounge in an inner room, while hurried calls were sent for physicians.

While the blood-sodden clothes were being removed, and before the physicians arrived, Mr. Frick talked calmly about the assault, and commented with a smile on the assassin's amazing muscular power; nor did his courage fail him when the surgeons began probing for the bullets. At first the doctors said there was little hope of recovery. The first bullet had entered the side of the neck, cutting the lobe of the ear, and had ranged backwards and downwards until it almost reached the shoulder. The second bullet had followed a similar course, but from right to left.

While the doctor was probing in the wounds Mr. Frick calmly directed him as to the place where the bullet would be found, and then as the instrument reached it, he remarked: "There! that feels like it, doctor." And while the probing, cutting, and sewing up of the wounds were going on, he dictated a cablegram to Mr. Carnegie, telling him that he was not mortally injured, and he signed several letters which he had previously dictated. He also completed the arrangements which he had begun earlier in the day for a loan; and signed all the necessary papers. The doctors said that it was the most magnificent exhibition of courage they had ever seen.

Most touching of all, and even more characteristic of the man, was his manner of greeting Mrs. Frick on his arrival home a few hours later in the ambulance. Mrs. Frick had been critically ill; and the excitement of the Homestead battle had rendered her condition precarious. Mr. Frick's first thought after the attack was of his wife; and he gave very emphatic orders that no alarming reports be permitted to reach her. Then he sent two of her relatives who had hastened to the office on hearing of the assault, to break the news to her gently, and to let her understand that his injuries were trifling. So well did they succeed that, as Mr. Frick was carried past her bedroom door, she was in no way alarmed. Telling the stretcher bearers to turn his head around so that he could speak to his wife, Mr. Frick addressed her by name, and called out a cheery inquiry after the youngest child. Then he assured her that he was not seriously hurt and would be in to see her before very long.

The fanatic who made this ferocious attempt on Mr. Frick's life had nothing to do with the strikers. He was of the usual type of European anarchist; and he had been only a few years in the country. He went from New York to Pittsburg specially to kill Mr. Frick. When asked why he selected Mr. Frick in particular, he exclaimed in astonishment: "Why, what would the company do without Mr. Frick? Carnegie is thousands of miles away, and he would not dare to oppose the men as Frick has done." So here again was an echo of Carnegie idealism. As for the undiscriminating criminal himself, he was sentenced to twenty-one years in the penitentiary for the assault, and one year in the workhouse for carrying concealed weapons.

The news of the attempted assassination created intense excitement at Homestead, where it was bulletined a few minutes after the occurrence. Crowds gathered at every street corner and in front of the telegraph stations and newspaper offices; and whenever a man received a message hundreds crowded around him to hear the latest news. The strikers heard of the attempt with mixed feelings. The more ignorant workmen rejoiced openly. "Frick's dead by this time and we've won the strike," shouted one. "The Carnegie Company don't amount to shucks without Frick," commented another, as he joyfully predicted the early collapse of the firm's resistance. But at the headquarters of the labor-union the news was received with dismay. While the leaders believed the strikers blameless of this particular horror, there already had been so much to set the public against them that they feared the discredit of this fresh act of violence would fall on them. And their alarm was justified. From one end of the country to the other, and across the oceans from distant lands, swept a wave of fierce indignation against the strikers and denunciation of their methods. Innocent of this particular crime, the strikers had to bear the disgrace of it.

On Mr. Frick himself the incident seemed to have no effect except for the pain and inconvenience it occasioned. His sorely wounded body suffered; but while nurses and attendants were prostrate under the intense heat of July, the patient made no complaint. From the first day he insisted on being kept informed of the progress of events. Newspapers, letters, and telegrams were read to him; and he dictated answers to many of the latter. His grasp on the strike situation was never relaxed for a moment. No move was made by the men that was not instantly telephoned to him; and nothing was done by the managers that did not emanate from him, or that was not previously submitted for his approval. Except that the contest was now conducted from Mr. Frick's Homewood residence instead of from his Fifth Avenue office, no difference was to be seen in the situation.

By this time the scene of disorder near Pittsburg had become the centre of interest for the whole world. No other war was being fought; no other event of universal interest was taking place; and the attention of the people of every land was focussed on the beautiful spot on the Monongahela which John McClure had so infelicitously named Amity Homestead. In every country columns were daily printed describing the happenings at the works and the military camp; and imaginary scenes at the bedside of Mr. Frick found their way into newspapers printed in many languages.

As if to keep this interest from flagging, a young soldier in the camp called for three cheers for Frick's assassin. His outraged commander immediately had him triced by the thumbs to a tent-pole and then drummed him, with his head half shaved, out of camp to the tune of the Rogue's March. The fellow had swallowed some tobacco juice while undergoing his punishment, and this had made him sick. So the sensation-loving journals exploited the incident as a brutal punishment; and this ran round the world as a valuable item of news.

There was one spot, however, where these items of news did not readily penetrate; and that was Rannoch Lodge, on beautiful Loch Rannoch. Here, thirty-five miles from the nearest railway and telegraph station, Andrew Carnegie, in accordance with plans previously made, denied himself to reporters and refused to answer telegrams or letters relating in any way to Homestead. Having delegated his authority to Mr. Frick, he knew that the measures they had jointly planned would be carried out to the letter, despite the efforts of anarchists or the protests of politicians of a less ruddy hue. And so he went fishing; and the London papers sought in vain to get an expression of opinion from him either on the Homestead battle or the attempt on Mr. Frick's life.

In the account of the Homestead strike which Mr. W. T. Stead published in 1900, after, as he claims, "talking on the subject with Mr. Carnegie this autumn," he repeats the story that the labor leaders "had applied to Mr. Frick for Mr. Carnegie's address in order to telegraph him—Mr. Carnegie being at that time absent in Scotland, and his address not being known to any one in this country except his business associates. Mr. Frick refused to give the address; whereupon Mr. Reid obtained it from our Consul-General in London, John C. New, and then cabled Mr. Carnegie, in which he accepted the terms proposed by Mr. O'Donnell, and urged that Mr. Frick be seen immediately with a view to effecting the settlement."

This statement is so incoherent that it is not clear who "accepted the terms proposed by Mr. O'Donnell." The idea sought to be conveyed is that it was Mr. Carnegie who accepted the terms of the strikers, since no one else mentioned in this strange narrative had anything to accept. To make this matter clear once for all Mr. Carnegie's cablegrams are here given as received in Pittsburg:

RANNOCH, July 28, 1892.

We have telegram from Tribune Reid through high official London Amalgamated Association reference Homestead Steel Works. The proposition is worthy of consideration. Replied "nothing can be done. Send H. C. Frick document." You must decide without delay. Amalgamated Association evidently distressed.

The next day this was modified by the following:

RANNOCH, July 29, 1892.

After due consideration we have concluded Tribune too old. Probably the proposition is not worthy of consideration. Useful showing distress of Amalgamated Association. Use your own discretion about terms and starting. George Lauder, Henry Phipps Jr., Andrew Carnegie solid. H. C. Frick forever!

And in his answer to Mr. Whitelaw Reid, Mr. Carnegie cabled that no compromise would be considered by him, and that he would rather see grass growing over the Homestead works than advise Mr. Frick to yield to the strikers.

The rest of the story quoted by Stead is fairly accurate. "Mr. Frick was obdurate. He refused to consider the matter at all, denounced the strikers as assassins, and declared that if Carnegie came in person, in company with President Harrison and the entire Cabinet, he would not settle the strike."

In regard to Stead's complaint that Mr. Carnegie's address in Scotland was not given to the strikers, he should have known, after he had "talked on the subject with Mr. Carnegie this autumn," that the latter had selected such an out-of-the-way residence as Rannoch Lodge for the very purpose of eluding the appeals of the workmen which it was foreseen his speeches and writings would call forth. And his silence during all the exciting happenings at Homestead was in accordance with plans made long before.

Mr. Carnegie's consistency at this time provoked much comment. Two days after the assault on Mr. Frick, the *St. James' Gazette* reported that "Mr. Carnegie has preserved the same

moody silence towards all the members of the American Lega-
tion here; and all other persons in London with whom he is
usually in communication have not heard a word from him since
the beginning of the troubles at Homestead." The publication went on to say that "the news of the shooting of Mr. Frick
has intensified the feeling of all classes against Mr. Carnegie.
A large meeting of the labor representative leagues was held in
this city yesterday, at which a resolution was adopted strongly
condemning the course of Mr. Carnegie in regard to the Homestead troubles. The resolution added that should Mr. Carnegie
insult British workmen by further philanthropic efforts in their
behalf, it was hoped that they would show their detestation of
him by contemptuously refusing to accept any offers of help
from him."

Now became prominent the contrast between Mr. Carnegie's
idealistic utterances and the doings at Homestead. Newspapers in every country and of every political color drew attention to the startling discrepancy; and not a few of them saw in
the violence of the strikers the logical outcome of the Carnegie commandment: "Thou shalt not take thy neighbor's job."
The host of critics, that arose with angry clamor, discovered
in Mr. Carnegie's practical philanthropy but the expression of
an unmitigated egotism; and many brutal and insensate taunts
were flung at him as he lay silent and self-contained in his
Highland shooting-lodge. It was altogether a pitiful exhibition. Even the London *Times* could not forego the chance to
fling a sneer. Commenting on the assault on Mr. Frick, the
writer concludes his editorial thus:

"Mr. Carnegie's position is singular. The avowed cham-
pion of trades-unions now finds himself in almost ruinous conflict with the representatives of his own views. He has probably by this time seen cause to modify his praise of unionism
and the sweet reasonableness of its leaders. Or, are we to assume that this doctrine is true in Glasgow but not in the United
States, or that it ceases to be applicable the moment Mr. Carnegie's interests are touched?"

A day or two later the representative of the Associated Press reported that he had driven from Kingussie to Rannoch Lodge, "and made repeated efforts to obtain an interview with Mr. Carnegie in order to obtain a statement from him of his views regarding the troubles at Homestead, Pa., and more especially concerning the shooting of H. C. Frick," but "his mission then proved fruitless. This morning, however, he was more successful," and Mr. Carnegie, "after persistent interrogation by the caller, finally said, 'Well, I authorize you to make the following statement : I have not attended to business for the past three years, but I have implicit confidence in those who are managing the mills. Further than that I have nothing to say.'"

The storm raised by the publication of this short interview proved how wise Mr. Carnegie had been in previously saying nothing. The tide of sympathy, which had swept from the strikers, now returned to them; and municipal bodies, workmen's unions, political clubs, vied with preachers, lecturers, and editors in England and America in fierce denunciation of one whose acts, it was said, "conform so little to his verbal utterances." Some of these expressions of contempt and hatred were puerile and stupid in their violence. "Count no man happy until he is dead," wrote the St. Louis *Post-Dispatch*. "Three months ago Andrew Carnegie was a man to be envied. To-day he is an object of mingled pity and contempt. In the estimation of nine-tenths of the thinking people on both sides of the ocean he has not only given the lie to all his antecedents, but confessed himself a moral coward. One would naturally suppose that if he had a grain of consistency, not to say decency, in his composition, he would favor rather than oppose the organization of trades-unions among his own working people at Homestead. One would naturally suppose that if he had a grain of manhood, not to say courage, in his composition, he would at least have been willing to face the consequences of his inconsistency. But what does Carnegie do? Runs off to Scotland

out of harm's way to await the issue of the battle he was too
pusillanimous to share.   A single word from him might have
saved the bloodshed—but the word was never spoken.   Nor has
he, from that bloody day until this, said anything except that
he 'had implicit confidence in the managers of the mills.'   The
correspondent who finally obtained this valuable information,
expresses the opinion that 'Mr. Carnegie has no intention of
returning to America at present.'   He might have added that
America can well spare Mr. Carnegie.   Ten thousand 'Carnegie
Public Libraries' would not compensate the country for the
direct and indirect evils re-
sulting from the Homestead
lockout.   Say what you will
of Frick, he is a brave man.
Say what you will of Car-
negie, he is a coward.   And
gods and men hate cowards."

In spite of the outward
show of indifference with which
Mr. Carnegie received these vicious
attacks, his sensitive soul suffered
keenly.   He afterwards told a repre-

"Fishing from morning to
night."

sentative of the Associated Press that
"the deplorable events at Homestead
had burst upon him like a thunderbolt from a clear sky.   They
had such a depressing effect upon him that he had to lay his
book aside and resort to the lochs and moors, fishing from morning to night."

Meanwhile Mr. Frick, propped up in bed, and swathed in
bandages, daily received the reports of the managers of the different works, dictated replies to letters and telegrams, and
allowed neither bodily pain nor a domestic bereavement to
slacken his grasp of the situation.   On Friday, August 5th,
thirteen days after the attempt on his life, he astonished his
business associates by suddenly walking into the office as if

nothing had happened. He left his home unattended, entered a street car, and without fuss or ceremony returned to the office and took his seat at his desk. It was characteristic of the man's simplicity. The previous day he had attended the funeral of his youngest child, born in the midst of this excitement and dead because of it. The mother's life was almost involved in the sacrifice.

CHAPTER XVI

THE AFTERMATH OF WAR

UNDER the protection of the state militia, workmen willing to accept the wages which the strikers refused were at once introduced into the deserted mills. Major-General Snowden, who was in command of the troops, took a firm hold of the situation the moment he arrived; and open defiance of law and order ceased at the sound of the first bugle-call. The impression had gone abroad among the strikers that the militia had come to prevent the landing of more Pinkertons. The illusion was dispelled in a single sentence of the commander: "The gates are open. Any one may go in if the company permits it." In three days a hundred men were at work; in two weeks nearly a thousand were inside the mill, and one of the regiments had left for home.

With the fatuity that had characterized the actions of the Amalgamated Association from the outset, a sympathetic strike was now ordered in the other Carnegie works. Although the scale had been signed at the Upper and Lower Union Mills and at Beaver Falls, the men at these establishments broke their agreement on July 14th, and left the mills in a body. Superintendent Dillon had both the Pittsburg mills running full with non-union labor within four weeks; and the unprofitable enterprise at Beaver Falls was allowed to remain idle for several months. Thus the Amalgamated Association unnecessarily lost three more mills at a time when it was fighting for its very existence.

The newspaper files of that period show that the industrial storm-centre at Homestead still held the attention of the world. At Little Rock, on July 16th, Carnegie was burnt in effigy. The same day the London *Echo*, once owned by Andrew Carnegie, demanded explanations of him as to the report that he had "fortified his works with barbed and electrically charged

Military camp overlooking the Homestead Works.

wire." The London *Financial Observer* of the same date preached a sermon on the text of Nero fiddling while Rome was burning.

"Here we have this Scotch-Yankee plutocrat meandering through Scotland in a four-in-hand, opening public libraries and receiving the freedom of cities, while the wretched Belgian and Italian workmen who sweat themselves in order to supply him with the ways and means for his self-glorification are starving in Pittsburg."

Pittsburg newspapers at the same time were gravely discussing the advisability of refusing Mr. Carnegie's recent gift of money for a library; and in both chambers of the American Congress denunciations of Frick, Carnegie, and Pinkerton were freely uttered. The world seemed topsy-turvy; and the strange doctrine that the strikers had a natural right to work in the

Carnegie mills at wages fixed by themselves was voiced in a hundred different forms. In some cases sympathy with the strikers took a practical form; as when the Fairport Fishing Company of Ashtabula offered them " 2,000 pounds of fresh or salt fish." A day later a Chicago bishop joined the *Financial Times* of London in abusing " Czar Carnegie."

On the 19th warrants were issued for the arrest of the principal leaders of the riot on a charge of murder; and the newspapers simultaneously reported that Mr. Dillon had 800 men at work in the Union Mills. The same day a special committee appointed by Congress to investigate the Homestead labor troubles held its first meeting; and work was resumed at the open-hearth department and the armor-plate mill. The governor of Pennsylvania also arrived at Homestead. On the 20th Keir Hardie, M. P., who had achieved notoriety by his bad manners and grotesque behavior in Parliament, sent the strikers' fund £100 which Andrew Carnegie had previously given him towards his election expenses; and Ben Butler came out in an erudite opinion on the possibility of extraditing Carnegie on a charge of murder. So laughter followed tears.

On July 22d the non-union men at Duquesne stopped work in sympathy with the Homestead strikers; but some of them regretting their action a few days later, a little riot occurred when they tried to get back into the mill. A few soldiers were sent over from Homestead; a dozen warrants were issued for the arrest of the ringleaders; and the trouble ended in a picturesque man-hunt on the hills and the sending of the manacled prisoners to Pittsburg. These men were all convicted of rioting.

The last day of this eventful month fell on Sunday. The scene in the works was thus described in the papers next morning:

" With for a church the biggest mill in America, boarded by a high fence and a protectorate of one hundred and fifty armed watchmen, with one thousand soldiers in easy reach, the non-union men in the Homestead plant gave thanks to God this morning. About four hundred of the new men had gathered in the beam-mill and found seats on rough, improvised benches. An orchestra from Pittsburg played 'Nearer, My God, to Thee,' and Chaplain Adams of the Sixteenth Regiment, standing where the sunshine glistened on his epaulets, preached a sermon that

The Sheridan cavalry and the Governor's troop going to the rescue of Battery B's cannon, which the strikers would not permit to be unloaded from the cars.
—*From Harpers' Weekly.*

touched many hearts, on a famed biblical character, Saul of Tarsus."

The same paper, under the caption "Everybody Condemned," tells of a conference on the Homestead situation of the Central Labor Union in New York.

By the 5th of August fifteen hundred men were at work at Homestead; and on the 8th the strike at Duquesne ended in a stampede for work in which more men were hurt than in the previous riot. About the same time the members of the congressional committee of investigation fell out among themselves, refused to sign their chairman's report, the minority of two became the majority, and of the other members each made a report for himself. Thus five reports were submitted by the committee; and it is from one of these expressions of individual opinion that Mr. W. T. Stead quotes a phrase in condemnation of Mr. Frick which has since been embodied in Alderson's authorized biography of Andrew Carnegie:

"The Committee of Investigation of the House of Representatives," says Mr. Stead, "roundly condemned Mr. Frick and his officers for lack of patience, indulgence, and solicitude, and they say:—

'Mr. Frick seems to have been too stern, brusque, and somewhat autocratic, of which some of the men justly complain. We are persuaded that, if he had chosen, an agreement would have been reached between him and the workmen, and all the trouble which followed would thus have been avoided.'"

This quotation, which, by the way, is garbled by Mr. Stead so as to omit a qualifying clause and to include an important word ("chosen") not used in the original, expresses the views of a single individual, Mr. Oates, and the other members of the committee who had heard the evidence refused to sign it. Mr. Stead's conclusion that "Mr. Frick, indeed, seems to have been the villain of the piece all through" is also adopted by Mr. Carnegie's biographer. In such ways history is made.

While the confused and contradictory reports of this committee of investigation contain little of value, the testimony of the witnesses examined by it has much in it that suggests the underlying causes of the strike and the violence offered to the company's watchmen. As this is a matter of public record it need not be repeated here. A single quotation from the testimony of Mr. T. V. Powderly, General Master Workman of the Knights of Labor, will serve as an illuminating example.

"Does your organization countenance the prevention of non-union men taking the place of striking or locked-out men?" Mr. Powderly was asked.

"We agree with Andrew Carnegie, 'Thou shalt not take thy neighbor's job,'" answered the chief of the Knights of Labor.

The report of the Senate Committee also made use of a quotation from Carnegie's *Forum* article ending with the same terse commandment, to illustrate the course which Mr. Frick ought to have followed in his treatment of the workmen! Under all this censure Mr. Frick remained silent, and to this day he has never said a word either in explanation or self-defence.

During all this time the strikers, overawed by the militia, had been fairly peaceable. A few assaults on non-union workmen were made whenever a small body of the latter was caught by night or in an out-of-the-way place; but the growing hopelessness of their position now made some of the old workers desperate. Superintendent Potter was stoned as he sat on his porch. The company's steamer was fired on by men concealed in a passing train. The house of a "scab" was set on fire; and an attempt was made to burn down a big boarding-house where non-union men were lodged. Dynamite was used in an attempt to injure one of the Union Mills. But these sporadic outbreaks had no effect beyond that of alienating the sympathy which the press and people of the country had so conspicuously bestowed upon the strikers a little while before. A butcher was boycotted for supplying the troops with ice; a school was deserted because the teachers were the daughters of an Association man who had wearied of the strike and gone back to work. The borough council was crippled because the unionists would not sit with the non-unionists. Through it all the condition of the works was slowly improving; and day by day more men were found at work. By the third week in September more troops had been sent away, and the strike was practically a thing of the past.

Organized labor, however, was slow to acknowledge its defeat. Up to this time the Knights of Labor had contributed

16

nothing to the cause of the strikers beyond a voluminous sympathy and some talk of a general boycott of Carnegie products. Now, in the hands of Master Workman Hugh Dempsey of District Assembly No. 3, it brought to the strikers' aid a weapon hitherto happily unknown in American industrial warfare. This was poison—a mixture of croton oil and arsenic varied with powders of antimony.   The hellish plot was carefully investigated by a jury presided over by one of the ablest judges of Pennsylvania; and the accused had the benefit of counsel of unquestioned force and influence.   The verdict of guilty, the sentence of the chief criminals to seven years in the penitentiary, the refusal of the board of pardons a year later to commute the punishment, may be taken as conclusive proof of the existence of this diabolical conspiracy, which brought dishonor to organized labor.

During September and October there was an alarming number of dysentery cases among the non-union men who got their meals inside the Homestead mills; but the sickness was at first attributed to bad water, careless habits, and the unaccustomed hardship of the work around the furnaces.   When the disorders failed to yield to the usual remedies, the doctors began to suspect a worse condition; and their suspicions were strengthened when the patients improved under treatment for antimony poisoning.   Some deaths taking place, the lesser criminals became panic-stricken, and hastened to confess that they had been bribed by Dempsey and an associate to put yellow powders into the soup and coffee served to the workmen.   After conviction one of these creatures withdrew his confession, acknowledged perjury, and the next day recanted again and swore that his first evidence was true.   It turned out that he had been tempted into a fresh conspiracy, which this time had for its purpose the pardon of the entire band of poisoners.   It is worthy of mention that the Knights of Labor stood by their fallen official with a steadfastness worthy of a nobler cause; and despite his sentence to the penitentiary kept him on their rolls.

On September 21st true bills were found against one hundred and sixty-seven participants in the Homestead battle—three for murder and the rest for aggravated riot and conspiracy. The next day Mr. Lovejoy, secretary of the Carnegie Company, was arrested at the behest of the Amalgamated Association on a charge of aggravated riot and assault and battery; and Mr. Frick and a dozen other officials of the company were included in the indictment.

With the exception of three ringleaders of the rioters, who were held on a murder charge, all of these persons were admitted to bail. The murder charges duly came to trial. In two cases the accused had no difficulty in proving an alibi; and the third, that of O'Donnell, resulted in an acquittal. Nine months later the cases against the Carnegie officials were dropped; and the same day an order of court was issued releasing from bail the strikers who were under indictment. Fifty-seven men in all had been arrested, of whom thirty-three were indicted for treason—the first cases of the kind in the history of the commonwealth—twenty-one for rioting, and three for murder.

On October 13th, after ninety-five days' service, the last of the soldiers left Homestead; and their withdrawal was at once followed by a recrudescence of violence. At this time the situation was as follows: Over two thousand workmen were in the mill, among whom were about two hundred of the former employees. A number of skilled workmen from Braddock, Duquesne, Pittsburg, and other places were among the non-union workmen. From day to day additions were being made to the forces in the mill, a limited number of them being Homestead men. The non-union men lived in and about the works. Business men of the borough generally admitted that the strike was lost to the Amalgamated Association. On the other hand, between two and three thousand idle workmen walked the streets, anxious, angry, or despairing; and in hundreds of homes near by, wives and mothers saw with dread the approach of a winter of suffering.   Yet, obedient to the clique that ruled the local lodges of the Association, these poor people watched strangers coming in, singly and by dozens, to take away their only chance of keeping their little home together. Here was "the terrible temptation" to violence which Andrew Carnegie wrote about in the *Forum ;* and many of them yielded to it.   Assaults on the new workmen became more frequent than ever; and even murder was done.   Every day brought its story of outrage.   Within two weeks of the withdrawal of the militia a new reign of terror had set in; and for their own defence many of the new workmen were sworn in as deputy sheriffs. At the same time a ringing protest against the prevailing outlawry was voiced at a public meeting of the peaceful citizens of Homestead, but with little avail.   The violence lasted as long as the strike had an official existence.   One was born of the other, lived with and by it, and could not die alone.

In the mean time many letters and cablegrams were received from Mr. Carnegie of the same tenor as those previously quoted. A paragraph from one of these, sent early in October, has some bearing on Mr. Stead's unfair statement that "the responsibility for the industrial war at Homestead lies upon Mr. Frick and Mr. Frick alone."   It is quoted in the following letter :

October 12th, 1892.

My Dear Mr. Carnegie :

.   .   .   .

I quote from a personal note received from you as follows :

"This fight is too much against our Chairman; partakes of personal issue.   It is very bad indeed for you—very, and also bad for the interests of the firm."   .   .   .   .   .

"There is another point which troubles me on your account, the danger that the public, and hence all our men, get the impression that it is all Frick.   Your influence for good would be permanently impaired.   You don't deserve a bad name, but then one is sometimes wrongly got.   Your partners should be as much identified with this struggle as you.   Think over this counsel.   It is from a very wise man, as you know, and a true friend."

I am at a little loss to know just why you should express yourself so. I know it is not from any other than a friendly interest, but, as you should know, it seems to me that I am particularly anxious that no action of mine should under any circumstances cause loss of any kind to the firm, and that I am not naturally inclined to push myself into prominence under any circumstances. It seems to me wherever it was possible to put any of our people forward I have not let the opportunity go by. That is to say, when they have been asked by any one whether some arrangement could not be made by which this thing could be fixed up they have had instructions to reply, on their own responsibility, that we could not under any circumstances agree to a compromise of any kind; that we held no resentments against any of our old men; that we did not care whether they belonged to a union or not, but that we would expect, if they wished to re-enter our employment, that they would apply as individuals, and if their positions were filled they would be offered other ones, provided they had not been guilty of violating the law &c. &c., and I think whenever any of our people here have had such an opportunity presented to them that they have most promptly acted, and thus identified themselves with the struggle.

I note the counsel you give, but I cannot see wherein I can profit by it, or what action could be taken by me that would change matters in respect to that which you mention.

. . . .

Yours truly,
H. C. FRICK.

To Andrew Carnegie, Esq.,
   care Messrs. J. S. Morgan & Co.,
      London, England.

A wise move was made about this time by Mr. Frick. He brought Mr. Charles M. Schwab from the Edgar Thomson works, and made him superintendent of Homestead in place of Mr. Potter, whom he promoted to the position of consulting engineer of all the Carnegie works. Mr. Schwab had graduated at Braddock under Captain Jones, and, displaying exceptional ability as a manager of men, had quickly won his way from one of the lowest positions in the yards to the highest in the office. His cheery friendliness made him especially popular among the workmen; and he had many admirers among the strikers at Homestead. Tactful and conciliatory, he at once set himself to win back the heads of departments and foremen; and before many days had passed had secured the best of them. The immediate consequence was that better work was done inside the shops, and the foremen were soon followed into the works by their favorites among the strikers.

"At bonny Ayr."

Meanwhile, around the Union Iron Mills and at Beaver Falls, some thousands of other workmen walked the streets in idleness, with feelings of anger and fear of the future, because of their sympathy with the men of Homestead. This was the aftermath of war.

During this eventful October, when the dead leaves were fluttering from the trees at Homestead, with dire whisperings of a winter of suffering for the strikers and their families, Andrew Carnegie was at bonny Ayr, the birthplace of Burns, where another library was being dedicated, with dinners, speeches, poems, and processions. A local bard on this occasion burst into song:

> " Independent and valiant from childhood to age—
> To pretence meeting scorn, to unrighteousness rage—
> In Carnegie ' the man and the brother ' we see
> Whom, ' for a' that and a' that ' Burns sang with such glee."

And simultaneously another poet, in distant Winona, sang in tuneful prophecy:

> " The mills of the gods grind slowly,
>   And they grind exceeding fine ;
> And in the ides of November
>   You'll find us all in line.
> Our bullets made of paper,
>   We'll plunk them in so hot
> That the G. O. P. will wonder
>   If they ever were in the plot.

>   For we are the people and
>   We'll occupy the land
>   In spite of the Carnegies'
>   Or Pinkerton's brigands."

In grace of diction, such as it is, the disciple of Burns has the advantage; but for blunt truth-speaking, he of Minnesota takes the palm. For the Homestead battle became a national issue in the presidential election a month later, and brought defeat to the Republican hosts. This was another of the sheaves gleaned from the crop sown on July 6th. One of the disappointed leaders—General Grosvenor of Ohio—stigmatized Mr. Carnegie as "the arch-sneak of this age," a judgment which Chauncey Depew ungraciously refused to reverse when it was submitted to him. "As a matter of fact," replied Mr. Depew, "the Homestead strike was one of the most important factors in the presidential contest, and led to a distinct issue in the campaign. It happened at a crisis and injured us irremediably. . . . The Republican leaders attempted early in the campaign to have the strike settled and cabled to Mr. Carnegie direct without consulting Mr. Frick. Every inducement was

"I TOO KNOW A GOOD THING!"

On the wall is a copy of Andrew Carnegie's congratulatory telegram to President Harrison on his second nomination: "The public knows a good thing when it sees it."

—From the Chicago Times.

made to bring Mr. Carnegie into the canvass, but he persistently declined to lend his influence or to pay one dollar to the campaign fund."

Another Republican leader was quoted by the New York *Times* as saying:

" Carnegie four years ago was the best friend the Republican party apparently had.   His contributions were heavy and spontaneous.   The Fifty-first Congress gave him all the protection he needed.   By this legislation he increased his profits fifty per

An Anti-Harrison cartoon, with Mr. Frick represented as bringing on his head the tribute he never paid.

cent.   The Homestead strike happened at the very worst moment for the Republican party.   Every argument was used to Frick and Carnegie to end it."

President Harrison naturally expressed himself more cautiously; but he nevertheless ascribed his defeat to the discontent and passion of the workingmen growing out of wages or other labor disturbances, which did not permit of that calm consideration by these workmen of the effect of the protective system upon his wages.   His exact words were:

" The facts that his [the workman's] wages were the highest paid in like callings in the world, and that a maintenance of this rate of wages, in the absence of protective duties upon the product of his labor, was impossible, were obscured by the passion evoked by these contests."

It is also certain that the farming vote was adversely affected by the broadcast publication of the high wages received by the Homestead workmen under a protective régime which left the

CHARGE OF THE MERCENARIES.
Mr. Frick is represented in the lead, with Mr. Carnegie following.
—From the New York World.

agriculturist on the outside. And so the Democrats rode into place on the Pinkerton barges; and the names of Frick and Carnegie became anathema maranatha to all good Republicans. It was a most unexpected aftermath.

For a few weeks longer the stubborn contest continued at Homestead, needlessly prolonging the suffering of the men and their families and breeding disorder in the township. One of the unhappy men was "goaded to suicide," as the newspapers expressed it. He had had no work since the strike. Before that he owned his home and had a well-paid position. His wife, "momentarily expecting to become the mother of a second child," was in "a most critical condition and may not recover."

Amid such happenings the public disorder was such as to lead to a demand for a return of the troops. Happily this met with no response; and on November 18th there was such a rush among the strikers for work that men were trampled in the crowd. Three days later the strike was reluctantly called off by the local lodges of the Amalgamated Association; and the three thousand workmen who had never belonged to the union, and had no rights of any kind in it, were permitted to seek work in the mill on any terms they could get. The struggle had lasted twenty weeks, had cost a score of lives, millions of dollars, and, so far as any one could then see, had benefited nobody.

Unconditional surrender !
—*From the Chicago Times.*

With the perspective afforded by lapse of time, however, it can now be seen that this titanic struggle was not in vain. Greatly as the suffering attending it must be deplored—suffering that ceased not with the official declaration of peace by the Association lodges, but stayed throughout the winter with the families of many of the strikers—it is nevertheless evident that the marvellous prosperity which, a year or two later, followed this struggle was made possible because of it. The mental and moral attitude of the workmen towards their employers and towards other workmen which found expression in the savagery of the attack on the company's watchmen, in the use of dynamite, burning oil, and the wounding of defenceless prisoners, belonged to a barbaric past, and was wholly incompatible with modern industrialism. The usurpation of the functions of government, the summary arrest and punishment of inoffensive citizens, and the displays of lawless arrogance by the Advisory Committee, implied a misconception of the mutual rights and duties of laborers and employers which could only be destructive of that harmonious co-operation essential to progress; and thoroughly imbued with false ideas as the workmen were, nothing but the most drastic measures would have sufficed for their correction.

One of the most intelligent of the strikers told the Senate committee of investigation that when the workmen found themselves "confronted with a gang of loafers and cutthroats from all over the country, coming there, as they thought, to take their jobs, why, they *naturally* wanted to go down and *defend their homes and their property and their lives with force*, if necessary, and that is the way the men felt at Homestead."

Confronted with such a theory of the natural rights of labor, the inflexibility of Mr. Frick, so thoughtlessly condemned at the time and often since, was the salvation of the workmen themselves, as they were afterwards among the first to admit. The talk of compromise with such ideas was foolish and injurious. There are some things that cannot be compromised. Insurrection is one of them. It is not possible to jump half-way down Niagara.

In January, 1893, all being quiet on the Monongahela, Andrew Carnegie returned from Europe; and on the 30th of that month he published a carefully prepared statement of his connection with the Homestead strike. Summarized, it is as follows:

"I did not come to Pittsburg to rake up, but to bury, the past, of which I knew nothing. . . . For 26 years our concerns have run with only one labor stoppage at one of our numerous works. . . . I desire now, once for all, to make one point clear. Four years ago I retired from active business; no consideration in the world would induce me to return to it. . . . I have sold portions of my interests and am gradually selling more to such young men in our service as my partners find possessed of exceptional ability and desire to interest in the business. I am not an officer of the company but only a shareholder.

To the numerous appeals which I have received urging me to give instructions in regard to recent troubles, I have paid no attention, but to all these people, and to any others interested

THE PITTSBURG PRESS.

LOCAL FORECAST.
Fair—Stationary Temperature.   PITTSBURG, FRIDAY EVENING, DECEMBER 9, 1892.   W.-PENNA.-W. V.
Fair and St.

IN HUMANITY'S NAME.

The Press Appeals for Aid for Suffering Homestead.

EXTREME DESTITUTION IN THE UNFORTUNATE BOROUGH.

What the Investigation of a Press Reporter Revealed.

WOMEN AND CHILDREN WHO WANT FOR BREAD.

The Work of Relief Far Greater Than the Local Committee Can Undertake.

PRIDE SEALS THE LIPS OF STARVING MEN AND WOMEN

The Press Starts the Relief Fund With a Contribution of One Hundred Dollars.

SOLOMON & RUBEN ADD ONE HUNDRED DOLLARS MORE.

in the subject, let me say now that I have not power to instruct anybody connected with the Carnegie Steel Co. Ltd. The officers are elected for a year and no one can interfere with them. . . . I do not believe in ruling through the voting power, even if I could. . . . When I could not bring my associates in business to my views by reason I have never wished to do so by force. As for instructing or compelling them under the law to do one thing or another that is simply absurd. I could not if I would, and I would not if I could. . . .

And now one word about Mr. Frick. . . . I am not mistaken in the man, as the future will show.   Of his ability, fairness and pluck no one has now the slightest question.   His four years' management stamps him as one of the foremost managers of the world—I would not exchange him for any manager I know.

People generally are still to learn of those virtues which his partners and friends know well.   If his health be spared I predict that no man who ever lived in Pittsburg and managed business here will be better liked or more admired by his employees than my friend and partner Henry Clay Frick, nor do I believe any man will be more valuable for the city.   His are the qualities that wear; he never disappoints; what he promises he more than fulfils. . . .

I hope after this statement that the public will understand that the officials of the Carnegie Steel Company, Limited, with Mr. Frick at their head, are not dependent upon me, or upon any one in any way for their positions, and that I have neither power nor disposition to interfere with them in the management of the business.   And further, that I have the most implicit faith in them."

A campaign pleasantry.

CHAPTER XVII

A RELUCTANT SUPREMACY

Ore-docks and vessels.

IT is something more than a coincidence that the day that marked the beginning of the Homestead strike saw the birth of the Carnegie Steel Company, Limited. On July 1st, 1892, for the first time in their history, the separate establishments whose growth we are tracing were brought into a single organization, and endowed with one mind, one purpose, one interest. Mr. Frick was too wise a general to enter a battle with his forces needlessly scattered; and while fences were being built around the company's works, their corporate strength was also concentrated and made instantly responsive to his will.

The consolidation of the different Carnegie interests had, however, long been contemplated by Mr. Frick. As early as February, 1890, he had discussed the project with Mr. Abbot, chairman of Carnegie, Phipps & Co., and had made it the subject of a written communication to Mr. Carnegie. But at that time there were obstacles of a financial nature. One concern was used to make paper for the other, as the phrase is. That is, one Carnegie company selling to another was able to discount the notes it received in payment; so that the transaction had all the banking advantages of an outside trade. On occasions, too, such notes could be discounted without any antecedent salè. In transactions of this kind Mr. Stewart, with his strong financial connections, had long proved very useful.

Mr. Stewart had died in 1889. His interest had been acquired by Mr. Frick, who, adding it to his previous holdings, thus became as large a stockholder as Mr. Phipps, and second only to Mr. Carnegie. At the same time Mr. Frick became chairman of Carnegie Brothers & Co., Limited, as well as a director in Carnegie, Phipps & Co. Having previously resumed the presidency of the coke company, which he had resigned under circumstances already related, Mr. Frick freely used its credit to finance the two steel companies and their subsidiary interests, and thus made it unnecessary to maintain their organizations separate. The consolidation of these interests would have come in the course of time as a measure of economy; but the combination was hastened by the threat of war with labor.

The sociologist will be interested in this illustration of the unifying effect of war in industrialism. Predatory competition, which is a form of warfare, has a similar consolidating effect; and the modern trust is its most conspicuous expression. The processes of industrial evolution often take a form that inevitably suggests the thought that even such great leaders as Mr. Frick, with their apparent independence and strong governing power, are little more than passive instruments through which natural forces operate. The changes which an industrial organism undergoes in its development are unquestionably governed by the same laws as those which mould the less complex forms of life, to which the doctrine of evolution is popularly limited; and it often appears that the strong personality of the greatest captain of industry can do little more than control the direction of this growth. His power is comparable to that of the gardener who fastens the young shoots of his peach tree to the southern wall, and causes it to spread out in the sunshine more than it would if left alone.

In the consolidation of July 1st, 1892, the Carnegie Steel Company, Limited, became the owner of the Upper and Lower

Union Mills, the Lucy Furnaces, the Edgar Thomson Steel Works, the mills at Homestead, the newly acquired property at Duquesne, the Keystone Bridge Works, the unprofitable and prolonged experiment at Beaver Falls, with a few other interests in ore and natural gas sprinkled about Western Pennsylvania. The capital was $25,000,000. It was a gigantic concern; but, as De Tocqueville says of the United States of his time, it was "a giant without bones." It had gristle, however, and this soon hardened into bones.

Having brought the separate establishments into a single organization, Mr. Frick now sought to harmonize their relations so that each plant would serve to supplement and round out the operations of every other. This he effected by the Union Railway, which he built to connect the principal works with each other and with all the different transportation systems entering the Pittsburg district. It was a masterly conception; for it unified the scattered works and made them as easy to operate as if they had been contiguous. At the same time it gave them unequalled transportation facilities through direct connection with every important railway system in Western Pennsylvania.

The advantages of easy exchange of products among the different works cannot be stated in figures; but they have their place in the phenomenal record of the firm's profits given elsewhere. The saving in switching charges alone paid interest on the cost of the railroad; and the company was allowed twenty-five cents a ton rebate on ore rates.

A further advantage was that the company thus regained possession of its own yards. Hitherto the different railroads running into the works had control of all tracks and sidings; and so tenaciously did they hold to these cheaply acquired rights that they often resisted the extension of a mill that involved the removal of a track. This cause of annoyance now came to an end; and a judicious rearrangement of tracks and sidings, so as to meet changed conditions, resulted in a great saving of yard space and expedited the handling of vast ton-

THE EDGAR THOMSON

THE HOMESTEAD S

THE DUQUESNE S

Plate X.

WORKS, BRADDOCK, PA.

RKS, MUNHALL, PA.

S, DUQUESNE, PA.

nages. The superiority of this system, by which the traffic was regulated by one organization instead of by several railroads, is readily seen when a statement is made of the total tonnage entering and leaving the works of the Carnegie Steel Company. In 1899 this amounted to 16,000,000 tons—as much as the combined total freight handled by the Northern Pacific, Union Pacific, and Missouri Pacific railways, with their 13,000 miles of track, 1,500 locomotives, and 50,000 freight-cars.

The next step in the progress of this great industrial aggregate towards completeness was that which gave it possession of the iron ore it needed. This was the only thing it had to buy of outsiders. So long as it did not itself produce everything it needed, it could not be considered a perfect industrial unit, such as it was Mr. Frick's ambition to make it. An accident helped him to a realization of his great plans; though they were nearly frustrated through the unexpected opposition of Mr. Carnegie.

The story of the way the Carnegie Steel Company acquired its great ore mines on Lake Superior lacks none of the romance that makes the history of Homestead and Duquesne so interesting. It is the story of a huge profit made with hardly a dollar of investment, and the accepting of an impregnable position in the industrial world with a reluctant and complaining consent. It is the amplified tale of the "most hazardous enterprise," told afresh; but where a thousand dollars was then involved, a hundred millions now hold our interest. Unfortunately it is a story that shatters all preconceptions of the genius necessary to achieve millionaireship; but that is merely incidental.

Among the boy companions of Thomas M. Carnegie was Henry W. Oliver. He had become one of the cleverest business men of Pittsburg, and had made several fortunes in iron and steel manufacture before he reached the maturity of mid-life. He was singularly far-sighted and enterprising, and a skilful financier. Some time in 1892 he formed a company, called after himself, to operate the Missabi Mountain mine on

17

the Mesaba range; his main object being to provide a cheap and uninterrupted supply of high-grade Bessemer ore for his own furnaces.

Mr. Frick, who had similar ideas for his own works, watched the experiment with interest; and presently he suggested to Mr. Oliver that an ore combination with the Carnegie Steel Company might be made mutually beneficial. Mr. Oliver was quick to see the advantage of such a union; permitting him, as

Group of miners near Lake Superior.

it would do, to bargain with independent miners and transportation companies on a basis of a high minimum. In other words, the enormous consumption of ore of the united plants would enable him to offer a guaranteed tonnage to railways and steamboat companies in exchange for low rates, as well as to make exceptional offers to mine owners willing to let their ores be worked on a royalty basis. He therefore viewed the suggestion with favor, and, after some negotiations, agreed to Mr. Frick's proposal to give the Carnegie Company one-half the stock of the Oliver Mining Company, conditioned on a loan of half a million dollars, secured by a mortgage on the ore properties, to be spent in development work. In this ingenious way Mr. Frick so arranged that the Carnegie ore interest would not cost a dollar.

The matter was at once brought to the attention of Mr. Carnegie, who laconically opposed it as follows, in a letter dated Rannoch Lodge, Kinloch-Rannoch, Perthshire, August 29th, 1892 :

"Oliver's ore bargain is just like him—nothing in it. If there is any department of business which offers no inducement, it is ore. It never has been very profitable, and the Massaba is not the last great deposit that Lake Superior is to reveal."

Mr. Frick, however, made the combination with Mr. Oliver; and, on his return from Europe, Mr. Carnegie expressed himself so vigorously in condemnation of it that there ensued the first coldness between himself and Mr. Frick.

Mr. Carnegie's attitude was not modified by the successful working of the arrangement; and during the next two years he repeatedly placed himself on record, with increasing emphasis, as being opposed to any venture in Lake Superior ores. Writing to the Board of Managers from Buckhurst Park, Withyham, Sussex, on April 18th, 1894, he says again :

"The Oliver bargain I do not regard as very valuable. You will find that this ore venture, like all our other ventures in ore, will result in more trouble and less profit than almost any branch of our business. If any of our brilliant and talented young partners have more time, or attention, than is required for their present duties, they will find sources of much greater profit right at home. I hope you will make a note of this prophecy."

Of course the managers made a note of the prophecy; and it afterwards furnished subject for many a subdued laugh at their meetings.

It subsequently transpired, however, that Mr. Carnegie thought his company was entitled to a larger share than one-half of the Oliver Mining Company's stock; and, to please him, Mr. Oliver consented to sell the Carnegies an additional interest of one-third, making their holdings five-sixths of the total stock. But he took care to safeguard his own interests by a contract under which the Oliver furnaces were entitled to one-

An open-pit mine.

sixth of all ore mined by the company. At this time the capital of the Oliver Mining Company was $1,200,000.

In 1896 Messrs. Oliver and Frick made the celebrated Rockefeller connection, by which they leased the other great mines on the Mesaba range on a royalty basis of only 25 cents a ton. This low price was given by the Rockefellers in consideration of a guaranteed output of 600,000 tons a year, to be shipped over the Rockefeller railroads and steamships on the Lakes, with an equal amount from the Oliver mine. This

amounted to 1,200,000 tons a year; and as the contract was to
run for fifty years, it meant a guarantee of 60,000,000 tons of
freight, at 80 cents a ton by rail and 65 cents a ton on the lakes
—a consideration great enough to justify the low royalty of 25
cents when other mine owners were getting 65 cents.   To the
Carnegie-Oliver iron interests it meant a visible saving of
$27,000,000.

This alliance with the Rockefellers had an unexpected result. It produced a panic among the other mine owners; and
stockholders in Boston, Chicago, Cleveland, and the Northwest
hastened to get rid of their ore properties at almost any price.
The demoralization extended to the ore markets; and Norrie,
which sold at $6 a ton in 1891, dropped to $2.65 on the docks
at Cleveland.

This was Mr. Oliver's opportunity; and backed by Mr.
Frick and some of the more enterprising Carnegie managers,
like Curry, Schwab, Gayley and Clemson, he hastened to secure
options on all the best mines in the Lake Superior region.   The
following is the argument he submitted to the Carnegie managers on July 27th, 1897:

NEW YORK, N. Y., July 27, 1897.

H. C. FRICK, Chairman,

DEAR SIR: I mail you my specific reports on the Norrie,
Tilden, and Pioneer mines.

I now address you mainly to impress my views that it should
be our policy to acquire all three of these properties.   We (I
mean the Carnegie and Oliver furnaces) have paid more than
our share of tribute to Cleveland and Northwestern miners.
Part of their receipts were profit, but a large part was wasted
in expenses that we will in the future save: in exploration, in
which we will benefit; in development of mines that have
proved failures; and in excessive freight rates to steamship lines
controlled by the Cleveland middle-men.   All this should stop.
I claim that we could produce and deliver our ore to Lake Erie
ports 20 to 30 cents per ton cheaper than it can be done by
those now in control of the mines we seek.   Our saving would

be in steady and more regular mining, in avoiding a line of high salaried officers, in procuring lower Lake freights, and in saving the Cleveland commission of 10 cents per ton. I am satisfied that the economies that we will practise in the lines above indicated will be fully equivalent, in the future, to any royalties we may pay. The Carnegie furnaces and the Oliver furnaces will require about four million tons of ore per annum. Our minimum, under my proposition, would stand as follows:

Mesaba	1,200,000
Norrie	700,000
Tilden	400,000
Pioneer	500,000
Total	2,800,000 Tons

On the above, the only cash obligation that we will have if my plan is carried out, is in the purchase of the Norrie stock. The Mesaba leases we can throw up on six months notice, and the Tilden and Pioneer leases on three months notice. The amount that we would invest in the Norrie is a very small item, considering the immense stake we have in the business and the fact that if we do not fortify ourselves on the plan that I have indicated, it would be easy for the mine owners to exact three to four millions of dollars, or even a greater sum, from us, as a profit on the ore we consume. A glance at the prices paid for ore the past 10 or 15 years will show that my estimate of the profits that we have paid them is extremely conservative

Excuse me for bringing to the attention of yourself and your associates the fact that the Carnegie Company never heretofore hesitated to invest millions of dollars to save 25c to 50c. per ton in the manufacture of pig iron. You destroy old plants and erect new ones to save a quarter of a dollar per ton. You are now engaged in building a railroad to the Lakes, at an immense expenditure of treasure and credit, with the ultimate object of making a saving (in which your competitors to a certain extent will share) of 25 to 30 cents per ton, and to protect Pittsburgh against high ore rates in the future. I propose at a risk of using our credit to the extent of $500,000, or possibly one million dollars, to effect a saving, in which our competitors will not share, of four to six million dollars per annum. All arguments to the contrary notwithstanding, I know I am right in these matters; as, in my judgment, with a knowledge of the nature of the ownership of the mines in the Northwest, no power can prevent their soon coming together and exacting the old time prices for ore.

On the Gogebic Range, the mines I have selected comprise over 80% of developed ore or " ore in sight." They comprise in this year's pool about 60% of the allotment, the allotment being made not on the basis of ore in sight, but on the basis of the preceeding year's shipments. They are the only mines on the Range that can mine iron ore at present prices and make money. The other mines with their small product and heavy general expenses, are not making one cent per ton. The result

An ore-train.

is that one or two of the smaller of these mines are being thrown up this year; and, with proper care and attention, if we were on the ground, we should be able to take up practically all of them.

Doubts may arise as to the quantity of ore in the properties we propose to take up. The question is, however, if the ore is not in the mines I propose to acquire, where can it be shown to exist, in properties available for lease or purchase, in the Ranges other than the Mesaba Range? I have selected as the properties we should acquire the mines that common report names as having the largest quantity and our special reports confirm that view. If there be not large quantities of ore in the properties we have under consideration, then there are no large deposits of Bessemer ore yet known, outside of the Mesaba Range, and the Chapin and Minnesota Iron Co's properties. In that case, Bessemer ores will shortly appreciate in value and we, with others, will have to pay the holders thereof a large advance on present prices.

An important point, in making the venture in the Gogebic region and securing a large body of ore, is the effect it will have upon the guarantee made us, by the Rockefeller party, that our ore shall be as low as any other Mesaba ore at Lake Superior ports. The possession of a large body of ore in the Gogebic Range will strengthen our position, in holding the Rockefeller people down to low freight rates from the Mesaba Range.

The three properties I propose to take up contain not only the largest body of ore in sight, but are practically the only mines excepting a few extra low phosphorus mines and the Chapin and Minnesota Iron Co., properties, that are this year, under their system of mining and expenses, producing ores at a profit. In addition to this, as showing their standing in the trade, they have been allotted, on the basis of last year's shipments, over 50% of the Gogebic output, and over 25% of the total, in a Pool of 4,250,000 tons, comprising all the Bessemer ores (including Chapin) produced in the Northwest, excepting only ores from the Mesaba Range.

A BUCYRUS SHOVEL AT WORK.
"Five cents a ton for labor."

I am not ignoring the strong position we hold on the Mesaba Range. With two exceptions, we possess the only steam shovel mines and the low cost of this ore is extremely gratifying. More Mesaba ore can be used in our mixtures, but it is not a wise policy to quickly exhaust the rich quarry we have on the Mesaba Range, taking off rapidly the surface ore. Although we are mining it at present for less than five cents per ton for labor, we must look to the future, when we will have to go deeper, pump water and lift the ore. We should rather prolong the period

Plate XI.

HENRY W. OLIVER

of cheap steam shovel mining, take in the other Range properties I suggest for mixture; and, by working one Range
against the other, keep down costs of freights. I desire to
impress upon you the fact, that if it had not been for our
Rockefeller-Mesaba deal of last year, with the consequent demoralization in the trade caused by the publication thereof, it
would not have been possible for us to now secure the other
Range properties I propose to acquire, either by lease or for any
reasonable price. We simply knocked the price of ore from
$4.00 down to say $2.50 per ton. Now let us take advantage
of our action before a season of good times gives the ore
producers strength and opportunity to get together by combination.

I trust that when you read this letter and my reports you
will not attribute the strong position I take to my usually
optimistic nature. It is true that I generally like to view the
bright side of affairs, but these practical matters I have digested
in a thoroughly judicial spirit, and my conclusions are the result
of great thought and most thorough investigation. You do not
hear of the many properties I have condemned and turned down
as being not worthy of your consideration. I have selected,
for the decision of my associates, only the very best. The
Minnesota Iron Company properties are out of the question;
the banns have been published and union with the Illinois Steel
Company is only a matter of time. All others, however, I
have, in one shape or another had before me. The Chapin is
too high in phosphorus and held by too stiff a crowd. Other
Menominee properties—(the Aragon, for instance, that was
sold the other day),—too small and expensive. I have not
recommended or tried to lead you into waste of money on ex-
plorations of virgin property. Mr. A. M. Byers told me that
he, with Kimberly, had worked for years, spending over a million of dollars, in sinking shafts through solid rock, hunting a
lost vein of ore, on the Ludington mine, which adjoins the
Chapin. Please recall that on the Mesaba Range I condemned
poor properties such as the Sauntry and others; that I stood
strongly against the Mahoning out of which they have great
difficulty this year in mining any but non-Bessemer ores, and
that I only brought before you, for approval, the magnificent
properties on the Mesaba Range that we are now operating.
Pardon me for mentioning the above. I only do it to impress
upon you the fact that I have analyzed this question most thoroughly. I have given months of thought to these questions,
where others have scarcely given minutes. I know I am right

and trust you and your associates will give me opportunity to prove it. The future will show that all my predictions will come true to the letter.   Yours &c
                                    HENRY W. OLIVER.

This document was sent by special messenger to Mr. Frick in London and by him transmitted to Mr. Carnegie in Scot-land. To the surprise and dismay of everybody concerned, Mr. Carnegie again opposed the project. From the fastnesses of his Highland retreat he again issued a laconic veto, with a quip and a chuckle at his partners' enthusiasm. Thereupon M. Oliver despatched the following cablegram :

G87CM697

THE CARNEGIE STEEL COMPANY, LIMITED.

PRIVATE TELEGRAPH SERVICE.

Telegram Sent from General Offices; Carnegie Building, Pittsburg, Pa.

Sent by	Received by	Time,

                              Dated.   September 25, 1897.
To CARNEGIE   LAGGAN
    I am distressed at indications here that Norrie options ex-piring on Monday, are to be refused. It would be a terrible mistake. The good times make it that I could not possibly secure these options again at fifty per cent., advance. The Norrie mine controls the whole situation. They have sold over one million tons this year. With the additional property we will get from the fee owners, we secure fifteen to twenty million tons of the ore that the Carnegie Company are purchasing this year five hundred and fifty thousand tons. I will guarantee, counting the surplus they have in their treasury, to return in profits every dollar we invest in two years. Do not allow my hard summer's work to go for naught.
                                    HENRY W. OLIVER
    chg. O. M. Co.

It will be seen from this that the Carnegies had just bought 550,000 tons of this very ore, which was yielding the mine owners $1 to $1.25 a ton profit. By instructions from Scotland

they had made this purchase just at the critical moment that
Mr. Oliver was negotiating for options on the shares of the
Norrie mine; and his task was made doubly difficult by the
fact. Before this the Norrie owners had sold only 150,000
tons, as against ten times that amount in previous years. Notwithstanding this embarrassing purchase, Mr. Oliver was able
to secure options from about four hundred stockholders, who
resided in every part of the country, and, one might say, in

Piles of iron ore ready for loading.

every part of the world. This was the "hard summer's work"
which was rendered futile by a word from Carnegie.

On receipt of Mr. Oliver's cablegram, however, Mr. Carnegie so far reconsidered his objections as to leave the decision
to the chairman and Board of Managers in Pittsburg; and these
gentlemen promptly authorized Mr. Oliver to close the deal.
This action was the pivotal point in the gathering together,
by the Carnegie-Oliver interests, of the great ore properties

which gave them their impregnable position in the iron industry of the country.   On the organization of the United States
Steel Company, the Carnegie-Oliver company owned two-thirds
of the known Northwestern supply of Bessemer ores—roughly,
500,000,000 tons, which Mr. Schwab has since valued at $500,-
000,000.   It would be difficult to find a parallel to this incident in any romance of American industrialism.

It is only fair to Mr. Carnegie to add that he afterwards so
far modified his estimate of Mr. Oliver as to offer him an interest in the Carnegie Steel Company.

The great value of the gift which Andrew Carnegie thus
reluctantly allowed Mr. Frick to accept for the company may
be further illustrated.   The first Mesaba mine secured by Mr.
Oliver is of such character that 5,800 tons of ore have been
mined and loaded into cars by one steam shovel in ten hours;
and the output for one month was 164,000 tons.   This was the
work of only eight men.   Three such machines, made by the
Bucyrus Company of South Milwaukee, mined from its natural
bed 915,000 tons of ore during the season of 1900, working day
shift only.   Some of the other great mines are of the same
character.   The method of mining is shown in the accompanying photographs.   Five tons of ore are lifted by the machine
each stroke; and five full-weight lifts will fill a car.   A 25-ton
car can be filled in two and a half minutes, which is at the rate
of 600 tons an hour.   Andrew Carnegie often says that Fortune
timidly knocks at every man's door at least once during his
lifetime.   The statement is too modest to fit his own case; for
Fortune has repeatedly battered down the barricades with which
he has tried to exclude her.   Nor has she been scared away by
the inscription above the Carnegie threshold, " Pioneering don't
pay!"

Having thus provided an unfailing supply of the best Bessemer ores at the mere cost of mining them, Mr. Frick at once
began to elaborate plans for their cheap and certain transportation to the furnaces.   A contract with the Bessemer Steamship

Company, a Rockefeller concern, ensured the regular delivery
of 1,200,000 tons a year at Lake Erie ports; and an agreement was simultaneously made with the Pennsylvania Railroad
for the land haul of some two hundred miles.   But this condition of dependence was unsatisfactory; and Mr. Frick boldly
talked of building his own railroad to the Lakes.   This brought
an offer from the president of the Pennsylvania Railroad of better facilities; and Mr. Frick proposed an arrangement under
which the Carnegie Steel Company should run its own ore
trains from Lake Erie, equipped with its
own locomotives and crew, over the
Pennsylvania tracks.   This plan was
well received by the officials of the
Pennsylvania Railroad; but before
anything definite had been
decided upon, a telegram was
received from Mr. Carnegie
in Florida, asking that all
negotiations be suspended
until the arrival of his letter.
When this came it was found
that he had entered into an
agreement with Mr. Samuel

"Battered down the barricades."

B. Dick, president of the Pittsburg, Shenango and Lake Erie
Railroad, to reorganize that company, which was on the verge
of bankruptcy, and to build an extension from its terminus at
Butler to a point on the Union Railroad at Bessemer.

This Pittsburg, Shenango and Lake Erie had had an eventful history, involving receiverships, reorganizations, and con-
solidations; and at this time it had little more than a right of
way and two streaks of rust, as the saying is.   It had certain
terminal facilities at Conneaut Harbor, however; and during
the previous year (1895) a quarter of a million tons of ore had
been handled there.   The Government was dredging the harbor,
and its facilities were capable of some improvement, though not

to the extent expected when this deal was made. The harbor has frequently been inconveniently crowded.

On July 25th, 1896, the first contract was let for the extension to Pittsburg; and simultaneously the work of renewing the old track was begun. One-hundred-pound rails were laid down, grades lowered, wooden trestles replaced with steel, and in other ways the road was so changed as practically to make it

Ore vessels in Conneaut Harbor.

a new one. A maximum south-bound grade of thirty-one feet per mile was secured over the entire route, an achievement of no small difficulty in the hilly parts of Western Pennsylvania. A steel bridge across the Allegheny two-thirds of a mile long was the most noteworthy engineering feature of this road; and the whole work of renewal and the building of forty-two miles of new track occupied only fifteen months. By October 4th, 1897, ore trains consisting of thirty-five steel cars, each carrying 100,000 pounds, were running from the company's own docks on Lake Erie over the company's own line to Bessemer, and there distributed over the company's Union Railroad to the blast-furnaces at Braddock, Duquesne, and Pittsburg. It was a long step in the progress towards self-sufficiency at which Mr. Frick had long been aiming; and it had cost nothing beyond an issue of bonds, which the volume of traffic furnished by the Carnegie Steel Company itself made gilt-edged.

The results of the operation of this road, now known as the Pittsburg, Bessemer and Lake Erie, and its docking facilities at Conneaut, as set forth by Mr. J. T. Odell, its former vice-president, are as follows:

"The lowest rate per ton per mile, the highest average length of revenue haul in proportion to its track mileage, the greatest density of tonnage in proportion to its freight-train mileage, the greatest average paying load, and the lowest 'ton-mile cost' of any road on the American continent reporting to the Interstate Commerce Commission. The average paying load of all its freight trains, including three branches, and with but little back loading, was, for the year ending December 31, 1899, 777 tons. It is confidently expected, when the south and north bound tonnage is 70 per cent. and 30 per cent. respectively, and the tonnage reaches 5,000,000 tons annually, as it promises, that the average paying load will be not less than 900 tons, or four and one-half times greater than the present average paying load of the country. The maximum weight of the paying load for the year was 1,580 net tons, with the average, as before stated, of 777 tons. Of the ore trains, each earned on a 3½-mill rate per ton per mile (gross ton) $5.13 per train mile. The road is laid with 100-pound rail and the track ballasted with furnace slag. The bridges will carry 6,600 pounds to the lineal foot. The standard locomotive is the consolidation pattern, having cylinders 22 by 28 inches and weighing 170,000 pounds on the drivers alone. The ore equipment consists mostly of steel cars, weighing 17 tons and carrying 50 tons of ore. The company is having built a few of what will prove to be the heaviest locomotives in the world, having cylinders 23 by 32 inches and weighing 217,000 pounds on the drivers. With these locomotives the total weight of an ore train, including the locomotive and light weight of the cars, will be about 2,600 tons.

"But it is not only in the operation of the road that greatest economy is obtained, but also in the transfer of the ore from the lake steamers to the trains. The steel company owns the entire harbor at Conneaut. Nine ships can be docked at the same time. Twenty-five thousand tons of all classes of freight can be handled every ten hours. The most modern machinery is used for handling ore and coal. A 6,000-ton ship can be cleared in fourteen hours, and in the same time from the moment the hatches are opened the ore can be at the furnaces at Pittsburg. A new steam shovel was completed last winter by which a train of 35 to 40 cars will be loaded with ore in two hours. A 40-ton car of coal can be unloaded and partly trimmed in the ship in thirty-six seconds. Most of the switching at Conneaut is done by the haulage system (a cable running between the rails at about 4 miles per hour). The operating officers believe that with this railroad the utmost limit of all that is possible in solving the problem of cheap transportation has been reached. Their achievement shows what remains to be done and can be done by the other railroads of this country in the same direction."

Ore-discharging machines at Conneaut.

The only gap that now remained was that on the Lakes. To fill it the company should operate its own line of steamers. While the contract with the Bessemer Steamship Company provided for the conveyance of 1,200,000 tons a year, the steel company was dependent upon the small fleet of ships owned by individuals to a greater extent than seemed desirable; and early in 1899 the Oliver Iron Mining Company purchased the Lake Superior Iron Company's fleet of six vessels, each capable of carrying 3,000 tons, as well as its ore properties on the Marquette range. Before taking over these steamers at the end of the year, certain changes in organization were made in conformity with the suggestions of Mr. Oliver, contained in the following letter to the Board of Managers of the Carnegie Steel Company:

Under our attorney's advice, taking in view the legal complications that might arise in a mining company being interested in navigation, we have settled that our venture in the purchase and building of vessels on the Great Lakes should be conducted

Ore docks.

under an organization distinct from the Oliver Iron Mining Company. We have taken out a charter and organized the

PITTSBURGH STEAMSHIP COMPANY.

The officers of the Company, the Board of Directors and the Stock interests are identical with those of the Oliver Iron Mining Company.

To finance the Company, I propose, first a paid up capital stock in cash of One million dollars ($1,000,000.00), and the issue of 5% gold bonds, interest payable semi-annually, of four million dollars ($4,000,000.00). The Union Trust Company of Pittsburgh to be the trustee of a mortgage covering all the vessels of the fleet, and to issue to the purchasers of the bonds interim certificates for eighty per centum of the cost of the vessels on the delivery to them of satisfactory bills of sale or chattel mortgage for each vessel as it is turned over by the seller or the builder of the vessel to the new Company; that is

18

to say, as fast as each vessel is delivered to the new Company, the bondholders advance 80% of its cost, and the stockholders the remaining 20% of its cost. On the completion of the fleet, as now projected, bonds in proper shape, reciting what vessels they cover, with proper requirements for insurance, etc., will be exchanged by the Trust Company for the interim certificates above recited. The cost of the vessels under contract (which is all we propose to acquire this season) aggregate about two million, nine hundred thousand dollars ($2,900,000.00).

Kindly advise me if the above plan is satisfactory to the Carnegie interests.

Bonds to be payable as follows:

Series " A," Five years	$1,000,000.00
Series " B," Ten years	1,500,000.00
Series " C," Fifteen years	1,500,000.00
Total	$4,000,000.00

In this way, on the very day of Mr. Frick's retirement from the chairmanship of the Carnegie Steel Company, the huge corporation became a complete industrial unit, owning everything it needed in its business, controlling every movement of its material, and in all its operations, from mining the crude ore to the shipment of the finished steel, paying no outsider a price.

Ore docks by night.

CHAPTER XVIII

THE WORKINGS OF THE CORPORATE MIND

In a Mesaba mine.

IN a former chapter reference was made to what was there called the mental evolution of the great industrial organism whose growth we are following, and a hint was given of the important part played in it by Mr. Frick. One of the most conspicuous directions of this mental growth was that involved in the systematization of the consultative work of the Board of Managers.

Although this board was the brain of a great body, its functions were long performed without regularity or method, and the results of its work were but imperfectly recorded. This is one of the most surprising features of this great business; for while the workings of every furnace and every machine were carefully watched and tabulated, the operations of the greatest machine of all, its brain, were spasmodic, unmethodical, and for the most part unnoted. The Board of Managers met by chance, there being no fixed time for its meetings. Consultations and deliberations were conducted in a haphazard way, and often no minutes of them were taken. If an important change was to be made, perhaps a meeting would be called; or it might happen that the managers most interested in it would have an informal meeting at the works, when the matter would be decided. The old minute-books of the various companies often show a gap of several months without an entry.

With the accession of Mr. Frick to the headship of the concern, this was promptly changed. A rule was made that the Board of Managers should meet every Tuesday at lunch, and that a full report of their subsequent deliberations should be kept. Similarly every Saturday, at noon, the different super-intendents and their assistants, some foremen, purchasing and sales agents and their principal assistants, to the number of

Superintendents at lunch.

thirty or more, met about a larger table, and, after lunching to-gether, talked over all matters of common interest. Here the unfriendly rivalry of former times gave place to a spirit of good fellowship and mutual helpfulness. Around the friendly board it was impossible for two important officers to refuse to speak to each other for five years, as happened more than once in the past. And such competition as grew up among them was that of friends animated by a common purpose—to do the best each could for the association.

Of course none but officials were ever admitted to these meetings; and the results of their deliberations were kept in profound secrecy. Except for the copies of the minutes sent to Mr. Phipps and Mr. Carnegie, the records were never seen by any one not entitled to attend the meetings in person. To give completeness to this narrative, however, and to illustrate in a practical way the workings of the corporate mind, the official record of one of these meetings is here given. Nothing has been changed in it, except that a long statement made by Mr. Frick is omitted. This concerned the proposed sale of the Carnegie-Frick companies, or in default of a sale, their consolidation. It is referred to elsewhere. In other respects the following is an exact reproduction of the official minutes of a meeting held in January, 1899. It is possible that many readers will find an intrinsic interest in the discussions of these "young geniuses"—some of whom, by the way, have already reached the dignity of grandsires.

At a meeting of the Board of Managers of

THE CARNEGIE STEEL COMPANY, LIMITED,

held at the general offices of the Association, Carnegie Building, Pittsburg, Pa., at 12:30 P.M., on Monday, January 16, 1899, there were present MM. Frick (chairman), Singer, Schwab, Peacock, Phipps, Clemson and Lovejoy (secretary); also MM. George Lauder, James Gayley and H. P. Bope. (Mr. Curry in Pasadena; Mr. Wightman in Florida.)

The minutes of the meeting of the Board of Managers held January 10th were read, and, on motion, approved.

The following communication from the president to the Board, under date of January 12th, was read:

"As reported by Mr. Phipps last week, we have finally closed for the purchase of the Bethlehem Plate Mills, which purchase the Board has already approved.

"The Mills, as you are aware, comprise a Slabbing Mill of the latest design; a 128" Plate Mill, complete in every particular; and a 42" Universal Mill of the latest and best construction. There are no changes in all these Mills we would suggest.

"We should have a capacity of 12 to 14,000 tons of Plates out of these Mills, besides some excess of Slabs which could be sold outside.

"It is estimated that the cost of putting these Mills in operation; foundations, buildings, furnaces, etc., will be approximately $500,000.00, and would like the Board to authorize this expenditure."

The following communication from W. E. Corey, general superintendent, Homestead Steel Works, to the president, under date of January 11th, was read:

"The building of ten (10) new Furnaces at Open Hearth No. 3 will cost about $80,000.00 per Furnace, or a total of $800,000.00. This, of course, includes all cranes, tracks, grading, filling in, etc., and also a stripper for the stripping of large Ingots for the new Slabbing Mill.

"Kindly authorize the expenditure of this money, and oblige."

The following communication from the president to the Board, under date of January 12th, was read:

"The demand for Open Hearth, instead of Bessemer Steel, is increasing each day. A careful calculation would indicate that ten (10) additional Open Hearth Furnaces are necessary for our Homestead Steel Works.

"Enclosed please find Mr. Corey's estimate and recommendation for same.

"We would propose making the Furnaces identical in every particular with those now built, which have been very satisfactory.

"Would recommend that the Board permit me to proceed with the erection of these Furnaces at once. They can be completed within about five months."

MM. Phipps and Clemson moved the authorization of an appropriation of $1,300,000.00, in accordance with the recommendations of the president.

Mr. Frick: "That cost appears high."
Mr. Schwab: "Mr. Corey admits that it is high, but does not want to get caught again with an insufficient appropriation. He will not waste money, and, if all is not needed, so much the better."

Mr. Frick: "We must have the Furnaces anyway, and may as well appropriate the outside cost. These are large amounts, but the whole matter has been thoroughly discussed outside of the Board Meetings, and all appear satisfied."

Mr. Schwab: "These Furnaces will increase our capacity 30,-000 tons of Open Hearth Ingots per month. This purchase renders it unnecessary to build the Plate Mill which was agreed upon, although no appropriation was authorized when we discussed the Car Works. There is no Plant I know of so well equipped as this. It is the latest and best in Plate Mills."

Mr. Lauder: "It is the right thing to do."

The motion was adopted; the vote being unanimous, and all present concurring.

The following communication from W. E. Corey to the president, under date of December 30th, was read:

"In line with my conversation with you concerning the changes in Beam Yard, beg to make the following report. In the first plan as proposed in my letter of November 18th, it will necessitate the expenditure of $40,000.00, and would enable us to make an average delivery of 10 days time on all Beam and Channel orders.

"Under this arrangement 30% of all Beams and Channels would be cut from stock, which would increase the cost per ton on Beams and Channels shipped from Homestead eight cents per ton.

"Now in going over this matter the second time, it seems to me that it would not be a paying investment to spend $40,-000.00 and increase the cost of production, if there is any other alternative.

"Now if our customers could be satisfied with an average delivery of 15 days on all orders, I would recommend that nothing be done towards this expenditure for another year, or until it is decided to move the Fitting Shop.

"I would, therefore, ask that you authorize an expenditure in the Beam Yard of $15,000.00, to be expended as follows: $6,000.00 each for two ten ton electric traveling cranes, one to be placed immediately outside the 40″ Mill at the roadway, and the other at No. 3 roadway to handle material from the small saw; $3,000.00 to be spent in moving small saw 40 feet due west from the present location, and making necessary change in tracks.

"This would enable us to make 15 day deliveries without increasing the cost of production.

"Kindly advise me at your earliest convenience what you think of this proposition."

Mr. Schwab: "These are only additional Cranes for the Beam Yard equipment we have now. While we save nothing by the expenditure, we save in time of filling orders."

Mr. Frick: "Money spent in expediting delivery is well spent, and especially now when we expect so large a business."

Mr. Schwab: "When this matter first came up in November, I was unwilling to recommend the expenditure of $40,-000.00, and referred Mr. Corey's letter back to him. When we rebuild the Fitting Shop, we can spend the $40,000.00 to very much better advantage. I would recommend the expenditure of $15,000.00."

On motion, (Peacock and Singer), the expenditure of $15,-000.00, as recommended by the president, was authorized; the vote being unanimous.

The following letter from W. E. Corey to the president, under date of January 11th, was read:

" Please find below an approximate estimate of expenditure for improvements at our Carrie Furnaces, as recommended by Mr. G. K. Hamfeldt, Superintendent.

Furnace with new shell, down-take, and dust-catcher with linings, incline with top arrangement, hoisting engine, and one coke and limestone bin, with track for stock yard, complete.....	$136,000.00
Extension and relining of two stoves....................	18,000.00
One compound condensing blowing engine, 40" × 72" × 60" × 84", with foundation, extension to Blowing Engine House, with foundations and Piping............	46,000.00
Weise Condenser, 3600 HP, complete	18,000.00
Total............... .,.....................	$218,000.00

"The detailed plans for same have not as yet been completed, but, as soon as completed, I will arrange with Mr. Gayley to go over them with Mr. Hamfeldt.

" Kindly advise me if you will authorize the expenditure of this money."

MM. Phipps and Clemson moved the authorization of an expenditure of $218,000.00.

Mr. Schwab: "This will put Carrie No. 2 in practically the same shape as our other Furnaces, and will make the Furnace equal to "F" or "G." It is in this direction we must go in making improvements."

Mr. Gayley (In reply to the chairman): "It should increase the product 100 tons per day."

Mr. Schwab: "We have no place to use the surplus steam at Carrie, and it will not pay us to compound the engines there at present. We can compound them later on, if it is found advantageous."

Mr. Singer: "This is a wise thing to do."

Mr. Peacock: "We should put all our Furnaces in good shape."

Mr. Gayley: "I am satisfied we need to do this."

Mr. Clemson: "It is a mistake to do anything else but keep our Furnaces in the best possible condition."

Mr. Lauder: "I think it is the right thing to do."

Mr. Phipps: "We all expected to do this when we bought the Plant."

Mr. Lovejoy: "It is in line with our policy, and should be done."

Mr. Gayley: "The Carrie Furnace Company intended to do a part of this work, if they had not sold."

Mr. Frick: "It is a large amount; but to our willingness to spend large amounts in improvements, we owe our success."

The motion was adopted; the vote being unanimous.

Mr. Schwab: "At a Meeting in New York of our principal Partners and Managers, it was decided that the following changes and new Interests should be made, commencing with January 1, 1899; subject to the approval of the Board and of the Shareholders.

"It is proposed to give $\frac{1}{9}\%$ to each of the following:

> W. B. Dickson;
> A. C. Case;
> John McLeod;
> Charles W. Baker;

and to give an increase of

> $\frac{1}{9}\%$ to James Gayley;
> $\frac{1}{6}\%$ to D. M. Clemson;
> $\frac{1}{9}\%$ to A. M. Moreland;
> $\frac{1}{9}\%$ to L. T. Brown;
> $\frac{2}{5}\%$ to J. E. Schwab."

On motion (Singer and Peacock), the following resolution was adopted:

"*Resolved;* That F. T. F. Lovejoy, Trustee, be and is now hereby directed, authorized and empowered to transfer out of Trust ' N ' certain Capital of this Association, to the persons and in the amounts named, as follows:

To James Gayley, $\frac{1}{9}$% or $27,777.78;
D. M. Clemson, $\frac{1}{6}$% or 41,666.67;
A. M. Moreland, $\frac{1}{9}$% or 27,777.78;

at its Book Value at the close of business December 31, 1898; subject to all of the conditions of the "Iron Clad Agreement," and subject also to confirmation at the next Meeting of the Shareholders; and

"*Resolved;* That having so done, F. T. F. Lovejoy be released and discharged from any further accountability as to his Trusteeship for the seven-eighteenths per centum of the Capital of this Association, the transfer of which is authorized hereby;"

the vote being unanimous.

On motion, (Singer and Peacock), the following resolution was adopted:

"*Resolved;* That F. T. F. Lovejoy, Trustee, be and is now hereby directed, authorized and empowered to transfer out of Trust ' N ' certain Capital of this Association, to the Trust Accounts and in the amounts named, as follows:

To Trust "W"   for L. T. Brown, $\frac{1}{9}$% of 1% or $27,777.77;
To Trust "AB"   for J. E. Schwab, $\frac{2}{9}$ of 1% or 55,555.55;
To Trust "AE"   for W. B. Dickson, $\frac{1}{9}$ of 1% or 27,777.78;
To Trust "AF"   for A. C. Case, $\frac{1}{9}$ of 1% or 27,777.78;
To Trust "AG"   for John McLeod, $\frac{1}{9}$ of 1% or 27,777.78;
To Trust "AH"   for Chas. W. Baker, $\frac{1}{9}$ of 1% or 27,777.78;

the same having been sold to the said persons at Book Value December 31, 1898; subject to all of the conditions of the ' Iron Clad Agreement,' and subject also to confirmation at the next Meeting of the Shareholders ";

the vote being unanimous.

Mr. Schwab: " As the members of the Board are aware, I go East tonight and sail for Southampton on Wednesday, expecting to be back here April 4th. During my absence, the plans for the new Car Works will proceed without any delay, and be ready with actual bids for all the machinery and other Contract items by April 1st, when an estimate of the cost will be given to the Board and an appropriation asked for. No expenditure will be necessary meantime."

(In reply to the chairman) :

" I have not figured closely on the cost at all, but would say in round figures the Works will cost from $750,000.00 to $1,000,000.00."

Mr. Peacock: " I think while we are on the subject of Car Works, it would be well to consider our present position with the new Steel Car combination. They have already approached us on the subject of a Contract, and would be willing to buy probably 1,000 tons of Steel per day, provided we stay out of the Steel Car business. I think, under a favorable Contract, I would favor this, especially since they are re-organized, and will be in good financial condition and safe to sell to."

Mr. Schwab: " I do not think anything should prevent our going ahead with our Car Works."

Mr. Clemson: " There is room for two, and they will have to come to us."

Mr. Phipps: " I would favor going ahead."

Mr. Lauder: " It would bear some thought, but, on the whole, I think I would go ahead with the Works."

Mr. Singer: " I think we should go ahead with our plans, but I am a little inclined to agree with Mr. Peacock. There is a great deal of detail connected with the Car business, and we will probably make as much money if we sell the Plates as if we turned the Plates into Cars and sold them."

Mr. Gayley: " I would go ahead with the Works."

Mr. Clemson: " I would build the Car Works, and would also look into the Steel Pipe business. I believe there is money in that."

Mr. Lovejoy: " I think we should go ahead with the Works, believing we can sell both Plates and Cars, and, having the Car Works, we can compel Schoen-Fox to buy from us."

Mr. Frick: " Is our Car as good as the Schoen or Fox car?"

Mr. Schwab: " I think it is better, but it is heavier. We expect to improve on it, and I believe we can make it as light as theirs, and, at the same time, a better and stronger Car."

Mr. Frick : "I am strongly in favor of going ahead. There will be room for both."

Mr. Clemson: "We brought in some good Gas Wells during the latter part of December, and are now in as good shape for Gas as we were this time last year. I will guarantee a sufficient supply of Gas for this year."

Mr. Frick : "That is very gratifying news."

At this point, Mr. Clemson withdrew from the meeting, having been called as a witness in a case pending.

A letter from Andrew Carnegie to the president, under date of December 30th, was read, as follows:

"Several times I have been upon the point of writing you about settling with James C. Carter, the lawyer here.

"We consulted him in regard to our claim against the Government for remission of fine imposed [for supplying defective armor-plate]. I suppose it is the general feeling that we had better not disturb that question, better just let it pass. If you find this to be so in the Board, then I should like a note to be written to Mr. Carter stating that we do not wish the case pursued any further and to send us his bill. His address is No. 277 Lexington avenue."

Mr. Frick : "Suppose Mr. Phipps should write to Mr. Carter in effect as follows:

"'We have not yet decided whether or not we wish to abandon our claim, but, should we decide to press it, we would wish to retain him. Meantime, however, as the case has been hanging fire for some time, we would be glad to have a bill for his services to date, which we will pay.'

"That complies with Mr. Carnegie's wish, and, at the same time, does not close the matter absolutely."

This met with general approval, and, on motion, the matter was so decided upon.

Mr. Frick : "I would like to ask Mr. Peacock if he is selling much Material today, and if he is getting advanced prices?"

Mr. Peacock: "I think the only increase in Billets sold, shown in our statements during the last four weeks has been where we have sliding scale Contracts. We have today nothing to sell but Structural Material, on which we are getting good prices.

"We have under consideration a Contract with the American Tin Plate Company of New Jersey, which has been agreed to, subject to the action of the Board."

The Contract was read in full, the features thereof being:

Quantity: 125,000 gross tons of Tin and Black Plates, Bars (not including Sheet Bars) per year, for a period of Five (5) years, from July 1, 1899, and thereafter until after One year's written notice, which may be given by either party, on or after July 1, 1903.

PRICE: When the Price of Pig iron per gross ton is:	The amount to be added to the price of Pig Iron for Sheet Bars shall be:
$ 8.99 or under	$5.45
9.00 to 9.99	5.60
10.00 " 10.99	5.75
11.00 " 11.99	6.00
12.00 " 13.99	6.25
13.00 " 14.99	6.50
13.00 " 14.99	6.75
15.00 " 15.99	7.00
16.00 or over	7.25

Price to be fixed monthly and averaged for six months.

Payments: Cash on the 20th of each month.
Deliveries: Approximately 10,416 tons per month.
Buyer may specify up to 10% Basic Open Hearth at 1.50 per ton advance.

Buyers may not re-sell without first putting Material through a process of manufacture.

Sellers agree, so long as the Buyers perform their part of this Contract "They will not sell to any competitive person or Company in the United States, Tin or Black Plate Bars of the character covered by this Contract;" and Sellers agree "Not to enter into competition with The Carnegie Steel Company, Limited, in any of the products which The Carnegie Steel Company, Limited manufactures, during the life of this Contract."

Buyers also agree, if their capacity be increased, Sellers shall have the privilege of selling the same proportion of the new requirements.

Any dispute as to price to be referred to A. H. Childs.

Mr. Frick : " Would it not be well to have all matters of dispute under this Contract referred to an Arbitrator? "

Mr. Peacock : " It might be, although our Attorneys advise us our position is better if we do not agree to defer all matters to an Arbitrator, since we would probably be compelled to appeal to the Courts to sustain the award of an Arbitrator, and we might as well fight out the whole thing in Court."

Mr. Frick : " I do not agree.   The decision of an Arbitrator is usually binding and conclusive among reputable business concerns."

All spoke in favor of the making of this Contract, and, on motion, (Schwab and Phipps), its execution was authorized; the vote being unanimous.

Mr. Peacock : " This represents 25% of their total requirements of last year."

Mr. Schwab : " It is more than double what we sold last year."

Mr. Peacock : " We have in process of negotiation a Contract with the National Transit Company for Plates, but it is not quite in shape to report to the Board.   It also is a sliding scale, and on $10.00 Pig, gives us $1.15 for Sheared Plates."

Mr. Schwab (In reply to the chairman) :
" That would give us $8.00 per ton profit."

On motion, (Phipps and Schwab), the making of this Contract was left with Mr. Peacock, with power to act.

MM. Gayley and Clemson, appointed as a Committee December 13th, made the following report:

" The Committee appointed to investigate the property of the Pittsburg & Conneaut Dock Company, at Conneaut Harbor, Ohio, to determine if land was available for the erection of a Blast Furnace Plant, would report as follows:

" A number of plans have been prepared to determine the best location, and with such plans before us a personal inspec-

CONNEAUT HARBOR

tion of the property was made during the past week. The plot selected is just east of the present coal unloading slip. The new drawbridge crossing the creek to the new dock will permit the largest ore vessels to pass. At a point on the creek 300 feet east of the drawbridge the vessels can turn into a slip, which will have to be dredged, which allows ample room for stock yards and furnace plant on the East side. By this arrangement, there is obtained on the Western side a strip of ground 400 feet wide which can be used by the Dock Company in further dock extensions, the length of such dock can be from 1,000 to 2,000 feet long as found necessary to dredge. There is provided in this arrangement ample room for a furnace plant between the slip and the hillside, and lengthwise will be found room for a number of furnaces. The low ground extending along the railroad for some distance affords an excellent space for disposal of slag for many years, or the slag can just as readily be conveyed to the upper end of the new dock and dumped into the lake, and in this way providing for dock extensions. There is sufficient flat land adjoining the furnace location, of which the Dock Company owns part, which if filled with slag would be suitable for Steel Works and other manufactories.

"The slip your Committee had in view for a furnace site comprised about 25 acres, with plenty of just as suitable property adjoining.

"The dock frontage at Conneaut for discharging ore is as follows:

Old Dock...................................	1,900 feet.
Direct unloading Dock	1,200 "
New Dock (under construction).................	1,100 "
Total.................................	4,200 "
New Dock can be extended.....................	1,100 "
Furnace Dock as outlined........	1,000 "
Making a Total of	6,300 feet.

and this can be increased by extensions into the lake and of the Furnace slip. The above figures are for ore unloading alone, and do not include the side of dock for coal or rail unloading.

"A Furnace at Conneaut Harbor making 300 tons of iron per day would require per annum 100,000 net tons of Coke and 40,000 gross tons of limestone."

Mr. Frick : "We will leave that report on the Minutes for consideration, and take up the matter at some future time."

Mr. Gayley : "We have made the following purchases of Manganese Ore :

"*Caucasian Ore :*

"Everitt & Company, 10,000 tons at 10¾ pence, shipment March to September.

"F. Haeberlin, 10,000 tons at 10⅝ pence, shipment
March to October.

"John Carr & Company, 6,000 tons at 10¾ pence,
shipment March to May.

"*Cuban Ore :*

"We have purchased from the Ponupo Mining & Transportation Company, their product for this year up to
25,000 tons at 24 cents per unit, at sea-board."

Mr. Gayley (In reply to the chairman) :

"We have several old Caucasian Ore Contracts at lower
prices than these, but find it difficult to get deliveries.
Making these Contracts, we will be able to get deliveries
under both the old and new Contracts. These prices on
Caucasian Ore are up about $1.50 per ton, while the Cu-
ban Contract has come down about $2.00 per ton. The
average increase in the cost of Ferro-Manganese this year
will be $1.50 per ton."

Mr. Peacock : "But we are getting from $4.00 to $5.00 per ton
more for Ferro than we did a year ago."

On motion, (Schwab and Peacock), the purchases reported
were approved, ratified and confirmed.

Mr. Gayley : "The Operations at Conneaut Dock, for the five
days ending January 13th, were as follows :

Receipts,	None.
Shipments,	11,359 tons.

(In reply to the chairman) :

"Everything at the Docks will be ready for next year's
business."

Mr. Frick : "It would be well to bear in mind the necessity of
getting the Cars under Contract with the Schoen Company
in time. Mr. Gayley might put a man on to look after
this."

Mr. Bope, as assistant general sales agent, submitted the
following report :

19

STATEMENT OF SALES OF STANDARD RAILS SINCE
NOVEMBER 18, 1898.

	Sales.	Options (minimum).	Totals.
Carnegie	326,623	46,000	372,623
Illinois	342,713	36,000	378,713
Cambria	65,266	......	65,266
Colorado	20,698	.....	20,698
Total	755,300	82,000	837,300

"All of our own sales above reported have been included
in our report of obligations following, although formal Contracts
for only 197,000 tons have been executed."

"The statement given below compares our estimated obligations (for the classes of material specified) at the opening of
business, Friday, January 6 and January 13, 1899:

Material.	Jan. 6th.	Jan. 13th.	Difference.
Rails	564,110	556,541	Loss 7,569
Billets, Blooms, Sheet Bars, etc.	445,227	433,739	Loss 11,488
Structural and Ship Material.	174,564	180,923	Gain 6,359
Axles and Bars	38,110	39,742	" 1,632
Plates	41,693	46,245	" 4,552
Total	1,263,704	1,257,190	Loss 6,514

"All in Gross Tons, based on our minimum obligations."

Mr. Phipps : "As the members of the Board are aware, we
have been building a foot-bridge over the Railroad at Duquesne, and are asked to sign a Contract, agreeing to keep
it in good order."

On motion, (Phipps and Schwab), the execution of such a
Contract was authorized; the vote being unanimous.

Mr. Phipps : "We have divided the Fawcett Land into Lots,
and a plan has been prepared showing 29 Lots, on each
side of the boulevard. This plan should be adopted, in
order that it may be recorded in the Court House."

On motion, (Schwab and Peacock), the plan submitted was
approved and adopted; the vote being unanimous.

Mr. Phipps : " Collections have been coming in so freely that we have found it advisable to anticipate our Ore payments, up to and including those for March."

Mr. Lauder : " Referring to the question of Lake freight on Ores : I think we can transport much cheaper than it is being contracted for, by building large barges and handling these by tugs in relays, running the business as a Railroad would transport cars. The barges should hold say 10,000 tons; two barges per day during the shipping season run-

Whaleback ore steamers in port.

ning regularly would give us our supply, and would, I believe, although I have not figured on it in detail, effect a saving of 40 to 50% in freight cost."

Mr. Frick : " In this connection, I was told by W. L. Brown that they transported ore from Escanaba to South Chicago for 17 cents. That should be looked up by Mr. Gayley, and we should also bear Mr. Lauder's suggestion in mind."

Mr. Schwab : " I think it practicable, but do not see where the great saving would come in."

Mr. Gayley : " The barges suggested are only 3,000 tons larger than those now in use. The traffic is a little uncertain on the Lakes and tugs might have to lie over and lose time. This is what keeps the rates higher than they would be otherwise. The suggestion is worthy of investigation, and I will take it up."

Mr. Frick here made the statement concerning the reorganization of the company, and asked: "Whom will you name as the Committee?"

On motion, (Schwab and Singer), MM. Frick, Peacock, Phipps (L. C.) and Lovejoy were appointed as the Committee, in charge of the Organization of THE CARNEGIE COMPANY, LIMITED; there being no dissent.

Mr. Frick : "The Committee will report progress to the Board from time to time; meanwhile, all should consider this, and be prepared to make suggestions on any points that occur to them.

"I may add that the question of Buying and Selling Value of Capital Stock in the new Company—that is, what will be paid to retiring Partners, or what will be paid by new Shareholders admitted—is having careful consideration, will be fixed on a fair basis, and will be set forth in an Agreement similar to our present ' Iron Clad Agreement,' to be signed when the new Company takes possession."

On motion, adjourned.

(Signed) LOVEJOY,
Secretary.

Approved at meeting held,

_____

_____

Chairman Board of Managers.

Copy to A. C., New York;
     H. P., Jr., Washington, D. C.;
     H. M. C., Pasadena.
17 January, 1899.

CHAPTER XIX

THE ZENITH OF PROSPERITY

IN 1889 negotiations were entered into by Andrew Carnegie with certain English bankers and capitalists with a view of selling out the iron and steel enterprises with which he was connected. At that time British investors were absorbing American industrial stocks with astonishing avidity; and Carnegie, believing the zenith of prosperity had been reached in his own business, thought the time an opportune one to sell out to the English. The project was resisted by Mr. Phipps, who had sold seven-eighteenths of his interest the previous year; but he finally yielded to his partner's insistence and gave a reluctant consent to the sale of the properties.

So far as could be seen at the time, Carnegie's lack of faith in the future was justified. Three years before, the profits of the several companies had amounted to nearly three million dollars. In 1887 they aggregated close on three and a half millions. Then in 1888 they dropped to $1,941,555; and it seemed a prudent measure to slip out of the business on what looked like the passing boom of 1889. The negotiations, however, had no satisfactory result; and Mr. Phipps, hearing of their failure, expressed his relief. Incidentally he gave expression to his opinion on the impropriety of selling out to a trust—an opinion that makes strange reading nowadays. Here is the beginning of the letter he wrote to Mr. Carnegie:

GRAND UNION HOTEL
Dresden, Saxony.
Nov. 1, 1889

DEAR ANDREW

Few pleasures on a foreign trip are equal to a friendly letter from home like yours of the 18th.

I am gratified that we are not to go out of business, and especially to make room for a trust, which is by no means a creditable thing. As you say the tariff would be repealed on rails and rightly so.

With Mr. Frick at the head, I have no fear as to receiving a good return upon our capital. Being interested in manufacturing keeps us within touch of the world and its affairs instead of being on the shelf. Of course I am anxious that you should not be worried by the business—only pleasantly interested. . . .

Yours truly
H. P. Jr.

It was a very fortunate thing for Carnegie, Phipps, and all the partners that the project failed; for in 1889 the profits of the year amounted to $3,540,000, the largest up to that date in the history of the various enterprises, despite the fact that rails were down to their lowest point, $29.25. Next year's profits were $5,350,000. The effect of Mr. Frick's management was beginning to be seen. In 1891, owing to dwindling prices and, in larger measure, to excessive cost of labor at Homestead, there was a falling off of a million dollars; and a still further reduction took place in 1892, the year of the strike. The profits this year were only $4,000,000. In 1893—panic year—a further reduction of a million dollars was recorded; and this marked the bottom. Thenceforward the annual balance sheets showed an ever-increasing profit, regular and slow at first, then by extraordinary leaps and bounds. Here is the gratifying record:

NET PROFITS OF THE CARNEGIE ASSOCIATIONS, CARNEGIE
BROTHERS & CO., LTD. (TO 1892), CARNEGIE, PHIPPS & CO.,
LTD. (TO 1892), AND THE CARNEGIE STEEL COMPANY,
LTD. (FROM JULY, 1892).

1889. ....$3,540,000*	1895 .... $5,000,000
1890................ 5,350,000	1896................ 6,000,000
1891....... 4,300,000	1897................ 7,000,000
1892................ 4,000,000	1898................ 11,500,000
1893................ 3,000,000	1899................ 21,000,000
1894................ 4,000,000	plus $4,500,000 reinvested.

These sums, added to those given on a previous page for the
years 1875 to 1888 inclusive, bring the aggregate net profits of
all the Carnegie associations to the impressive total of $93,-
391,005.41. In the year 1900—the last of its separate existence—the Carnegie Steel Company made a profit of nearly
$40,000,000, and a sum was taken from the Contingency Fund
to bring it up to this even figure.

It is believed by the Carnegie officials, and with some show
of reason, that this magnificent record was to a great extent
made possible by the company's victory at Homestead. From
that time on the firm profited by the heavy investments it had
made in labor-saving machinery; and costs got so low that one
year when the Carnegies made over four million dollars, their
chief competitor, the Illinois Steel Company, had upwards of a
million dollars' loss. The following year the Carnegies made
over five millions, while the Chicago company made only $360,-
000. By 1897 the cost of steel rails on cars at the Braddock
mill was only $12 a gross ton!

One of the most marked economies in production resulted
soon after the Homestead strike, when Mr. Frick created a posi-

---

* At this date a change was made in the method of accounting, by which the
odd sums were dropped from Profit and Loss and put into a "Contingency Fund."
Later any amount under half a million was so disposed of ; and, on the other hand,
when the Profit and Loss account showed an odd sum of more than half a million,
enough was borrowed from the Contingency Fund to make the total balance in
even millions. That is why, on another page, the profits of the association are
given to within a cent, while here they are stated in even millions.

tion, without any distinctive name, for Mr. P. R. Dillon, who
had done such excellent work at the Union Iron Mills and at
Beaver Falls.   His duties were advisory, covering mechanical
as well as labor equipment, and extended to every department
of the company's service.   By skilful adjustments he increased
the capacity of one group of workers after another, here adding
a man, there taking two away; in one place gearing up the
machinery, in another reducing it, until a high degree of mechanical perfection was reached, and there was not a superfluous wage-earner in the shops.   At Homestead alone five
hundred men were thus saved; and in all the Carnegie works

The Carrie Furnaces.

the reductions amounted to over fifteen hundred workmen.
And this without diminishing the output of a single group.
Indeed, the better practice thus resulting soon brought back the
displaced men; and the tonnage of the works increased more
rapidly than ever before.   The increase between 1893 and 1894
amounted to almost as much as the entire output of the works
in 1888, and exceeded it the following year.

During these years and those immediately following them
the growth of the several works was nothing less than phenomenal.   No great expansion was possible at the older establishments, such as the Union Iron Mills and the Lucy Furnaces;
but at Braddock, Homestead, and Duquesne additions were
made every year greater than the entire plant had been a short

time before. At Homestead one set of open-hearth furnaces was rapidly added after another, and new mills erected to finish the increased output of steel. In one case only sixty days intervened between the turning of the first sod and the casting of an ingot on the same spot. The two Carrie furnaces, just across the river, were bought by Mr. Frick with his usual issue of bonds, and the bonds liquidated out of profits. Later two other furnaces were added; and these great stacks have broken the world's record for yearly tonnage. At Duquesne the same nervous activity was displayed. Four huge blast-furnaces were built to supply the metal required by the extensive open-hearth plant that soon supplemented the two Bessemer converters which Mr. Frick found there when he bought the works. At the Edgar Thomson works almost every year witnessed an addition to its great battery of blast-furnaces, until Kloman's little Escanaba stack was but as a single letter in half the alphabet. Here, expressed in gross tons of steel ingots made, is the great record of the growth of the combined business of these plants under the management of Henry C. Frick:

1888	332,111	1894	1,115,466
1889	536,838	1895	1,464,032
1890	660,071	1896	1,375,249
1891	797,286	1897	1,686,377
1892	877,602	1898	2,171,226
1893	863,027	1899	2,663,412

The import of these statistics is seen by a comparison. In 1885 Great Britain led the world in the production of steel. Her total output for that year was 695,000 tons *less* than the product of the Carnegie Steel Company in 1899.

During this period the H. C. Frick Coke Company, while still supreme in its field, had not expanded with anything like equal rapidity. This was partly because it was already great enough to supply the Carnegie demands twice over, and partly bceause its profits and credits had been used to develop the steel company. Beginning as early as 1888, during the Edgar

Thomson strike, the credit of the coke company had been continuously used to strengthen the steel companies; and ambitious as Mr. Frick was to put the latter concerns at the head of the steel-producing establishments, not only of America, but of the world, he let the profits of his own special business go into blast-furnaces and open-hearth plants, when his personal prominence would have been furthered by putting them into coal lands and new ovens.

In 1899 the H. C. Frick Coke Company owned 40,000 of the 60,000 acres of unmined coal land in the Connellsville re-

Shoveling ore from its native bed into cars.

gion, 20,000 acres of surface land, 11,000 coke-ovens, 2,500 railroad-cars, and 3,500 dwellings. Its capital was $10,000,-000, of which Andrew Carnegie personally owned a little over one-quarter, the Carnegie Steel Company about the same, and the rest was held by Mr. Frick and a number of smaller owners, of whom the principal ones were Mrs. T. M. Carnegie and Mr. John Walker. It was in no way affiliated with the Carnegie Steel Company, except that it worked in harmony with it. At times the necessities of the latter conflicted with its proper interests, and then these had to give way to the Carnegie control.

Ten years having elapsed since the failure of the attempt to sell the works to English investors, new schemes of a like character were made in 1899. For a long time past Mr. Carnegie had lived principally abroad, and Mr. Phipps had withdrawn from active participation in the affairs of the company. Mr. Frick's had been the guiding hand that had led the concern to a prosperity surpassing the dreams of the most sanguine of his colleagues; and in all plans for the future his continued leadership seemed a necessity. But Carnegie was loath to resign in favor of one whose prominence threatened to overshadow his own; and the plans he made for his own final withdrawal invariably included the simultaneous resignation of Frick. And Frick, full of energy and not yet fifty years of age, had no thought of resigning; so that the plans never got beyond the nebulous stage until the shock of litigation forced them into some degree of definiteness. The result was an illustration of what Herbert Spencer calls "a consolidation effected by war."

Before dealing with this sensational suit and the causes leading up to it, a more detailed reference should be made to some of these earlier schemes of consolidating the steel and coke businesses, and selling them to outsiders. This will serve to correct the prevalent idea that the sale which was finally made to Mr. J. Pierpont Morgan for the United States Steel Corporation was due entirely to commercial conditions, and not to any desire on the part of the Carnegie people to be rid of their property.

Early in January, 1899—to be specific, on Thursday, the 5th of that month—a meeting was held at the house of Andrew Carnegie in New York, attended by Messrs. Hy. Phipps, Frick, Schwab, Lovejoy, Peacock, and Lauder, for the discussion of two questions. The first was the price that should be named for the properties of the Carnegie Steel Company and the H. C. Frick Coke Company in response to certain overtures to purchase which had been made by a syndicate of New York and Chicago capitalists. The second question was whether the two companies should be consolidated in case of a failure to sell them, and on what terms. Both matters were carefully considered; and a decision to sell having been reached, the price of $250,000,000 was fixed upon for the steel company's stock, "carrying with it all that is on its books," including the shares in the coke company. Payment was to be made one-half in cash and one-half in fifty-year five-per-cent. gold bonds.

When these terms were laid before the syndicate they were rejected. While the members did not say so, they had evidently expected to make a partial payment in stock.

A consolidation of the coke and steel business was then decided upon; and on January 14th Andrew Carnegie wrote his wishes to his cousin, George Lauder, as follows:

"Mr. Rodgers, Standard Oil and Federal, said truly, 'Too big a dog to wag so small a tail.' Now H. C. F. and I talked over the matter. He will proceed to get plan, new charter, bonds, etc., as proposed.

I wish you and Peacock and Lawrence, Clemson, Lovejoy, Gayley, etc., to decide whether you wish to buy the other Frick Coke Company Stocks at $35,000,000.00, which Frick now wants; or prefer to let things stand as they are with the present fixed rate on Coke.

The Frick Company price was $30,000,000.00, if $75,000,-000.00 Mortgage Bonds only made by C. S. Co., and you may prefer to do this, or might make the Mortgage $100,000,000.00, and only issue $75,000,000.00 now, and provide only the other issue for new property to be acquired, which would be the same thing practically as the $75,000,000.00 Mortgage.

I am just as willing to keep my Frick Company Stock as to sell it to C. S. Co., and I suppose H. C. F. is. He can make it pay us more than the interest on the $35,000,000.00.

You should consult all the Managers, including Singer, and let each state frankly his preference. Also ask Schwab if he has not gone; if he has, I will see him here.

It is a matter for all of you to decide, not for me. As I told you, C. S. Co. paying in Bonds makes it easy payments—

no cash—which is different from heavy yearly payments to make. Personally am glad to have this year to ourselves to show what we can do. If we wish to sell out, believe me, we can do so ourselves for more than $250,000,000.00."

The reference to the proposed purchase of "the other Frick Coke Company Stocks at $35,000,000" is misleading. The price was to include all the stock of the coke company, as is shown by the Frick plan to which Mr. Carnegie refers. The clause relating to this reads:

"The [projected] Carnegie Company Limited shall purchase all the property and business of the H. C. Frick Coke Company, the Youghiogheny Northern Railway Co., Youghiogheny Water Co., Mt. Pleasant Water Co., Trotter Water Co. and the Union Supply Co. Ltd. subject to all their debts, obligations and engagements, or all of the Capital Stock of said Companies as shall in the consummation of the general purpose of this agreement be subsequently deemed most desirable by the Committee hereinafter designated, for the sum of Thirty-five million dollars ($35,000,000) to be paid as hereinafter stated."

In other words the entire business of the Frick Company and all its dependencies was offered at $35,000,000. This is exactly half the price paid for it a year later in settlement of the famous litigation.

Mr. Frick's plan, thus referred to, of a company with a capital of $60,000,000 and a bond issue of $100,000,000, was not acceptable to Mr. Carnegie, who drew up a prospectus in substitution of it, and sent it with the following letter to his colleagues in Pittsburg. The phraseology of these documents is not very clear; but in the prospectus the retirement of Mr. Frick is distinctly provided for:

"WE (THE CARNEGIE STEEL COMPANY, LIMITED, and the H. C. FRICK COKE COMPANY) [shall] make this year, under the lowest prices on record, say close to $15,000,000.00.

We had only six months of Carrie Blast Furnaces; not six months work of the big new Blooming Mill; no Armor deliveries, except for three months; a loss of nearly $1,000,000.00 profit.

Had these been running as now our net would have been beyond $15,000,000.00.

For 1899 :

We, with half product, sold 1,200,000 tons, orders on our books, at higher prices of at least $1.00 deliveries..............................$1,200,000.00

We have of Armor—going to work for years ahead—another............................ 1,000,000.00

Carrie Blast Furnaces; the Blooming Mill all he year, another.......................... 500,000.00

If we get $1.00 more pull on the remaining 1,200,000 tons. 1,200,000.00

                                                            ————————————

                                                            $3,900,000.00

Our increased product of Furnaces and Mills give us a big increase, but there is a gain of....$4,000,000.00

Which might easily be $5,000,000.00.

Frick Coke is now making at the rate of a $1,000,000.00 more per year; even better prospects.................................... 1,000,000.00

                                                            ————————————

                                                            $5,000,000.00

The Light Rail Mill begins say July 1st; our new Mines this year will increase profits there; our big new Universal Mill goes into operation say May 1st.

Mr. Fricks estimate of.................$15,000,000.00

Frick and Superior Mines over........... 5,000,000.00

                                                            ————————————

                Net for 1899...................$20,000,000.00

Just as likely to be above as below, I think more so, but say $20,000,000.00.

In 1900 :

We had the big Plate Mill; Steel Car Shops; new Axle Plant; Car Wheel Foundry; all arranged for—came in early in 1899;—also two new Blast Furnaces at Carrie.

For 1900, therefore, present conditions are good for $25,-000,000.00. These conditions are very low. Prices liable to advance $2.00 to $5.00 per ton.

The first would give us $ 5,000,000.00 more, 30,000,000.00
The second   12,500,000.00 more, 37,500,000.00

I am certain that in two years hence we shall be on the basis of $25,000,000.00 net yearly, even at low prices.

We have to supply the world—note last week's British advices—less Ore this year and last from foreign points; great scarcity; prices wild; coke put to 15/6 [fifteen shillings and sixpence] at Works, best grade; *bad to get* at that; near $3.75 per ton and scarce. Impossible to increase supply of either Coke or Ore.

Since we reach Atlantic ports at $1.00 per ton, we have the trade of the world.

I favor holding on for two or three years; no question but we can sell our property at $400,000,000.00.

200,000,000 Bonds @ 5%   = $10,000,000.00
200,000,000 Stock @ 6%   =   12,000,000.00
                                _____
                                $22,000,000.00
              Surplus.....................   3,000,000.00

We shall beat this—why then not wait. If you wish to sell now then here is the plan.   A. C."

(PROSPECTUS)

THE CARNEGIE STEEL COMPANY, LIMITED, and the H. C. FRICK COKE COMPANY.

In pursuance of a decision of long standing, the four principal owners of The Carnegie Steel Company, Limited, and the H. C. Frick Coke Company (MM. Carnegie, Phipps, Frick and Lauder) now retire from active business. To enable them to do so, and with the approval of all the younger Partners, the partnership has been changed to a corporation—Capital $300,-000,000.00.

One half...........$150,000,000.00 Gold Mortgage Bonds;
Preferred Stock, 6%....75,000,000.00
Common Stock,.......75,000,000.00

All the Bonds and Preferred Stock will be taken payment by the four outgoing Partners.

Part of the Common Stock will be held by the present younger Partners; part is now offered to the public.

Applications from Pittsburg and Western Pennsylvania,

especially in Manufacturers of Iron and Steel, will be given preference, the desire being to enlist as many experienced business men at home as possible.

All the present Partners agree to continue in the service for Five (5) years. MM. Carnegie, Phipps, Frick and Lauder also agree to remain for that period in their present positions as Consulting Partners.

The Partners have agreed to make good any deficiency in the Net Earnings, should such occur during said five years, in the amount necessary to pay interest on Bonds and upon Preferred Stock, and 6% upon Common Stock.

To meet this liability there has been deposited with . . . . Trust Company, $20,000,000.00 of Bonds, contributed pro rata by the Partners.

The present earnings of the Companies exceed the sum required for the payment stated and leaves a satisfactory surplus for contingencies. Additional Works now in progress, which the demand of the ever growing business required, will add to the earnings. The property of the new Company embraces all the property of the two former Companies; everything is included—real estate, railroads, coke lands (38,000 acres unmined), mills, furnaces, houses, offices, water rights, mines, and everything of every description.

The debts of the Company, including all Mortgage Bonds, etc., are more than covered by the quick assets—the Stock of Material, and the Bills Receivable, and the Cash on Hand. The Company starts with . . . . Working Capital.

(SIGNATURES)

This prospectus is true; nothing kept back.

These different plans of consolidation and reorganization were still under consideration when, towards the end of March, overtures were made by ex-Judge W. H. Moore of Chicago for the purchase of the Carnegie-Frick properties, with the view of combining them. This time an effort was made to get a price on Andrew Carnegie's individual holdings of stock in the two companies, carrying as they did control; but, for the sake of appearances, Mr. Carnegie refused to deal with outside parties, and stipulated that the negotiations should be conducted in the names of his principal partners, Phipps and Frick. Accordingly these gentlemen joined the syndicate, with the understanding that Moore and his friends should finance the entire scheme.

Carnegie demanded a million dollars for a ninety days' option on his entire interests at a price of $157,950,000; and he afterwards raised this bonus to $1,170,000. The increase was met by Messrs. Phipps and Frick each contributing $85,000, Carnegie agreeing to return these sums to them later. The other members of the steel and coke companies required no bonus for an option on their shares except the nominal sum of one dollar. These agreements were signed on April 24th.

If the sale had been consummated it would have been on the basis of $250,000,000 "for the entire ownership of first party [Andrew Carnegie] and associate owners and interests in all the properties and assets of The Carnegie Steel Co. Ltd., except its holdings in the stock of the H. C. Frick Coke Co., and allied interests, namely: about thirty (30) per cent. of the whole of the said H. C. Frick Coke Co., in which thirty per cent. in said H. C. Frick Coke Company interests the said second parties [H. C. Frick and Henry Phipps, Jr.] may take first party's interest on the basis of Seventy millions of dollars ($70,000,000) for the whole of the said H. C. Frick Coke Co. properties and allied interests." And "as to the first party's individual holdings of stock in the H. C. Frick Coke Co. and allied interests, this shall be upon the basis of Seventy millions of dollars for the entire property and assets of the H. C. Frick Coke Co. of which stock the holdings of the said first party is about twenty-five (25) per cent. of the whole."

To quote still further from the original option, "the first party agrees to take as part payment for his interests as above one hundred millions of dollars ($100,000,000) in five per cent. fifty year, gold bonds, to be executed by such individual corporation or limited partnership association, as may be designated by the second parties, or their assigns, which bonds shall be secured by a mortgage upon all the real estate of the Carnegie Steel Co. Ltd. and to be a first lien thereon, except so far

20

as the same shall be now encumbered, and which shall cover all of the stocks, interests and securities covered by this option."
. . . "The remainder of the consideration for the sale of the interests hereby optioned is to be in cash."

In this way Carnegie would have been so secured that he would virtually have had a first mortgage on all the partnership assets, thus gaining a preference over all his partners.

An instrument of a like tenor and purport was signed by other members of the Carnegie-Frick companies, without any forfeitable bonus.

At the time this option was bought the money market was in such condition that no difficulty was anticipated by Judge Moore in raising the necessary funds to carry out his plans, huge as these were. He represented that he would have the co-operation of the National City and the First National Banks of New York. The death of Roswell P. Flower, however, and the forced liquidation of the many industrial securities that he had been supporting, brought on a panic that was as disastrous as it was unexpected. Occupied in protecting existing obligations, bankers and capitalists had little disposition to engage in fresh ventures; and realizing the impossibility of safely launching a great enterprise in such troubled waters, Messrs. Frick and Phipps went to Scotland to try to get an extension of their option. At Skibo Castle Mr. Carnegie refused to extend the option, and the negotiations came to an abrupt end.

An interesting document was drawn up at this time which is worth including here, presenting as it does at a glance the imposing magnitude of the business whose growth we have traced from the little Kloman forge in the basement at Girty's Run. It is the draft of a prospectus prepared by the Moore Syndicate, but never published. It marks the zenith of the Carnegie Steel Company's prosperity. Supplementing it is a letter from Mr. C. M. Schwab, of considerable interest.

(PROSPECTUS)

A limited amount of the stock of the "CARNEGIE STEEL COMPANY" is now offered to the public, on the following basis:

The corporation which it is planned to form with the name "Carnegie Steel Company," will have, through a charter to be obtained under the laws of Pennsylvania, appropriate powers for acquiring, producing, manufacturing and dealing in steel, iron, ore, coal and coke, and all things made of steel or iron, with all other powers deemed convenient, and will have an authorized capital of two hundred and fifty million dollars ($250,000,000), divided into two million five hundred thousand (2,500,000) shares of the par value of one hundred dollars ($100) each.

Each subscriber will agree to take and pay for the number of shares for which he may subscribe, or such smaller proportionate number as may be allotted to him in the event of over-subscription, of the full-paid stock.

The price is to be one hundred dollars ($100) in cash for each share of stock, and is to be paid into such depository as may be designated by the Managers in control of the subscription lists, within ten days after notice calling for such payment shall be delivered or mailed to the subscriber; but ten dollars out of every one hundred dollars of subscription may be made payable immediately on allotment, if so stated in the notice thereof. If the stock certificates cannot be delivered when payments are completed, receipts will be issued calling for the stock when ready.

The corporation is to be vested with fifteen million dollars ($15,000,000) in cash and also with the cash and other available assets of The Carnegie Steel Company, Limited, and the H. C. Frick Coke Company, and, subject to a Bonded Debt of one hundred million dollars ($100,000,000) in 50 year 5% Gold Bonds, with the properties of The Carnegie Steel Company, Limited, and the H. C. Frick Coke Company, which include the following:

The Edgar Thomson Works, at Bessemer, Pa., including:
Edgar Thomson Blast Furnaces,
Edgar Thomson Foundry,
Edgar Thomson Steel Works.
The Duquesne Works, at Duquesne, Pa., including:
Duquesne Blast Furnace,
Duquesne Steel Works.

The Homestead Steel Works, at Munhall, Pa., including:

Bessemer Steel Department,
Open Hearth Steel Department,
Finishing Mills,
Armor Plate Department.

The Carrie Blast Furnaces, at Rankin, Pa.
The Lucy Blast Furnaces, in Pittsburg, Pa.
The Keystone Bridge Works, in Pittsburg, Pa.
The Upper Union Mills, in Pittsburg, Pa.
The Lower Union Mills, in Pittsburg, Pa.
The H. C. Frick Coke Company's Coal and Coke properties in Westmoreland and Fayette Counties, Pa., including:

About 40,000 acres of unmined coal,
20,000 acres of surface lands,
11,000 coke ovens;
2,500 railroad cars,
3,500 dwellings.

The Larimer Coke Works, at Larimer, Pa.
The Youghiogheny Coke Works, at Douglas, Pa.
All the capital stock of the following Companies:

The Union Railroad Company,
The Slackwater Railroad Company,
The Youghiogheny Northern Railway Company,
The Carnegie Natural Gas Company,
The Youghiogheny Water Company,
The Mount Pleasant Water Company,
The Trotter Water Company,
The Pittsburg and Conneaut Dock Company.

Over one-half the capital stock of the Pittsburg, Bessemer and Lake Erie Railroad Company.

43.6 per cent. of the capital stock of the Pennsylvania and Lake Erie Dock Company.

One-fourth of the capital stock of the New York, Pennsylvania and Ohio Dock Company.

Five-sixths of the capital stock of the Oliver Iron Mining Company, owning:

All the stock of the Metropolitan Iron and Land Company,
All the stock of the Pioneer Iron Company,
Over 68 per cent. of the stock of the Lake Superior Iron Company,
Over 98 per cent. of the stock of the Security Land and Exploration Company,
Other ore properties in negotiation which will be included if acquired.

One-half of the capital stock of the Pewabic Company.

Three-fourths of the capital stock of the Pittsburg Limestone Company, Limited.

Other interests in Ore Mines, Transportation Companies, Dock Companies, Valuable Patents, and Companies owning Patents, etc.

These Furnaces, Steel Works, Coke Works, and other properties are in full operation, their latest complete months' products being as follows:

BLAST FURNACES.

		PRODUCT—GROSS TONS.	
Names.	Stacks.	Mar., 1899.	Apr., 1899.
Edgar Thomson Furnaces..........	9	90,585	88,937
Duquesne Furnaces	4	70,261	63,012
Carrie Furnaces	2	18,935	19,447
Lucy Furnaces	2	6,031	9,100
Total.......................	17	185,812	180,496

STEEL WORKS.

	PRODUCT—GROSS TONS.	
Names.	Mar., 1899.	Apr., 1899.
Bessemer Steel—		
Edgar Thomson Steel Works................	66,427	62,381
Duquesne Steel Works.....................	53,189	48,849
Homestead Steel Works	31,282	30,219
Total........	150,898	141,449
Open Hearth Steel—		
Homestead Steel Works	90,088	70,714
Total Steel Ingots.....................	240,986	212,163

ROLLING MILLS.

		PRODUCT—GROSS TONS.	
Names.	Kind.	Mar., 1899.	Apr., 1899.
Edgar Thomson Steel Works..	Rails	179,256	159,344
Duquesne Steel Works	Billets.....	29,315	29,223
do	Sheet Bars........	14,556	11,478
do	Splice Bars...	4,207	3,409
Homestead Steel Works.....	Blooms and Billets.	95,635	82,977
do	Structural.........	22,043	22,179
do	Plates.............	8,651	8,818
Upper Union Mills	Structural	12,106	11,028
do	Plates.............	8,455	7,466
Lower Union Mills	Structural	4,374	3,947
do	Plates.............	3,543	3,429

COKE WORKS.

Names.	SHIPMENTS—NET TONS.	
	Mar., 1899.	Apr., 1899.
H. C. Frick Coke Company	506,870	477,640
Larimer Coke Works	5,030	5,090
Youghiogheny Coke Works	2,860	1,850
Total Coke	514,760	484,580

OTHER DEPARTMENTS.

	Kind.	PRODUCT—GROSS TONS.	
		Mar., 1899.	Apr., 1899.
Edgar Thomson Foundry	Castings	5,465	5,439
Duquesne Steel Works	Finished Splices	4,114	3,470
Homestead Steel Works	Armor	446	621
do	Rivets and Bolts	125	105
do	Castings	152	200
do	Fitted Work	1,958	1,928
do	Columns	635	411
Upper Union Mills	Rivets and Bolts	21	20
do	Fitted Work	346	713
Lower Union Mills	Axles	2,629	1,664
do	Forgings	108	103
do	Spring Steel	638	731
Keystone Bridge Works	Bridge Work	3,394	2,933
do	Castings	274	348
do	Rivets	116	143

As has been the fixed policy of the "Carnegie" Associations during the past twenty years, Improvements, Extensions and Additions are constantly being made. Blowing Engines are being added at Edgar Thomson, Duquesne and Carrie Blast Furnaces, which will increase the product of Pig Iron 175,000 tons per annum. Ten Open Hearth Furnaces, a 30 inch Slabbing Mill, a 128 inch Plate Mill and a 42 inch Universal Plate Mill are building at Homestead Steel Works, and will be completed in June and July next, increasing the product of Steel Ingots 350,000 tons per annum, and of Plates 300,000 tons per annum. A Steel Axle Works, at Howard, near the Homestead Steel Works, will be completed by November next, with a capacity of 100,000 tons of Car Axles per annum. Many other minor Improvements are under way, all with a view to increasing product, decreasing cost or expediting shipment.

The present output of these Works is at the annual rate of 2,200,000 gross tons of Pig Iron, Spiegeleisen and Ferro-manganese; and 2,800,000 gross tons of Steel Ingots, with adequate finishing capacity.

The Improvements now approaching completion will increase the output to the annual rate of 2,375,000 gross tons of Pig Iron, Spiegeleisen and Ferro-manganese; and 3,150,000 gross tons of Steel Ingots, with sufficient finishing capacity to turn this Steel into Rails, Billets, Structural Shapes, Plates, Railroad Forgings and other Merchantable forms.

The Net Earnings of the business which will be transferred to the "Carnegie Steel Company" were

> For March, 1899....................$1,652,038.75
> For April, 1899.................... 1,888,227.72

Owing to the magnitude of the business, and the immense tonnage of the various products, it is necessary that long time contracts be made, far in advance of the time of delivery. The result is that present shipments are at prices far below present rates, the rates at which contracts are being made for future delivery. Had current prices been obtained for the shipments during these two months, the Net Earnings would have been

> For March, 1899..................$3,182,574.95
> For April, 1899.................... 4,325,922.78

and with present market prices and the increased product resulting from the Improvements named, an average single month's Net Profit will largely exceed the above; justifying the expectation that the "Carnegie Steel Company" will pay annually, under almost any condition of business:

> 5% on $100,000,000 Bonds.......... $5,000,000.00
> And at least
> 6% on $250,000,000 Stock.......... 15,000,000.00
> ————————
> $20,000,000.00

and leave an ample surplus for extra Dividends, as well as for other Improvements and Additions which will still further increase the Net Earnings and the rate of Dividends on the Stock, besides providing a fund for retiring the Bonds at maturity. The Carnegie Steel Company has been, is, and will be in an absolutely independent position, owning the sources of supply: Ore, Coal, Coke, Limestone and Natural Gas; the Transportation Lines for bringing the raw materials to the Works; the Docks for handling Ore; the Coke Works, Blast Furnaces, Steel Works and Finishing Mills, each advancing the product to a higher grade, until it is ready for the markets of the World, with every intermediate profit saved for the benefit of its Stockholders.

The efficient Organization which had brought the "Carnegie" Associations to their present unassailable position will remain intact. Nearly all of the former Shareholders in The Carnegie Steel Company, Limited, and the H. C. Frick Coke Company, all of whom were actively engaged in the business, have taken Stock in the "Carnegie Steel Company," and many other Officers and Employés, Superintendents, Foremen, Heads of Departments, Sales Agents, Workmen and Clerks, have subscribed for Stock in the new Company, demonstrating their faith in its future and ensuring the same bold yet conservative management which has rendered possible such an aggregation of capital as this; making large profits, yet earning them; controlling the market, yet never abusing its power; encouraging the wider use of Steel by the reductions made in its Cost, yet paying the highest wages in the World. Such has been the past, such is the present and such will be the future of the Carnegie Steel Company.

PITTSBURG, PA., May 15th, 1899.

MY DEAR MR. FRICK:

You ask me to give my views as to the probable future earnings of the Carnegie Interests, and as to the proposed reorganization on a basis of $100,000,000 Bonds—$250,000,000 preferred stock and $275,000,000 common stock.

Permit me to say that commencing in 1879 as Engineer, constructing the works, ten years as General Superintendent of our principal works and over two years as President, I feel that I know the properties and their possibilities as well, or better than any one in or out of the concern.

While we have been highly successful in the past, as every one knows, I believe we are only now getting in shape to be truly successful and truly profitable. Our April profit and loss sheet shows earnings slightly over $1,500,000.00 with rails netting us only $17.50 and billets $16.00. Lowest prices we ever had on an average were $16.50 for rails and $14.50 for billets, so you see we have reaped very little of the advantages of increased prices. With prices anywhere near to-day's selling prices we would easily make over $3,000,000.00 per month,

THE CARNEGIE STEEL COMPANY, LIMITED.

Office of Secretary.

BALANCE SHEET, MARCH 1, 1900.

ASSETS.			
CASH:- Treasury,		1,287,427.66	
Works,		19,293.43	
Sales Agencies,		25,302.50	1,332,023.59
BILLS RECEIVABLE,			7,174,804.02
MORTGAGES RECEIVABLE: Employes,			239,845.44
ACCOUNTS RECEIVABLE: Current,		16,381,884.06	
Securities,		517,324.30	16,899,208.86
STOCKS: Finished Product,		2,755,203.92	
Materials for Use,		7,087,964.76	
Ore at Lake Ports,		1,952,212.31	
Ore at Mines,		16,470.00	11,811,850.99
AVAILABLE ASSETS,			37,457,732.90
WORKS and PROPERTIES:-			
Edgar Thomson Works,	10,429,594.67		
Duquesne Steel Works,	2,333,406.35		
Duquesne Furnaces,	5,626,211.91		
Homestead Steel Works,	16,644,201.84		
Carrie Furnaces,	1,079,588.69		
Howard Axle Works,	717,476.87		
Lucy Furnaces,	1,251,869.99		
Keystone Bridge Works,	713,160.11		
Upper Union Mills,	1,000,000.00		
Lower Union Mills,	700,000.00		
Larimer Coke Works,	200,000.00		
Youghiogheny Coke Works,	160,000.00		
City Farm Lots,	960,664.50		
Verona Land,	40,000.00		
Liberty Farm,	225,000.00		
Oliver Land,	310,313.81		
Fawcett Land,	25.00	42,396,513.74	
1900 IMPROVEMENTS:-			
Edgar Thomson Furnaces,	50,489.15		
Edgar Thomson Steel Wks.,	31,441.69		
Edgar Thomson Foundry,	10.50		
Duquesne Furnaces,	13,324.48		
Duquesne Steel Works,	304,635.24		
Homestead Steel Works,	240,666.98		
Carrie Furnaces,	204,070.56		
Howard Axle Works,	102,542.90		
Lucy Furnaces,	3,415.57		
Keystone Bridge Works,	1,663.18		
Upper Union Mills,	6,537.12		
Lower Union Mills,	- -	958,797.35	
STOCKS & BONDS, Investments,		14,940,405.50	58,295,716.59
UNDIVIDED CAPITAL,		77,710.72	
DUE FROM PARTNERS,		5,585,642.22	5,663,352.94
TOTAL ASSETS,			101,416,802.43
LIABILITIES.			
MORTGAGES PAYABLE:-			
Edgar Thomson Works,	209,945.00		
Duquesne Steel Works,	995,000.00		
Duquesne Furnaces,	200,000.00		
Homestead Steel Works,	103,250.00		
Carrie Furnaces,	600,000.00		
Howard Axle Works,	273,275.85		
Keystone Bridge Works,	50,000.00		
Liberty Farm,	150,000.00		
Oliver Land,	153,000.00	2,734,470.85	
BILLS PAYABLE: Current,	4,360,174.73		
Stewart,	375,000.00		
Borntraeger,	271,423.56	5,006,598.29	
ACCOUNTS PAYABLE: Current,	2,469,650.44		
Ore,	240,130.21	2,709,780.65	
SPECIAL DEPOSITS,		3,776,276.27	
LIABILITIES PAYABLE,		14,227,126.06	
SPECIAL FUNDS:-			
Contingent Fund,	557,143.50		
Contingent Special,	711,810.00		
Relining Fund,	211,328.85		
Coal Extinguishment Fund,	15,822.45	1,496,104.80	
DUE TO PARTNERS,		4,113,657.38	
SURPLUS,	£6,579,914.19		
CAPITAL,	25,000,000.00	81,579,914.19	101,416,802.43

Photographic copy of last balance sheet before consolidation.

and then our new works to be started in two months will, I estimate on present prices, bring us an additional profit of $600,000.00 per month or total of $3,600,000.00 per month.

As to the future even on low prices, I am most sanguine. I know positively that England cannot produce pig iron at actual cost for less than $11.50 per ton, even allowing no profit on raw materials, and cannot put pig iron into a rail with their most efficient works for less than $7.50 per ton. This would make rails at net cost to them of $19.00. We can sell at this price and ship abroad so as to net us $16.00 at works for foreign business, nearly as good as home business has been. What is true of rails is equally true of other steel products. As a result of this we are going to control the steel business of the world.

You know we can make rails for less than $12.00 per ton, leaving a nice margin on foreign business. Besides this, foreign costs are going to increase year by year because they have not the raw materials, while ours is going to decrease. The result of all this is that we will be able to sell our surplus abroad, run our works full all the time and get the best practice and costs in this way.

As to the works, any competitor will tell you that we are far ahead of any one, and, if the plans which we have for the future, are carried out we will be farther ahead than ever. I have no fears for the earnings in the future. I believe they will much exceed any estimate we have made, provided, however, that the same methods of organization and operation as now exist, are fully carried out in the future.

It must not be run as other concerns are run, but as it is now conducted. This is most important. I believe the earnings will fully justify the capitalization and as a proof of my belief in this, I am quite willing to take every dollar I own in the stock of the new concern on the basis proposed.

Very truly yours,

C. M. Schwab,
President.

Mr. H. C. Frick, Chairman,
   Building.

The third attempt to sell the Carnegie properties to the public having thus failed, the partners returned to their schemes of consolidation and reorganization. This time Mr. Frick and the junior members took up the task; and they made elaborate plans for a new company with a capital of $250,000,-000 and no bonds. This company was "to purchase from the Carnegie Steel Co., Ltd., for $195,312,500 all its properties real, personal and mixed, excepting its holdings in the stocks of the H. C. Frick Coke Co." . . . and "from the H. C. Frick Coke Co. and its subsidiary companies named above, for $54,-687,500 all their properties, real, personal and mixed; the total consideration, $250,000,000, to be paid in instalments as the stock subscriptions became due." Provision was made for "Andrew Carnegie to loan to each 'Debtor Partner' an amount sufficient to enable him to pay his indebtedness to either selling company." "All the stock" was to be "placed in a trust for ten years, during which time no stock shall be sold excepting" from one owner to another, or by authorization of a three-fourths vote of stock in value and stockholders in number, or in the event of death of any member. This plan, representing the "unanimous views of every subscriber hereto, after full discussions of all suggestions had at meetings held September 11, 19, and 25," was commended to "the favorable consideration of the senior members." "We would not favor any plan that would contemplate bonding the property," they concluded. Ten signatures followed.

Of course nothing came of it. It is surprising that anything should have been expected of a plan that did not "contemplate bonding the property." Andrew Carnegie had placed himself on record with sufficient emphasis to leave no doubt in any reasonable mind as to the kind of security he wanted. So this plan joined the other liquid ideas that the corporate mind had secreted during the preceding years.

CHAPTER XX

CARNEGIE'S ATTEMPT TO DEPOSE FRICK

IN chemical experiments it often happens that before the process of crystallization can be started in a saturated solution, a blow must be given to the vessel containing it. This was evidently the condition of the ideas that had long been floating in and out of the minds of the partners concerning consolidation and reorganization: it required the shock of a rupture between Carnegie and Frick to jar the fluid schemes into solidity. And in conformity with the run of forty years' uninterrupted Carnegie luck, this shock, which threatened at first to have a shattering effect, further welded the corporate interests, doubled the already enormous wealth of the principal partners, and made the little ones all millionaires.

It was not inconsistent with its previous history that the Carnegie enterprise should reach its final and perfected form through strife. Born of a quarrel, it throve on contention. Each stage of its growth was marked by some dispute; and that it ever became a Carnegie concern, rather than a Miller, Coleman, or a Shinn creation, was solely due to the consolidating effect of timely "ejectures," as Carnegie euphemistically named the expulsion of partners.

The proposed "ejecture" of Frick, however, was not the simple matter it had been in previous cases. The man whose stubborn nature had passed through the annealing process a dozen times was not the one to accept an arbitrary dismissal; and the fight he now made was as notable, and was as keenly watched by the country, as was the contest with labor that had given him the real headship of the great organization he managed.

In tracing the causes of this attempted "ejecture," the one just named was probably the first. Since the earliest days it had been the basis of Andrew Carnegie's policy to tolerate no rival. In every previous case the growing prominence of partners had been checked before it had become dangerous. The genius of Kloman, the strong personality of Coleman, the masterful competency of Shinn, each in turn was forced to yield to the superior money power of Carnegie, and to find, as one of the old partners graphically puts it, "a top fence-rail of its own to crow from." Phipps, willing to stand in the shadow and indifferent even to the honors that were peculiarly his, inspired neither jealousy nor fear. Lauder was only Carnegie's echo. Singer conscientiously attended the Board meetings, and his ambition was more than satisfied with the prerogative of making the motion for dividends. Stewart was a good-natured and most useful treasurer, who could always get money on a pinch. Abbot, publicly greeted by Carnegie as "that young Napoleon of business" one day, was exiled almost the next. The business genius of T. M. Carnegie might have made him dangerous, but he died young. Of them all Frick, young, forceful, self-contained, tenacious, ambitious, and rich, was more than a rival; he was an equal from the start. And when he emerged from the Homestead contest with the admiration of the country, while Carnegie had only mystified the people, his leadership was everywhere acknowledged.

The first effort to diminish Frick's prominence was made in 1895. At this time he was trying to unify the coke-producing interests in one great company. He had almost succeeded; but there remained one third-rate operator who refused to join the combination on any reasonable terms. The character of this person was such that he was hardly tolerated amongst honest men, except when they met him at church; and Frick had ceased to seek his co-operation. Then Carnegie secretly took up the negotiation, and arranged a scheme by which this individual, with his twelve hundred ovens, should assume the headship of the coke combination, while Frick with his ten thousand ovens, should modestly drop into a subordinate place. The project died with apoplectic suddenness as soon as it was proposed to the man most interested; and Carnegie acquired a new view of his partner. Thereupon the office of president of the Carnegie Steel Company was created, and Mr. Leishman was put in with that title, Mr. Frick remaining chairman as before.

To the outside world it looked as if Mr. Frick had been deposed from his headship by this proceeding; but every clerk in the office and every man in the mills knew that this was not so. The power that ruled every department, from the highest to the lowest, was Frick; and the president had merely such outside prestige as the chairman did not value.

The cause of disagreement between Carnegie and Frick that had most influence in producing the final rupture was the divergent views they held concerning the price the steel company should pay for coke. While Carnegie controlled a majority of the coke company's stock, through his personal holdings and those of the firm, there were a few outside shareholders whose interest it was that the steel company should pay the full market price for its fuel; and to protect these minority stockholders, Frick always made as good a contract as he could with the steel company. Carnegie, on the other hand, wishful to keep all costs down, tried to obtain specially low rates on coke for his firm. This matter eventually brought about the final rupture.

Before this happened, however, another source of ill feeling grew out of the failure of the Moore Syndicate to complete the purchase of Carnegie's interest at a price of $157,950,000. For unfortunately the news of this option had been made public; and the newspapers of England and America overwhelmed

Carnegie with their comments and congratulations, just as though the huge transaction had been completed. When, through the collapse of the money market, the syndicate found itself unable to finance a deal calling for a hundred millions in cash in ninety days, Mr. Carnegie's chagrin was all the greater because of the premature applause to which he had been treated. And his annoyance was very natural. With excessive zeal his friend Stead had rushed a book through the press entitled " Mr. Carnegie's Conundrum: £40,000,-000. What shall I do with it?" and bearing on its title-page the famous Carnegie dictum: "The man who dies rich dies disgraced!" Under the circumstances it was an anticlimax. Furthermore, an enterprising advertiser of soap or some such detergent placarded England, where Carnegie was then staying, with offers of prizes for the best answer to " Mr. Carnegie's Conundrum "; and daily reports were published in the newspapers of the thousands of answers re-

"Offensive advice gleaming from bill-boards."

ceived. The position in which the millionaire philanthropist was thus placed was most undignified. He could not take up a paper without seeing in the form of an advertisement some idiotic suggestion as to how he ought to spend the forty million sterling he had failed to receive. He could not take a walk without the same offensive advice gleaming from a hundred bill-boards; and supersensitive as he always was to ridicule, his displeasure not unnaturally fell upon the partners whom he regarded as primarily responsible for this absurd notoriety. So when they came to him for an extension of their all-too-short option, he not only refused it, but in contravention of his agreement with them, kept the $170,000 which they had contributed as their share of the $1,170,000 paid him as a bonus for

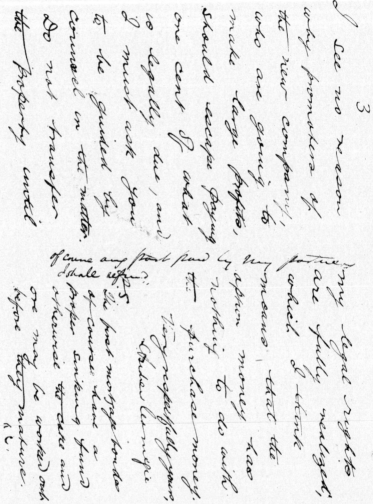

Photographic copy of letter from Mr. Carnegie in England to his trustees in Pittsburg. In his own hand are the words: Of course any part paid by my partners I shall refund.

the option. Here is a photographic reproduction of a portion of the letter in which he made this agreement.

The culmination of these animosities was reached in October, after Mr. Carnegie's return from Europe. It came about in this wise.

One day, during the previous spring, Mr. Phipps called on Mr. Carnegie in New York and was greeted with great effusion. "Harry," said Carnegie, "Frick has just left; and I've made a splendid contract for coke. It is a three years' agreement to give us coke at $1.35 a ton."

"And if the market price drops below $1.35?" queried Mr. Phipps.

Mr. Carnegie was surprised. He had not thought of that. A day or two later, when Mr. Phipps called again, he said:

"Harry, I've fixed that coke matter. We are to have the same price as others if it drops below $1.35."

It afterwards turned out that the way he had "fixed" it was that he had told Lauder to notify Schwab that a clause must be added to the contract, under which the Carnegie Steel Company would pay the same price for coke as any other buyer, provided that price was less than $1.35.

"Is that what Mr. Carnegie demands?" asked Mr. Frick, on receiving the message through Mr. Schwab.

"It is," replied the latter.

"Then the arrangement is all off, and must be taken up anew."

This answer was communicated to Mr. Carnegie; but he did not mention the matter to Mr. Frick, although he allowed others to give him to understand that he considered the agreement as amended by himself binding on the coke company.

During the early summer the price of coke was low, and there was no disposition shown by the Carnegies to have the alleged contract enforced; but when prices advanced an attempt was made to settle with the Frick Company at $1.35 a ton. Insisting that the coke company had no contract with the steel company, President Lynch had all shipments billed at market rates; and when Mr. Lawrence Phipps, on behalf of the steel company, refused to pay more than $1.35 a ton, he was

21

notified that no further orders would be filled until payment for past purchases was made at the rates charged. To remove all doubt as to where the coke company stood, a meeting of the Board of Directors was held on October 25th, 1899, and the following resolution was passed:

"*Resolved,* That the president be authorized and instructed to notify the Carnegie Steel Company, Limited, that the existence of any contract is denied and that no claim to settle in accordance with the terms of the alleged contract for past, present or future deliveries of coke to the said Carnegie Steel Company, Limited, will be recognized or entertained by this Company."

It was at this critical juncture that a disagreement of a more personal nature occurred between Messrs. Frick and Carnegie, and brought down the tottering fabric of their friendship with

"Set the city of Chicago on fire."

a crash that wrought the final transformation of the Carnegie Steel Company, alienated lifelong friends, gave the public the secret confidences of the corporation, and Pittsburg a new batch of millionaires. It seemed a little thing to produce such momentous changes; but then, it was only Mrs. O'Leary's cow that set the city of Chicago on fire.

At the meeting of the Board of Managers on December 11th, 1899, Mr. Schwab made reference to the contemplated purchase by the Carnegie Company of a tract of land situated on the Monongahela River belonging to Mr. Frick; and he mentioned "a hitch in the negotiations." This tract had been acquired by Mr. Frick in partial exchange of other land; and Mr. Lawrence Phipps, who was familiar with land values in that neighborhood, had valued it at $4,000 an acre. The land was wanted by the company; and Mr. Frick offered it to the firm at $3,500. As Mr. Schwab remarked at the meeting, "there is no doubt about our needing this land before long "; and Mr. Frick had shown his habitual foresight in securing it. For some reason, however, Mr. Carnegie disapproved of the purchase after he had sanctioned it; and insinuated that Mr. Frick was making a profit on the transaction. This coming to Mr. Frick's ears, he withdrew his offer. This was the "hitch" to which Mr. Schwab referred. Later fresh troubles arose; and Mr. Frick sold the land to other parties for half a million dollars more than he had asked the Carnegie Steel Company.

The insinuation, with its implications, was indignantly resented by Mr. Frick. He did not meet the covert attack by a return innuendo, but by an open minute spread upon the records of the Carnegie Steel Company. This, dated November 20th, was as follows:

In submitting Mr. Moreland's report, I would like to call attention especially to low prices we are to receive for rails through the greater part of next year—almost $8.00 per ton below the present market price, and very little above what old rails for re-melting are selling for. This will seriously affect our labor at Edgar Thomson, which is based on the price we receive for rails.

Mr. Carnegie continually referred, while here, to the low prices obtained under sliding scale contracts, entirely ignoring the fact that he alone was to blame for creating the atmosphere in which these sliding scale contracts, and other contracts, were made, by insisting last fall, against the almost unanimous protest of his partners, on selling rails far into the future at $16.00 and $17.00 per ton. It was fair for Sales Department to assume that if those were his views as to the prices which were to prevail for rails, they should be well satisfied with the much better prices they were themselves obtaining for other products under sliding scale contracts they were then making; although, it must be said for Mr. Carnegie, that he gave as his reason for wanting such low prices for rails, that it was for the purpose of breaking up eastern Rail Companies.

I learn that Mr. Carnegie, while here, stated that I showed cowardice in not bringing up question of price of coke as between Steel and Coke Companies. It was not my business to bring that question up. He is in possession of the Minutes of the Board of Directors of the Frick Coke Company, giving their views of the attempt, on his part, to force them to take practically cost for their coke. I will admit that, for the sake of harmony, I did personally agree to accept a low price for coke; but on my return from that interview in New York (within the next day or two) President Schwab came to me and said that Mr. Lauder said the arrangement should provide that, in case we sold coke below the price that Mr. Carnegie and I had discussed, the Steel Company was to have the benefit of such lower price. I then said to Mr. Schwab to let the matter rest until Mr. Carnegie came out (he told us he intended to come), and we would take up the question of a coke contract. He changed his plans, and did not come out. I saw him in New York, before he sailed, and told him that Mr. Lauder had raised that question, and suggested that he write Mr. Schwab, and let Messrs. Schwab and Lynch take up the question of a coke contract. Mr. Schwab, I believe, never heard from him on the subject, and Mr. Lynch, President of the Frick Coke Company, very properly, has been billing the coke, as there was no arrangement closed, at a price that is certainly quite fair and reasonable as between the two Companies, and at least 20 cents per ton below the average price received from their other customers. We have By-Laws, and they should govern. If not, why do we have them? It is the business of the Presidents of the two Companies to make contracts of all kinds. Mr. Carnegie has no authority to make a contract that would bind this Company. Neither have I any authority to make any contract that would bind the Frick Coke Company; and, at any rate, why should he, whose interest is larger in Steel than it is in Coke, insist on fixing the price which the Steel Company should pay for their coke? The Frick Coke Company has always been used as a convenience. The records will show that its credit has always been largely used for the Steel Company, and is to-day, to the extent of at least $6,000,000.00. The value of our coke properties, for over a year, has been, at every opportunity, depreciated by Mr. Carnegie and Mr. Lauder, and I submit that it is not unreasonable that I have considerable feeling on this subject. He also threatened, I am told, while here, that, if low price did not prevail, or something was not done, that he would buy 20,000 acres of Washington Run coal and build coke ovens. That is to say, he threatened, if the minority stockholders would not give their share of the coke to the Steel Company, at about cost, he would attempt to ruin them.

He also stated, I am told, while here, that he had purchased that land from me above Peters Creek; that he had agreed to pay market price, although he had his doubts as to whether I had any right, while Chairman of the Board of Managers of the Carnegie Steel Company, to make such a purchase. He knows how I became interested in that land, because I told him in your presence, the other day. Why was he not manly enough to say to my face what he said behind my back? He knew he had no right to say what he did. Now, before the Steel Company becomes the owner of that land, he must apologize for that statement. I first became interested in that land, as I told you, through trading a lot in Shady Side that I had owned for years. The land is six miles away from any land owned by the Carnegie Steel Company. Steel Company does not need it now, and will not need it for a long time in the future, if at all; but, of course, if they owned it, it might keep another large works from being built, or enable Steel Company to go into competition with some other large industry.

Harmony is so essential for the success of any organization that I have stood a great many insults from Mr. Carnegie in the past, but I will submit to no further insults in the future.

There are many other matters I might refer to, but I have no desire to quarrel with him, or raise trouble in the organization; but, in justice to myself, I could not at this time, say less than I have.

A copy of this was sent in the usual way to Mr. Carnegie in New York. He waited in silence to see if the Board of Managers would approve the minutes at their next meeting; and when they did so he at once came to Pittsburg, called a meeting of the members of the Board, and demanded that they sign a request to Mr. Frick for his resignation. He said he would not use it unless he had to; but that he wanted to be fortified with it. Armed with this he called upon Mr. Frick, whom he found willing to resign in the interests of harmony.

Accordingly the next day Mr. Frick tendered his resignation and it was accepted by the Board. Here are the minutes of the meeting:

"At a meeting of the Board of Managers of The Carnegie Steel Company, Limited, held at the General Offices of the

Association, Carnegie Building, Pittsburg, Pa., at 12:30 P.M., Tuesday, December 5, 1899, there were present MM. Schwab (president), Peacock, Phipps, Morrison, Clemson, Gayley and Lovejoy (secretary); also MM. Andrew Carnegie, Henry Phipps, George Lauder and W. H. Singer.

The following communication was read:

'December 5th, 1899.

GENTLEMEN:

I beg to present my resignation as a member of your Board.
Yours very truly,

H. C. FRICK.

To

THE BOARD OF MANAGERS,
The Carnegie Steel Co., Ltd.,
Pittsburgh, Pa.'

On motion, (MM. Clemson and Peacock), the resignation was accepted, with the sincere thanks of the Board of Managers, both as such and as representing the Shareholders; for efficient, zealous and faithful service as a member of this Board from January 14, 1889, to the present day; the vote being unanimous, and all present concurring."

The difficult position of the junior partners in this crisis is graphically stated in the following extract from a letter written by Mr. C. M. Schwab, the day before Mr. Carnegie's arrival in Pittsburg:

SUNDAY, Dec. 3rd, 1899

. . . I just returned from New York this morning. Mr. Carnegie is en-route to Pittsburgh to-day, and will be at the offices in the morning. Nothing could be done with him looking towards a reconciliation. He seems most determined. I did my best. So did Mr. Phipps. I feel certain he will give positive instructions to the Board and Stockholders as to his wishes in the matter. I have gone into the matter carefully and am advised by disinterested and good authority that, by reason of his interest, he can regulate this matter to suit himself—with much trouble no doubt, but he can ultimately do so. I believe all the Junior members of the Board and all the Junior Partners will do as he directs. Any concerted action would be ultimately useless, and result in their downfall. Am satisfied that no action on my part would have any effect in the end. We must declare ourselves. Under these circumstances, there is nothing left for us to do but obey, although the situation the board is thus placed in is most embarrassing.

No one can read this letter without sympathizing with Mr. Schwab. On the one hand Carnegie, the majority stockholder, could force him to vote for Frick's expulsion or ruin him if he resisted. On the other hand, Schwab's obligations to Frick and their friendship for years made his subservience to Carnegie almost impossible. This is undoubtedly what he himself felt; for he had always freely admitted his great obligations to Mr. Frick. Indeed, he had frankly attributed his success to him. "If I have anything of value in me," he once wrote, Mr. Frick's "method of treatment will bring it out to its full extent"; and he "regarded with more satisfaction than anything else in life—even fortune—the consciousness of having won" Mr. Frick's friendship and regard. It can be well imagined that it was with great reluctance that he afterwards allowed himself to be forced by Carnegie into active opposition to his chief.

With Mr. Frick's resignation from the chairmanship of the Board the dispute seemed ended; Mr. Carnegie returning to New York apparently satisfied. A month or so later, however, he returned to Pittsburg with an elaborate scheme for the complete "ejecture" of Mr. Frick. Before describing this, the further course of the coke controversy should be outlined.

When Mr. Carnegie was in Pittsburg in December he quietly began to lay his plans for war. His first move was to try to win over Mr. John Walker.

Mr. Walker was one of the minority stockholders of the coke company; and as trustee for the minor heirs of his old partner Wilson, he had kept a large part of their fortune in the Frick Coke Company. He was, therefore, doubly interested in the controversy. Mr. Walker's high commercial standing, his

fine judgment and excellent fighting qualities, made him an adversary to be conciliated if possible; and Mr. Carnegie, during
this visit, sought to detach him from Mr. Frick.

Some ten years before this, when Mr. Walker was chairman of Carnegie, Phipps & Co., a personal difference had
arisen between him and Carnegie, and he withdrew from the
firm. Carnegie now offered him a position on the Board of the
steel company and an interest in it, in exchange for his holdings in the coke company. As this involved abandoning his
friend Frick in a fight which the latter had entered into to safeguard the interest of all minority stockholders, including his
own and those of the widow and orphans of Carnegie's old boy
companion—for Wilson was one of The Original Six—Mr.
Walker declined the offer. He thereby failed to make several
millions of dollars which would otherwise have been his.

It afterwards transpired, however, that Mr. Walker had been
mistaken in supposing that Mr. Carnegie wished to sacrifice
the interests of *all* the minority stockholders in the coke company. For at this time Mr. Carnegie told Mr. Schwab to quietly
notify Mr. Walker that if he would withdraw his opposition to
the coke contract, the matter would be so arranged that he and
those he represented should receive the same profits from their
coke investments as they would if the steel company paid full
price for its fuel. Mr. Schwab, however, did not dare himself
to make such an offer to a man like Mr. Walker; and he asked
another member of the Board of Managers to do it. This gentleman also declined, as did every other member of the Board
to whom the matter was submitted; and Mr. Walker lost the
opportunity of declining the bribe. And if he reads this book
he will probably learn for the first time of Mr. Carnegie's
benevolent intentions.

Failing thus to win Mr. Walker to his side Mr. Carnegie
promptly included him in the fight, which he now carried right
into his adversary's camp.

It will be remembered that the majority—a little more than

half—of the coke company's stock belonged to Carnegie and the steel company. On the 9th of the following January (1900) the usual stockholders' meeting was held; and, by the power afforded by their large holdings, the Carnegies increased the Board of Directors from five to seven, dropped Messrs. John Walker and Giles B. Bosworth from the Board, and elected to the directorate six of the managers of the steel company. Four of these, Messrs. Gayley, Moreland, Clemson, and Morrison, had not previously been stockholders; but to qualify them to serve as directors, each had now five shares put in his name. The others were Lauder, Lynch, and Frick.

On January 24th the majority in the new Board voted to the Carnegie Steel Company a contract for all the coke, at $1.35 a ton, that that company could use in its furnaces for five years, commencing January 1st, 1899, amounting approximately to 2,500,000 tons a year, or about one-third of the entire product of the H. C. Frick Coke Company; and this agreement, previously prepared and executed by the Carnegie Steel Company, was signed by Mr. Lynch, president of the coke company, under his own protest and that of Mr. Frick. The market price of coke was then $3.50 a ton.

This surprising contract, being made retroactive, required the coke company to refund to the Carnegies a sum of $596,000 paid on account of coke sold during the previous year. The further loss to the coke company at prevailing prices was $1.65 a ton, or something like $4,000,000 a year. This is probably the most astonishing thing that ever happened in the course of the Carnegie Steel Company's amazing history.

As soon as the minority stockholders heard of these proceedings they sent the following protest to the president and Board of Directors of the H. C. Frick Coke Company, and received the appended reply:

GENTLEMEN: I have been informed that your Board of Directors on Jan. 24th, 1900, passed a resolution intended to ratify an alleged contract with the Carnegie Steel Company, Ltd., whereby your company is to supply to the latter all the coke it may require for use in its furnaces for five years, commencing Jan. 1, 1899, for $1.35 per ton, delivered on cars at your works, and that your company has signed a written memorandum of such contract.

As a stockholder in your company, I protest against any such contract, and I demand that you do nothing in recognition thereof, and especially that you do not ship or bill any coke to the Carnegie Steel Company, Limited, thereunder; and that you do not settle with said company for coke shipped to it since Jan. 1st, 1899, at the price named in said contract, or at any price other than the market price at the time of delivery. I deny that such contract was ever made until you attempted to do so on Jan. 24th, 1900. This contract is for many reasons unfair and fraudulent and against the minority stockholders of the H. C. Frick Coke Company. It is made by those who represent the majority of stockholders, really in the interest of such majority, as against the interests of the H. C. Frick Coke Company and the minority stockholders therein. The market price of coke on Jan. 24th, 1900, was at least $3.50 per ton, and yet this contract, covering almost one-third of all coke manufactured by the company, fixes a price of $1.35 per ton. In many other respects it unfairly and dishonestly favors the majority stockholders of the coke company to the loss of the minority stockholders.

The Carnegie Steel Company, Limited, and Andrew Carnegie (who owns more than one-half of the interest in the steel company) own together more than one-half of the stock of the H. C. Frick Coke Company. A majority of the present Board of Directors of the coke company are managers and partners in the Carnegie Steel Company. It was this majority who forced this contract in favor of the Carnegie Steel Company, Limited, on Jan. 24th, 1900.

I demand that you rescind the said action of your board in favor of said contract; that you take such further action as may be necessary to rescind and annul said contract. If you refuse to act, then I ask that you call a meeting of the stockholders of the coke company to take action and pass upon the questions herein raised, and upon the requests I now make.

Please advise me promptly what your company proposes to do in the matter, as it is my intention to take proper legal steps to prevent your so doing, if you intend carrying out such pretended contract.   Yours truly,

S. L. SCHOONMAKER.

PITTSBURGH, Feb. 6th, 1900.

Mr. S. L. Schoonmaker, New York City.

MY DEAR SIR: I beg to advise that I received your communication of 1st instant, addressed to the President and Board of Directors of the H. C. Frick Coke Company, and I submitted the same to the Board at a meeting held Feb. 6th, 1900, when the following motion was adopted:

'That the President be instructed to carry out the contract between the H. C. Frick Coke Company and The Carnegie Steel Company, Limited, dated January 1st, 1899, and all its terms and provisions, and that he inform Messrs. Walker and Schoonmaker that he is so directed by the Board.'

Very Truly Yours,

THOS. LYNCH,

President.

Thereupon suit was brought by Mr. Walker and the other minority stockholders to enjoin the coke company from selling, shipping, and delivering any coke to the steel company under the pretended contract.

In the mean time important events were happening in the council-chambers of the steel company. The peaceful acceptance of Mr. Frick's resignation as chairman of the Board proved but a lull in the storm. In New York Mr. Carnegie was devising a plan for the rehabilitation of an extinct iron-clad agreement, so as to make it applicable to the new situation. Then, in January, he returned to Pittsburg, called a meeting of the Managers, and had them go through the ritual he had prepared.

At one of their interviews about this time Mr. Frick had offered to sell his interest in the company to Mr. Carnegie at a price to be fixed by arbitrators. This being refused, he offered to buy Carnegie's on the same terms. Mr. Carnegie gasped with astonishment. It was the most direct challenge of his supremacy which he had ever received. The proceedings of the Managers, under Carnegie's direction, now contemplated the forcible seizure of the Frick interest at book values. How

inadequate these were will be seen from the following statement of some of them, side by side with the profits made during the previous year:

	Net profit, 1899.	Book value, Nov. 1st, 1899.
Edgar Thomson Furnaces	$3,829,716.68	
" " Steel Works	614,518.51	$10,258,703.98
" " Foundry	370,866.80	
Duquesne Blast Furnaces	2,983,094.79	5,089,967.52
" Steel Works	1,104,728.39	2,057,745.83
Homestead Steel Works	4,564,413.63	11,909,199.55
Carrie Furnaces	820,638.65	829,625.42
Lucy Furnaces	1,303,524.37	1,251,869.99
Keystone Bridge Works	13,682.68	717,776.49
Upper Union Mills	1,091,857.88	1,000,000.00
Lower Union Mills	438,052.03	700,000.00
Scotia Ore Mines	1,695.74	
Larimer Coke Works	17,276.56	
Youghiogheny Coke Works (loss)	35.73	
Sundries—including		
H. C. Frick Coke Company....$1,253,853		
Oliver Iron Mining............ 1,067,000		
Carnegie Natural Gas.......... 420,000		
Union Railroad 100,000		
Etc., etc	3,845,949.36	
Borrowed from Contingency Fund	50,570.80	
Net earnings for year	$21,000,000.00	

While the Board was still in session Mr. Carnegie went out
to see Mr. Frick, to demand his stock at these book values.
Mr. Frick, who had remained outwardly unmoved amid all the
horrors of the Homestead battle and cool in presence of the
assassin, felt outraged by the intrusion of Andrew Carnegie on
such a mission; and his anger burst out like a flame.   Carnegie hastily retreated, and returned to the Board room white with
emotion; and later, when the affair came into the courts, he
made an affidavit charging Mr. Frick with an ungovernable
temper.

The further course of this affair, in which, at the instigation
of Mr. Carnegie, all the partners except Messrs. Hy. Phipps,
Lovejoy, and Curry joined, is summarized in Appendix A from
Mr. Frick's own narrative, which formed part of a bill in equity
filed in the Court of Common Pleas a month or so later.   The

revelations of the stupendous profits of the steel industry contained in this plea set the country agog, so that interest in the contest itself became almost secondary.   Every newspaper in the land printed long extracts from the pleadings; and columns of comments were published on the amazing exhibition of industrial efficiency thus presented.   Had the Moore option been valid at this time there would have been no difficulty in raising a hundred million dollars.   In other lands the litigation and the secrets it revealed attracted the same general attention. Everywhere the hope was expressed that the suit would be allowed to reach the courts.   It was pointed out that " what legislative bodies and committees of inquiry had failed to accomplish might be reached if the secrets of the great corporation were passed in review through the courts "; and it was not only sensation-loving and curiosity-seeking people who wanted to know more, but legislators and publicists of every kind.

The Carnegie answer was filed on March 12th.   It claimed that the plan for forming the limited partnership, which Frick had declared to be a general one, was devised by Frick himself, and that he acquired much of his interest through the working of the so-called iron-clad agreement.   It was denied that on December 31st, 1899, the association had assets or property, which in its legal capacity it could transfer, worth $250,000,-000.   While it was admitted that Mr. Frick proved a valuable member to the company, it was asserted that " notwithstanding his ability" he "is a man of imperious temper, impatient of opposition, and disposed to make a personal matter of every difference of opinion, even on questions of mere business policy.   At times, moreover, he gives way to violent outbursts of passion, which he is either unwilling or unable to control. He demands absolute power and without it is not satisfied." The answer maintained that the refusal to submit their differences to arbitration was because the company proposed at all times to maintain the integrity of the iron-clad contract.

There were no disclosures, however. The Carnegies had had more than enough of them; and even while this answer was being prepared efforts were made to stop the litigation. With a studied display of indifference the principal Carnegie officials absented themselves on alleged vacations; but their movements were conducted with method. Andrew Carnegie went golfing in Florida, but stopped in Washington long enough to transmit through Mr. Lawrence Phipps the first overture for .

THE GREAT SHERIFF'S PUZZLE—How to find Carnegie and his forty partners.

—From a Pittsburg paper.

peace. The terms accompanying this were refused and others suggested; and these in turn were rejected by Carnegie. This rejection resulted in Mr. Frick's obtaining sixty per cent. more in the final settlement than he otherwise would have had. Then Mr. Hy. Phipps took a hand in the negotiations; and, having previously reached an understanding with Mr. Carnegie, he had little difficulty in winning the adhesion of Messrs. Frick, Lovejoy, and Walker to a scheme of consolidation and reorganization that should safeguard the interests of all and restore an

outward semblance of peace to the association.　Five days after
the filing of the Carnegie answer a peace conference met at Atlantic City, when the Carnegie Steel Company underwent the
last metamorphosis before its final absorption in the United
States Steel Corporation, and dollars began to rain down upon
the partners faster than they could count them.

CHAPTER XXI

THE FAILURE OF THE IRON-CLAD

THE settlement of this historic litigation out of court before any evidence was taken left the public in doubt as to the legal value of the document known as the iron-clad agreement. As this agreement had an important influence on the history of the several Carnegie organizations, some account of it and its failure to work the "ejecture" of Mr. Frick is called for in this narrative; especially as it is not likely that any frank statement concerning it will ever be made elsewhere.

In 1884 the practice was inaugurated of rewarding exceptional services of employees by crediting them with an interest in the association; Messrs. Curry, Moore, Borntraeger, and Abbot being the first to receive this favor. The book value of the interests thus assigned was charged against recipients; and the shares were held by the company as security until the indebtedness had been paid off. Usually the profits alone sufficed to liquidate the debt.

During the next three years other employees were similarly rewarded; and to meet this new condition of debtor partners a plan of automatic ejecture was devised, so that no junior partner need be kept in the association any longer than his favor lasted. This was the iron-clad agreement of 1887. It was an excellent device; for while serving as an incentive to further efforts, such a revokable interest also kept the "young geniuses" in a properly humble frame of mind. But there was no thought of applying this iron-clad to the other partners, whose interests were paid up. That was an afterthought.

In 1892, on the consolidation of the several companies, a new iron-clad agreement was drawn up. Concerning this document Mr. Henry Phipps afterwards made the following statement:

"When the consolidation papers were agreed to by Mr. Carnegie and me, at his place near Windsor, England, in 1892, it was understood that the 'Iron-clad' should only apply to debtor partners, or employees, which was the intent of the paper of 1887. Of course much was left to the honor of the Managers, who were then, and in whom it was not unreasonable for me to impose implicit confidence. Never has it been used, to my knowledge, and I am confident the agreement would never have been made an engine of oppression and robbery. This information was again vouchsafed me when I signed a paper relating to my death, and Carnegie said this was only to apply to debtor partners, or employees, which was the intent of the paper of 1887. 'But,' I replied, 'there are clauses in the agreement that are unjust,' and he replied, 'Harry, I am ill, and am going abroad, and fix it to your satisfaction.' On such a promise, so clear and explicit, I would have done anything for my friend, and especially in his condition.

I am very sorry to say that since then he has shown no willingness to correct the agreement as promised."

In apparent conformity with this understanding, limiting its application to debtor partners, this iron-clad of 1892 was not signed by Messrs. Carnegie, Phipps, and Lauder. Most of the other partners signed it, but not all. Under its terms some interests of deceased or retiring members were bought by the company; but no "ejecture" took place.

In 1897 a new and more stringent agreement was drawn up, intended to reach other than debtor partners; and this was signed by Andrew Carnegie and sent from abroad on October 3d, with a letter to the Board of Managers, saying:

"I have signed the paper making these corrections, because

22

I wished you to have something that will keep the Firm right so far as my interest is concerned; but, of course, you will get all the signatures upon one corrected paper, by and by."

This, however, was never done. Andrew Carnegie's was the only signature ever appended to this document. Concerning it Mr. Phipps wrote on October 4th from London:

" Please inform the Chairman, President and Board of Managers that I refuse to sign the ' Iron-clad ' or any paper of a similar character, and that I shall resist the buying of the Company's Stock as the proposed Agreement contemplates, and thereby creating liabilities of which we have quite sufficient. Any business man will admit, and no one will deny, that such debts are foreign to the purpose for which our Company was formed.   Better *new* capital than *no* capital, which would be the position in which we would be in if any such project were consummated.   Besides the act would be clearly illegal.

For these and other good reasons, I beg that no action in the matter be taken."

So the attempt to extend the provisions of the iron-clad failed, and the situation remained as before.

A futile effort was afterwards made to reach a provisional agreement; and nothing more was attempted until Mr. Carnegie tried to secure the "ejecture" of Mr. Frick. This he sought to accomplish in an original and ingenious way. Having secured the resignation of Mr. Frick from the chairmanship of the company, Mr. Carnegie appeared before the Board of Managers on January 8th, 1900, and offered and had passed the following resolution:

" *Whereas*, as appears by the Minutes of October 19, 1897, a proposed Supplemental Agreement, dated September 1, 1897, to the original Agreement, appearing in the Minutes of January 18, 1887, was signed by Andrew Carnegie, conditioned upon all members signing the same, but was objected to by Henry Phipps, who refused to sign the same; and consequently, that it has not been signed by several other members of the firm, and is, therefore, of none effect; Now, therefore, be it

Resolved: That the Resolution of October 19, 1897, approving said Supplemental Agreement, passed in the hope that Mr. Phipps would upon reflection withdraw his opposition and all members sign, is hereby rescinded; and the Board decides that no further steps be taken with the proposed Supplement, thus leaving the original Agreements in full force."

The minutes then relate that

" Without a motion, the Secretary was directed to obtain to the Supplemental 'Iron-clad Agreement,' dated July 1, 1892, the signatures of the present members of this Association who have not signed the same, it having not been presented for signature to the members admitted while the aforesaid Supplemental Agreement of September 1, 1897, was being drawn up, considered, revised and after its adoption."

In other words, by expunging a minute on the books of the Carnegie Steel Company, it was sought to revive an agreement made thirteen years before by the members of an entirely different corporation, Carnegie Brothers & Co. Then an attempt was made to graft onto this Carnegie Brothers' agreement "a supplemental iron-clad" of the Carnegie Steel Company eight years old, which had never been signed by the principal owners. To make this double-decked instrument effective, there were now added the signatures of Carnegie himself and of some members who had no existence at the time the agreement was signed by Mr. Frick, against whom all this ingenuity was directed. And it was on these proceedings that the Carnegie Steel Company rested its case against Henry C. Frick in the greatest lawsuit ever commenced in the State of Pennsylvania.

The document itself, called " the Supplemental Iron-clad " for the first time in the minutes of the meeting of January 8th, 1900, reads as follows:

This agreement, Made this first day of July, A.D., 1892, and on certain dates thereafter, as shown, between The Carnegie Steel Company, Limited, party of the first part, and each one of the members of that Association who has hereunto affixed his name, party of the second part, witnesseth :

(I) That the party of the second part, for and in consideration of the execution and delivery of this agreement by each of the other active members of said Association, The Carnegie Steel Company, Limited, and in consideration of the sum of One Dollar in hand paid by the party of the first part, the receipt whereof, by the signing hereof, is hereby acknowledged, as well as for other good and valuable considerations, to him moving, does hereby covenant, promise and agree to and with the party of the first part, that he, the party of the second part, at any time hereafter when three-fourths in number of the persons holding interests in said first party, and three-fourths in value of said interests, shall request him, the said party of the second part, so to do, will sell, assign and transfer to said first party, or to such person or persons as it shall designate, all of his, the said party of the second part, interest in the Limited partnership of The Carnegie Steel Company, Limited. The interest shall be assigned freed from all liens and encumbrances or contracts of any kind, and this transfer shall at once terminate all the interest of said party of the second part in and in connection with said The Carnegie Steel Company, Limited.

(II) The request of the requisite number of members and value of interests shall be evidenced by a writing signed by them or their proper Agents or Attorneys in Fact; and a copy thereof shall be either served upon the party whose interest it is proposed to buy, or mailed to him at his post office address; at least five (5) days before the day fixed in said request to make said transfer and assignment.

(III) The party of the first part covenants and agrees that it will pay unto the party so selling and assigning, the value of the interest assigned, as it shall appear to be on the books of said The Carnegie Steel Company, Limited, on the first day of the month following said assignment.

Said payment shall be in manner as follows :

If the interest assigned shall not exceed two (2) per centum of the Capital Stock at par, the same shall be paid for as follows :

One-fourth cash within ninety (90) days of the date of the assignment, and the balance in two equal annual payments from the date of the assignment, to be evidenced by the notes of said first party.

If the interest assigned shall exceed two (2) per centum, but shall not exceed four (4) per centum of the Capital Stock at par, then the same shall be paid for as follows : One-fourth cash in six months after the date of the assignment, and the balance in three equal annual payments from the date of the assignment, to be evidenced by the notes of the said first party.

If the interest assigned shall exceed four (4) per centum, but shall not exceed twenty (20) per centum of the Capital Stock at par, then the same shall be paid for as follows: One-fourth cash within six months after the date of the assignment, and the balance in five equal annual payments from the date of the assignment, to be evidenced by the notes of said first party.

If the interest assigned shall exceed twenty (20) per centum of the Capital Stock at par, then the same shall be paid for as follows: One-fourth cash within eight months from the date of the assignment, and the balance in ten equal annual payments from the date of the assignment, to be evidenced by the notes of said first party.

All deferred payments shall bear interest at six per centum per annum, payable semi-annually.

(IV) This agreement, and the option the party of the second part hereby gives to the party of the first part, is hereby declared to be irrevocable, and that it may be carried out in good faith, and notwithstanding any effort on the part of the party of the second part to evade it, the party of the second part does hereby appoint the person, who, at the time when he is called upon to act, is Chairman of the party of the first part, the Attorney in Fact for said party of the second part, for him and in his name, place and stead to assign and transfer the said interest in said The Carnegie Steel Company, Limited, whenever under this agreement it would be the duty of said party of the second part so to do.

This appointment is also irrevocable; is coupled with the interest of said party of the second part in said The Carnegie Steel Company, Limited, and will justify and warrant the said Attorney in Fact to act for the said party of the second part in the premises just as efficaciously after the death of said party of the second part, or after said party of the second part has attempted to revoke this power of attorney or evade his agreement, as if said party of the second part were alive and living up to it in entire good faith.

(V) Death shall not revoke, alter or impair any of the terms of this contract, but the first party shall, after the death of the party of the second part, have the following time to elect to buy his interest on the terms hereinbefore set out:

If the interest does not exceed four (4) per centum, four months.

If the interest exceeds four (4) per centum, but does not exceed twenty (20) per centum, eight months.

If the interest exceeds twenty (20) per centum, twelve months, and the said party of the second part to this agreement does hereby direct his personal representatives, after the death of him, the said party of the second part, to approve, join in and perfect any transfer his said Attorney in Fact may make, and the said Executor or Executors or Administrator or Administrators of the party of the second part shall carry out this contract, and all its provisions, just as if said representatives had themselves made this agreement.

(VI) This agreement is hereby declared to be a lien and encumbrance upon the interest of said party of the second part in said The Carnegie Steel Company, Limited. No attempt of the said party of the second part voluntarily to sell, pledge or mortgage, and no proceedings adversely against the said party of the second part by execution, process of law, or Equity of any kind, bankruptcy or insolvency, shall in any way, shape or form affect, impair or alter this agreement, or any part of it, or take from under its operation the respective interest of said party of the second part from the clog hereof.

Both the parties hereto agree and declare that it is the settled policy of The Carnegie Steel Company, Limited, and of the party of the second part, in entire good faith, and with all effort on our part to carry out its true spirit and meaning, this agreement; being satisfied that if we do so, it will be greatly to the benefit of The Carnegie Steel Company, Limited, and to the party of the second part as a member thereof; and that any effort on the part of said party of the second part to evade any of the provisions of the same will most properly prove his unfitness to be connected with said The Carnegie Steel Company, Limited.

In witness whereof, the party of the first part has hereunto set its common seal, attested by the signatures of its Chairman and Secretary, and approved by two of its Managers; and the party of the second part has hereunto set his hand and seal the day and year first above given.

THE CARNEGIE COMPANY, LIMITED,
By H. C. FRICK,
Chairman.

Attest: Approved:
(SEAL) F. T. F. LOVEJOY,   J. G. A. LEISHMAN,
Secretary.   Manager.
F. T. F. LOVEJOY,
Manager.

Then follow a number of signatures, some made "on the day and year first above given," namely, July 1st, 1892, and others, including Andrew Carnegie's, nearly eight years later.

On the strength of this agreement the following notice was now served on Mr. Frick, Mr. Schwab having been delegated by Mr. Carnegie to obtain signatures to it:

"Under the provisions of a certain Agreement between The Carnegie Steel Company, Limited, and the partners composing it, known as and generally referred to as the 'Iron Clad' Agreement, we, the undersigned, being three-fourths in number of the persons holding interests in said Association, and three-fourths in value of said interests, do now hereby request Henry C. Frick to sell, assign and transfer to The Carnegie Steel Company, Limited, all of his interest in the capital of The Carnegie Steel Company, Limited, said transfer to be made as at the close of business January 31, 1900, and to be paid for as provided in said Agreement.

Done at Pittsburg, Pa., this 10th and 11th days of January, 1900.

C. M. Schwab.	Andrew Carnegie.
Gibson D. Packer.	Geo. Lauder.
D. G. Kerr.	A. M. Moreland.
H. E. Tener, Jr.	James Gayley.
A. C. Case.	D. M. Clemson.
Jno. McLeod.	Thos. Morrison.
Lewis T. Brown.	L. C. Phipps.
Geo. E. McCague.	Chas. L. Taylor.
W. B. Dickson.	Jno. C. Fleming.
E. F. Wood.	W. W. Blackburn.
Geo. Megrew.	H. P. Bope.
J. E. Schwab.	James Scott.
Homer J. Lindsay.	W. H. Singer.
Alexr. R. Peacock.	W. E. Corey.
Millard Hunsiker,	Geo. H. Wightman.
per C. M. Schwab,	J. Ogden Hoffman.
(Power Attorney).	Chas. W. Baker.

I hereby certify that the foregoing is a true and correct copy of the Original now in file in this office.

This 15th day of January, 1900.

F. T. F. Lovejoy,
Secretary."

It will be noticed that Mr. Lovejoy simply signed it in his official character as secretary of the company.   Mr. Curry was on his death-bed; but he was asked to sign it and refused.   " Mr. Frick is my friend," said Mr. Curry.   " And am I not also your friend? " Mr. Carnegie asked.   " Yes; but Mr. Frick has never humiliated me," was the pathetic answer of the dying man.

Mr. Henry Phipps not only refused to sign the demand, but joined Mr. Frick in protesting against the action of the Board. These protests are as follows:

To THE CARNEGIE STEEL COMPANY, LIMITED:

I have read a copy of the minutes of the Board of Managers of the Carnegie Steel Company, Limited, dated January 8th, 1900, handed to me Friday afternoon, January 12th, 1900, and I desire particularly to call your attention to certain actions of the Board regarding the so-called agreements as to partners' interests, dated 1887, 1892 and 1897;

I dissent from some of the statements of alleged facts therein contained, and I, certainly, do not agree, but object to and deny, that the said action of the Board of Managers on January 8th, 1900, and, indeed, any action of the Board of Managers, could or did re-instate the so-called agreement of 1887.

As I have heretofore stated, I am opposed and object to any attempt not only to force from any partner his interest in our Company, but, also, to the right of our Company to use its capital in the purchase of any such interest.

HENRY PHIPPS, JR.

PITTSBURGH, January 15, 1900.

To THE CARNEGIE STEEL COMPANY, LIMITED.

On Friday evening, January 12th, 1900, for the first time I learned that the Board of Managers of your Company secretly and without notice to me, at a meeting on Monday, January 8th, 1900, passed a resolution offered by Andrew Carnegie, rescinding a former resolution of October 19th, 1897, touching the agreement of September 1st, 1897, and at the same time your Secretary was directed to procure the signatures of the present members of the association who had not signed the same to what is now for the first time in your minutes called " the Supplemental Iron Clad agreement dated July 1st, 1892."

This is to notify you that all the said action on January 8th, 1900, was taken without my knowledge or consent and I do hereby protest against and object to the same. In some respects the recitals or statements therein contained are untrue in fact. The action did not and could not as the resolution asserts, re-instate the so-called agreement of 1887. At the instigation of Andrew Carnegie you now speciously seek without my knowledge or consent and after a serious personal disagreement between Mr. Carnegie and myself, and by proceedings purposely kept secret from me to make a contract for me under which Mr. Carnegie thinks he can unfairly take from me my interest in The Carnegie Steel Company, Limited. Such proceedings are illegal and fraudulent as against me, and I now give you formal notice that I will hold all persons pretending to act thereunder liable for the same.

H. C. FRICK.

PITTSBURGH, January 13th, 1900.

No attention was paid to these protests, and on February 1st the following letter was sent to Mr. Frick:

THE CARNEGIE STEEL COMPANY, LIMITED,

General Offices; Carnegie Building,

PITTSBURG, PA., February 1st, 1900.

Mr. H. C. Frick,
   Building.

DEAR SIR:—I beg to advise you that pursuant to the terms of the so called "Iron Clad Agreement" and at the request of the Board of Managers, I have to-day acting as your attorney in fact executed and delivered to The Carnegie Steel Company, Limited, a transfer of your interest in the capital of said Company.

Yours truly,
C. M. SCHWAB.

Such is the interesting story of the famous iron-clad agreement, and Mr. Carnegie's attempt to use it for the "ejecture" of Mr. Frick.

CHAPTER XXII

THE ATLANTIC CITY COMPROMISE

ONE of the junior members of the Carnegie Steel Company, recently speaking of these events, unconsciously adopted the circus simile used by one of a former generation of partners, elsewhere quoted, in explanation of the apparent willingness with which he and his colleagues joined Carnegie in the effort to depose Frick. "We were simply a band of circus horses," he said, "and we all jumped as the ring-master cracked his whip."

Although several of the junior partners protested at a secret meeting, only one of the well-trained band, besides Curry, openly shied and refused to jump at the crack of the ring-master's whip. This was Secretary Lovejoy. Entering the Carnegie employ in 1881 as a telegraph operator, he had won his partnership through his unusual ability as an accountant; and for many years he had filled the responsible office of secretary to the entire satisfaction of his seniors. In particular he had won the confidence of Mr. Frick; and during the Homestead strike had ably served as the chairman's chief assistant. Frankly admitting his obligations to Mr. Frick, he took a unique position in the fight; and refused to be cajoled or threatened away from the side of his chief. He and Curry were the only ones of the thirty odd "young geniuses" to openly deny that a majority of shares necessarily carried with it a surplus of wisdom and

Plate XII.

equity. He also accentuated his isolation by filing a separate answer in the Equity Suit, in which he advanced in terse phraseology an original argument against the validity of his colleagues' acts.

The independence thus shown by Mr. Lovejoy greatly facilitated an amicable adjustment of the difficulty; for Andrew Carnegie refused to treat with Frick in any way, and it became necessary for the latter to find some one to represent him who had the ability to cope with the combined forces of his opponents. From this difficult position Lovejoy emerged with credit.

The first peace conference was held at Andrew Carnegie's residence in New York on Saturday, March 17th, 1900. It was attended by Messrs. Carnegie, Henry Phipps, Schwab, and Lovejoy. The long-talked-of consolidation of the Carnegie and Frick companies was now finally agreed upon; and the preliminaries settled for a compromise of the personal differences of the leading partners. Fearing that the newspapers would suspect what was going on if the whole Board of Managers suddenly appeared in New York, it was arranged to continue the conference on Monday at Atlantic City; and Carnegie telegraphed to Pittsburg, telling the members of the Board to leave on Sunday night for the New Jersey resort. To disarm suspicion they were instructed to take their wives with them.

Mr. Frick had remained in Pittsburg; but he was kept informed of the progress of the negotiations over the telephone by Mr. Lovejoy. He was satisfied with the plans outlined, provided no details inimical to his interests were introduced; and Lovejoy spent most of the night drafting the agreement.

On Monday this agreement was read to the assembled board at Atlantic City. In general it was acceptable to Carnegie and his adherents; but one clause provoked bitter opposition and jeopardized the whole plan. It appeared that Carnegie had registered a vow never to recognize Frick as a partner; and to maintain his consistency he demanded that Frick's interest should not be given direct to him, but through the hands of a trustee.   This was the only thing in the agreement that was productive of discord; and concerning it Carnegie displayed such heat and persistence that Lovejoy, rather than imperil the settlement, conceded the point.

The next day the amended agreement was adopted; and just as the last signatures were being affixed Mr. James B. Dill arrived by special train from New York to draw up the new company's charter.   The same afternoon the conference ended; and Schwab celebrated the conclusion of peace by a banquet at the Bellevue Hotel, Philadelphia, which he had ordered by telegraph.

The agreement thus reached reads as follows:

MM. Schwab, Carnegie, L. C. Phipps, Morrison, Clemson, Gayley and Moreland, representing The Carnegie Steel Company, Limited, and Henry Phipps, representing John Walker and others of the H. C. Frick Coke Company, agree as follows:

All the business of The Carnegie Steel Company, Limited, and the H. C. Frick Coke Company to be merged substantially as shown in paper "A" of June 3rd, 1899, attached hereto, adjustments to be made up to April 1st, 1900, which will bring the two concerns into the same relative positions as to bookvalues as they occupied April 1st, 1899.

In the matter of the dispute between the two companies as to prices of coke, neither party shall be held to be right or wrong, both shall be considered equally so, therefore the difference will be split in two, each party yielding one-half of its claim.

	ANDREW CARNEGIE.
	HENRY PHIPPS.
F. T. F. LOVEJOY.	C. M. SCHWAB.
Witness: JAS. BERTRAM.	L. C. PHIPPS.
	THOS. MORRISON.
	JAMES GAYLEY.
	D. M. CLEMSON.
	A. M. MORELAND.

The same parties representing The Carnegie Steel Company, Limited, and F. T. F. Lovejoy representing H. C. Frick, under full authority so to do, agree as follows:

The Carnegie Steel Company, Limited, will hand over to said Lovejoy Six per cent of the Stocks and Securities it obtains under this merger, said Lovejoy to receipt for the same in full of all claims of said Frick against the Company or any of its members. To this receipt the signature of H. C. Frick will also be appended, and H. C. Frick will thereupon withdraw his suit against the Company. Meanwhile all legal proceedings to remain in statu quo.

The Committee to carry out the details of this Agreement is to consist of C. M. Schwab, G. D. Packer, F. T. F. Lovejoy and A. M. Moreland, who shall act by unanimous consent, but that failing, all differences if any will be referred to Judge J. H. Reed, whose decision shall be final.

The plans for carrying out this Agreement are more fully set forth in paper marked " B " herewith appended and made part of this Agreement.

We, the undersigned, pledge ourselves to carry out the spirit of this agreement in good faith and with every desire to bring it to a successful conclusion.

L. C. PHIPPS.	ANDREW CARNEGIE.
THOS. MORRISON.	H. PHIPPS.
JAMES GAYLEY.	C. M. SCHWAB.
D. M. CLEMSON.	

Witness: JAS. BERTRAM.
    F. T. F. LOVEJOY.
    A. M. MORELAND.

STATEMENT "A," SHOWING ACCOUNTS OF STOCKHOLDERS IN THE CARNEGIE STEEL COMPANY, LIMITED, AND THE H. C. FRICK COKE COMPANY, AFTER THE ACCEPTANCE OF CERTAIN OPTIONS ON THE STOCKS, GIVEN APRIL 24, 1899.

Stockholders.		Personal Account. C. S. Co., Ltd.	Value of C. S. Co., Ltd. Stock.	Value of H. C. F. C. Co. Stock.
Andrew Carnegie,	Cr.	$4,025,055.76	$146,250,000.00	$30,039,898.09
Henry Phipps,	Cr.	151,092.98	27,500,000.00	7,652,354.74
H. C. Frick,	Cr.	50,911.89	15,000,000.00	16,604,529.50
George Lauder,	Cr.	107,487.38	10,000,000.00	1,187,237.97
C. M. Schwab,	Dr.	1,168,024.90	7,500,000.00	618,575.66
W. H. Singer,	Cr.	358,916.61	5,000,000.00	773,031.18
H. M. Curry,	Dr.	81,486.59	5,000,000.00	771,183.88
L. C. Phipps,	Dr.	656,173.70	5,000,000.00	412,627.36
A. R. Peacock,	Dr.	726,017.98	5,000,000.00	412,259.46
F. T. F. Lovejoy,	Dr.	110,593.76	1,666,666.67	138,029.63
Thos. Morrison,	Dr.	185,067.94	1,666,666.67	137,843.16
Geo. H. Wightman,	Dr.	248,119.44	1,666,666.67	137,661.73

Stockholders.		Personal Account. C. S. Co., Ltd.	Value of C. S. Co., Ltd. Stock.	Value of H. C. F. C. Co. Stock.
D. M. Clemson,	Dr.	$258,754.79	$1,666,666.67	$137,661.73
James Gayley,	Dr.	186,619.70	1,527,777.78	126,401.58
A. M. Moreland,	Dr.	233,044.75	1,527,777.78	126,220.15
Chas. L. Taylor,	Dr.	96,982.26	1,250,000.00	103,337.01
A. R. Whitney,	...	....	1,250,000.00	102,974.15
W. W. Blackburn,	Dr.	29,091.29	833,333.33	69,012.29
Jno. C. Fleming,	Dr.	23,510.01	833,333.33	69,012.29
J. Ogden Hoffman,	Dr.	62,231.06	833,333.33	69,012.29
Milld. Hunsiker,	Dr.	94,791.77	833,333.33	69,012.29
Geo. E. McCague,	Dr.	108,797.58	833,333.33	69,012.29
James Scott,	Dr.	106,888.16	833,333.33	69,012.29
H. P. Bope,	Cr.	13,285.95	277,777.78	22,883.14
W. E. Corey,	Dr.	140,577.43	833,333.33	68,649.43
Jos. E. Schwab,	Dr.	176,301.22	833,333.33	68,649.43
L. T. Brown,	Dr.	107,002.79	555,555.55	45,766.29
D. G. Kerr,	Dr.	43,197.23	277,777.78	22,883.14
H. J. Lindsay,	Dr.	43,197.23	277,777.78	22,883.14
E. F. Wood,	Dr.	48,690.11	277,777.78	22,883.14
H. E. Tener, Jr.,	Dr.	48,690.11	277,777.78	22,883.14
Geo. Megrew,	Dr.	48,690.11	277,777.78	22,883.14
G. D. Packer,	Dr.	48,690.11	277,777.78	22,883.14
W. B. Dickson,	Dr.	63,805.55	277,777.78	22,883.14
A. C. Case,	Dr.	63,805.55	277,777.78	22,883.14
John McLeod,	Dr.	63,805.55	277,777.78	22,883.14
Chas. W. Baker,	Dr.	63,805.55	277,777.77	22,883.14
Undivided,	Dr.	271,731.30	1,250,000.00	102,974.24
Mrs. L. C. Carnegie ...		....	....	5,018,026.81
John Walker..........		....	....	1,434,398.29
Thomas Lynch........		....	....	640,794.18
Vandervort Estate......		....	....	521,794.83
Borntraeger Estate		....	....	360,103.45
G. B. Bosworth........		....	....	355,497.51
J. G. A. Leishman.....		....	....	360,085.87
Robt. Ramsay		....	....	194,355.37
John Pontefract		....	....	194,355.37
S. L. Schoonmaker.....		....	....	194,355.37
Mrs. C. A. Wilson		....	....	92,631.07
Miss H. R. Wilson		....	....	40,166.20
John Walker, Gdn......		....	....	40,161.36
Miss C. B. Wilson		....	....	40,110.99
John T. Wilson........		....	....	40,082.89
Miss E. C. Wilson		....	....	39,425.79
Totals ....Dr.		$901,434.95	$250,000,000.00	$70,000,000.00

Interest adjusted to June 1, 1899.

Pittsburg, June 3, 1899.

MEMORANDUM " B," covering details agreed upon at Atlantic City this 19th March, 1900, by each and every of the persons whose names are attached hereto; each agreeing with the others that he will do all in his power in good faith to carry out this agreement and to induce every other Stockholder in the Companies named to join in this agreement, being convinced that it will be for the best interests of all concerned:

The business of The Carnegie Steel Company, Limited, the H. C. Frick Coke Company, and all the Companies subsidiary to each, or either, to be consolidated, thus:

All of the lands, works and other properties now owned and operated by The Carnegie Steel Company, Limited, to be sold and transferred to the Carnegie Steel Company, an existing Pennsylvania Corporation, saving and excepting the Stocks held by it in certain other Corporations, to wit, the H. C. Frick Coke Company, with all its subsidiary Companies, the Oliver Iron Mining Company, the Union Railroad Co., the Pittsburg, Bessemer & Lake Erie R. R. Co., and all Stocks in other Companies, now held by The Carnegie Steel Company, Limited, which are considered permanent investments and not merely securities; payment therefor to be made in Stock of the Carnegie Steel Company, the Capital whereof shall be increased to ($50,000,000) Fifty Million Dollars.

The Stock now held by The Carnegie Steel Company, Limited, in the H. C. Frick Coke Company, the Youghiogheny Northern Railway Co., the Youghiogheny Water Co., the Mt. Pleasant Water Co., and the Trotter Water Co., to be distributed among the Shareholders of The Carnegie Steel Company, Limited, in proportion to their several interests, said Shareholders to be charged for said Stocks at their respective book values as at April 1st, 1900.

F. T. F. LOVEJOY.

ANDREW CARNEGIE.
HENRY PHIPPS.
CHARLES M. SCHWAB.
LAWRENCE C. PHIPPS.
THOMAS MORRISON.
JAMES GAYLEY.
DAVID M. CLEMSON.
ANDREW M. MORELAND.

A Corporation to be formed under the laws of New Jersey, having the name and title The Carnegie Company, with $160,-000,000 Capital Stock, which Company shall acquire all the stock of the Carnegie Steel Company, the H. C. Frick Coke

Co., all their subsidiary Companies, and the Stocks of all other Companies now held by The Carnegie Steel Company, Limited, which are held as investments; by purchase, paying to the Stockholders therefor as follows:

For all of the Stock in the Carnegie Steel Company, and for all of the Stocks now held by The Carnegie Steel Company, Limited, saving and excepting the Stocks held by it in the H. C. Frick Coke Co., the Youghiogheny Northern Rly. Co., the Youghiogheny Water Co., the Mt. Pleasant Water Co., and the Trotter Water Co., One hundred and twenty-five million dollars in Stock of The Carnegie Company and a like amount in Bonds of said Company, as hereinafter described:

For all of the Stock in the H. C. Frick Coke Co., the Youghiogheny Northern Rly. Co., the Youghiogheny Water Co., the Mt. Pleasant Water Co., the Trotter Water Co., and the Union Supply Co., Limited; Thirty-five million dollars in Stock of The Carnegie Company, and a like amount in Bonds of said Company, as hereinafter described.

Preliminary to the foregoing, adjustments shall be made as follows:

A Dividend shall be declared by The Carnegie Steel Company, Limited, of such amount as shall be necessary to make the "Book Values" of the Stocks of The Carnegie Steel Company, Limited, (exclusive of its holdings in the H. C. Frick Coke Co. and its subsidiary Companies) on the one hand, and of the H. C. Frick Coke Company and all its subsidiary Companies on the other, relatively the same on April 1st, 1900, as they were on April 1st, 1899, when the values of $250,000,000 and $70,000,000, respectively, were first established.

After The Carnegie Steel Company, Limited, shall have distributed among its shareholders its holdings of Stock in the H. C. Frick Coke Co. and its subsidiary Companies, adjustments shall be made between all the Stockholders in the H. C. Frick Coke Co., so that each shall hold his proper and proportionate amount of Stock in the subsidiary Companies; such adjustments to be made at the respective "Book-values," April 1st, 1900, of the said Stocks.

The Bonds to be issued by The Carnegie Company shall be in such form as shall be agreed upon by the Committee hereinafter named, under the directions of the General Counsel, and shall embody the following:

Bonds payable in One hundred years; interest payable in New York, semi-annually, at five per cent per annum, free of all Tax; to be in such amounts, $1,000, $5,000 and $10,000,

as may be found best; to be divided into four series of $40,-
000,000 each so as to make interest fall due February 1st and
August 1st; March 1st and September 1st, May 1st and November 1st, June 1st and December 1st of each year; secured
by a Mortgage or Deed of Trust covering all the Stocks held
by The Carnegie Company in all the subsidiary or operating
Companies; after Five years a Sinking Fund of one-half of one
per cent. on said Bonds to be established; Bonds to be subject
to be drawn for redemption out of Sinking Fund at any time at
1.05 after five years. In case of default in the payment of
interest, the principal may become due and payable. No personal liability on Bonds; to be registered or not, at holder's
option; with such other provisions as are usual or advised by
counsel for the proper protection of the Bondholders.

Each Stockholder in The Carnegie Company whose interest
has not been fully paid up shall have the right and privilege at
his option, of selling to The Carnegie Company, at par, sufficient of his Bonds to liquidate his indebtedness, or of deposit-
ing as collateral security for such indebtedness, Bonds or Stock
of The Carnegie Company in proportion to his indebtedness;
three times in Stock or one and one-half times in Bonds, at his
option.

Stock in The Carnegie Company shall be reserved to the
amount of $3,200,000 for the purpose of selling interests in
said Company to deserving officials and employees, carrying out
the plan heretofore established by Carnegie Brothers and Co.,
Ltd., which is declared to be an essential feature of the new
Company.

Signed in duplicate; one copy being intrusted to A. M.
Moreland, Secretary of The Carnegie Steel Company, Limited,
and the other copy to F. T. F. Lovejoy.

ANDREW CARNEGIE.
HENRY PHIPPS.
C. M. SCHWAB.
L. C. PHIPPS.
THOS. MORRISON.
JAMES GAYLEY.
D. M. CLEMSON.
A. M. MORELAND.
F. T. F. LOVEJOY.

Witness: JAS. BERTRAM.

We, the undersigned, Shareholders in The Carnegie Steel
Company, Limited, having read the foregoing Agreement, do

23

now hereby, by the signing hereof, fully approve the arrangement and join in the same as to our interest.

GEORGE LAUDER,

pr. ANDREW CARNEGIE.

GIBSON D. PACKER.

We, the undersigned, Stockholders in the H. C. Frick Coke Company, having read the foregoing Agreement, do now hereby, by the signing hereof, fully approve the arrangement and join in the same as to our interest.

MRS. LUCY C. CARNEGIE, EX.

by ANDREW CARNEGIE.

Five days after the signing of this agreement a charter was obtained of the State of New Jersey, incorporating the Carnegie Company for the purpose of acquiring all the stock of the Carnegie Steel Company, the H. C. Frick Coke Company, all their subsidiary companies, and the stocks of all companies hitherto held by the Carnegie Steel Company. It is worth noticing that the committee charged with the carrying out of the agreement ignored that part of it which, at the instance of Mr. Carnegie, excluded Mr. Frick; and his name appeared third on the list of incorporators of the new company, as a subscriber for 15,484 shares.

On March 30th the committee made its report concerning the adjustment of the relative book values of the two merging companies as follows:

PITTSBURG, PA., March 30, 1900.

To THE BOARD OF MANAGERS OF
    THE CARNEGIE STEEL COMPANY, LIMITED.

The Committee appointed by the Shareholders of The Carnegie Steel Company, Limited, and the H. C. Frick Coke Company, for the purpose of carrying out the plans of Re-Organization of the Carnegie Interests, beg leave to report:

In the matter of the adjustment of the relative Book Values of The Carnegie Steel Company, Limited, and the H. C. Frick Coke Company with its subsidiary Companies:

At April 1st, 1899, the relative Book Values were as follows:

The Carnegie Steel Company, Limited 3.27986
H. C. Frick Coke Company and Allies. . . . 1.

Based on careful estimates of March Profits of all the Companies whose Stock is included, the same relative Book Values, at April 1, 1900, show a surplus for distribution to Shareholders of The Carnegie Steel Company, Limited, of. .$16,277,464.69

To this should be added the holdings of The Carnegie Steel Company, Limited, in the Stock of the H. C. Frick Coke Company and its subsidiary Companies, carried on the Steel Company's books at. 5,585,174.39

Total for distribution. $21,862,639.08

This Committee would, therefore, recommend the declaring by The Carnegie Steel Company, Limited, of a final Dividend of 88% or $22,000,000.00, payable as follows:

To cover the Value of the Stock of the H. C. Frick Coke Company and its subsidiary Companies charged to Partners in accordance with the Re-Organization Agreement. $5,585,174.39

3%, payable in Cash on demand by either "Paid-up" Partners or "Debtor" Partners whose interests were purchased not later than January 1, 1899. . . . . 750,000.00

Balance payable at such times and in such instalments as this Committee shall decide after consultation with the principal Partners and the Treasurer. 15,664,825.61

Total. $22,000,000.00

Respectfully submitted,

C. M. Schwab.
G. D. Packer.
F. T. F. Lovejoy.
A. M. Moreland.

The following is a correct list of stockholders and bond-holders of the Carnegie Company, as formed or organized after the Frick-Carnegie suit:

Capital.....................................$160,000,000.00
Bonds......................................$160,000,000.00
Par Value of Stock, $1,000.00 per Share.

	Shares of Stock.	Bonds.
Andrew Carnegie.......................	86,382	$88,147,000
Henry Phipps	17,227	17,577,000
Henry C. Frick.......................	15,484	15,800,000
George Lauder........................	5,482	5,593,000
Charles M. Schwab....................	3,980	4,061,000
Henry M. Curry	2,829	2,886,000
William H. Singer	2,830	2,886,000
Lawrence C. Phipps..................	2,654	2,707,000
Alexander R. Peacock	2,653	2,707,000
Lucy C. Carnegie	2,459	2,510,000
Francis T. F. Lovejoy..............	884	902,000
James Gayley........................	885	902,000
Thomas Morrison.....................	885	902,000
Andrew M. Moreland	885	902,000
Daniel M. Clemson..................	885	902,000
George H. Wightman	884	902,000
John Walker......	722	737,000
Charles L. Taylor....	663	677,000
Alfred R. Whitney..................	663	677,000
John C. Fleming....................	442	451,000
William W. Blackburn...............	442	451,000
J. Ogden Hoffman	442	451,000
Millard Hunsiker........	442	451,000
George E. McCague..................	442	451,000
James Scott	442	451,000
William E. Corey	442	451,000
Joseph E. Schwab...................	442	451,000
Thomas Lynch......................	317	323,000
Henry P. Bope	295	301,000
Lewis T. Brown	295	301,000
Robert T. Vandervort	255	260,000
John B. Jackson...................	176	179,000
John G. A. Leishman	176	179,000
Giles B. Bosworth.................	176	179,000
David G. Kerr	147	150,000
Homer J. Lindsay.................	147	150,000
Ezra F. Wood....................	147	150,000
Hampden E. Tener, Jr.............	147	150,000
George Megrew....................	147	150,000
Gibson D. Packer.................	147	150,000
William B. Dickson	147	150,000

	Shares of Stock.	Bonds.
Albert C. Case............	147	$150,000
John McLeod........	147	150,000
Charles W. Baker	147	150,000
Janet E. Ramsay.........	95	97,000
John Pontefract....................	95	97,000
Sylvanus L. Schoonmaker	95	97,000
Azor R. Hunt	74	75,000
Alva C. Dinkey....	74	75,000
P. Toesten Berg	74	75,000
Charles McCreery	74	75,000
Caroline A. Wilson	45	46,000
Helen R. Wilson......................	19	20,000
Clara B. Wilson......................	19	20,000
John T. Wilson......	19	20,000
Edna C. Wilson......................	19	20,000
James G. Hunter	19	19,000
Emil Swenson........	19	19,000
James J. Campbell	19	19,000
Frederic H. Kindl....	19	19,000
James B. Dill.........	1	......
Andrew M. Moreland, Trustee	3,189	......
Total..	160,000	$160,000,000

Thus was reached the final metamorphosis of the Carnegie
Steel Company. In the new organization Mr. Frick was
omitted from the directorate, as was also Mr. Carnegie. Mr.
Lovejoy was also dropped. But outwardly peace prevailed;
and the only remaining trace of a past conflict is the Society
of Carnegie Veterans, formed of the loyal band of Carnegie
adherents. No former partner is eligible for membership
in this association who did not take part in the attempt to depose Mr. Frick. Once a year these young geniuses hold a banquet; and, amid palms and electric mottoes to the glory of him
who made them rich, recount their battles and congratulate each
other on the outcome of their victory. And the dear departed
shades of Kloman, Shinn, Coleman, T. M. Carnegie, Stewart,
Curry, and others long forgotten, would listen in vain for a word
of recognition of their share in these triumphs.

CHAPTER XXIII

THE BILLION-DOLLAR FINALE

THE absorption of the Carnegie Company by the United States Steel Corporation has been invested with much dignity and lofty circumstance by numerous writers in reviews and magazines; and owing to its magnitude, running into hundreds of millions, the transaction has struck the popular imagination and acquired a world-wide interest. To those who watched the incident from the inside, who saw the framework of the scenery and the elaborate mechanism of the stage effects, who attended the rehearsals and heard the subdued tones of the prompter, there was a certain grim humor in a performance which those in front watched with bated breath. But despite its lack of spontaneity, the proceeding had the dignity conferred by magnitude; and its brilliant success made it impressive even to those who heard the creaking of the machinery.

The time is not yet ripe for a full and frank description of the events leading up to this important consolidation; but a rough outline of them may be given.

About a year before Mr. Frick resigned the headship of the Carnegie Steel Company he appointed a committee, with Mr. Clemson as chairman, to report on a project he had formed of building a tube works at Conneaut, the Lake Erie terminus of the Bessemer Railroad. There being little freight from Pittsburg to the Lake port, the ore trains returned for the most part empty; and to utilize this profitless haul, various plans had been discussed by Mr. Frick and his colleagues for the building of blast-furnaces and other works at Conneaut that would call for Pittsburg coal and coke. One of these schemes is out-lined in the minutes of the meeting of the Board of Managers held on January 16th, 1899, previously quoted; and at the same meeting Mr. Clemson made a remark which showed that, after making the investigation authorized by Mr. Frick, he was in favor of also starting the tube works.

It is probable that these works would have been built by the Carnegie managers but for the attempt made the same year to sell out to the Moore Syndicate; it being thought undesirable to antagonize, while such a deal was pending, the important finan-ciers who were interested in the National Tube Company, with which the new works would have come into competition. But there was no idea, at this time, of holding the tube project as a threat over anybody. It was a simple business plan growing out of the need for filling the empty ore-cars on their return to Conneaut.

After the reorganization of the steel company consequent on the withdrawal of Mr. Frick, it was seen by Mr. Carnegie that this tube project might be revived and utilized to force the purchase of at least his own holdings in the Carnegie Company, and perhaps of the whole concern. So the plan was gone over afresh, amplified and made definite, and then given to the newspapers by the Carnegie press agent and by Carnegie interviews. Thus it was published the length and breadth of the country as the settled purpose of the steel company. Here are two of these statements: the first as furnished by the Car-negie press agent, and the second in a characteristic interview with Andrew Carnegie. The Pickwickian humor of the latter will not be lost on the reader who recalls the discussion of the Carnegie managers in 1899 concerning the Conneaut project, quoted in the eighteenth chapter of this book.

"It has been determined by the Carnegie Company, in order to utilize this now profitless haul, to establish at the lake ter-minal, where it already owns great docks and has ample facilities for handling ore and for the lake shipment of the finished product, an extensive pipe and tube manufacturing plant, representing an investment of $12,000,000. The projected works will stretch over a mile along the lake front, and will be the most extensive and complete plant of the kind in existence. Electric power will be mainly used for driving the machinery, and the system of operation will be continuous, the ore being unloaded from vessels at one end and worked through successive stages of iron and steel-making in a direct line to the finished pipe and tube at the other end."—*World's Work.*

"Immediately following the Carnegie Company announcement of the location of a tube plant at Conneaut Harbor, Ohio, rumors were set afloat throwing some doubt on the sincerity of the company's intention to carry out the announced plans. In the iron trade there was an attempt to find a reason for the location of the plant at Conneaut rather than in the Pittsburg district. Regarding the reasons for going outside of the Pittsburg district Andrew Carnegie was quoted last week as follows: 'In the first place I am bound to say that Conneaut was not considered until the Pennsylvania Railroad, without consulting, doubled our export rates . . . which led our people to take up the question: How can we escape from the grasp of this arbitrary railroad combination? A study of the subject convinced every one that we could do so by taking to water. When I returned from Europe it was to find all agreed that this was the method of relief. . . . Our establishment at Conneaut will benefit Pittsburg, because we shall give the Pittsburg railroads an object lesson. A very small proportion of our freight will go by rail from these works. We are already in the shipping business, and have only to add half a dozen small steamers to our fleet to ply to the important lake cities, distributing steel and loading up with scrap, of which we shall use an enormous quantity.' . . .

Asked whether the proposed plant was supposed to be a blow at the National Tube Co., Mr. Carnegie replied that at one time the original National Company purchased billets from his company, but later decided to work its own blast furnaces and make its own billets. Continuing he said: 'As I understand the policy of the Carnegie Steel Co., it is to co-operate in every way with its fellow manufacturers in the industrial world, and not to push itself into any new field save in self-defence. We did not leave the National Tube Co. They left us, which they had a perfect right to do, of course. Now we are ready to shake hands and co-operate with them in the most friendly spirit. We are better for them than a dozen small concerns, conducted in a small, jealous way. We believe there is room enough for the two concerns," etc.—*Iron Trade Review*, January 17th, 1901.

In the conversion of the heathen, missionaries have found it useful to describe the condition of the damned before presenting a picture of the joys of the blessed. It was on some such principle that the threat of industrial war was thus made by the Carnegies before the blessings of co-operation and consolidation were set out before the vision

"In the conversion of the heathen."

of the alarmed financiers of the country. The panic produced by the double threat of the Carnegies to build a rival tube works and to enter into competition with the great Pennsylvania Railroad has been graphically described by a recent magazine writer:

"Either project as a threat would have been alarming. The two together as imminent and assured accomplishments produced a panic. And a panic among millionaires, while hard to produce is, when once under way, just as much of a panic as is a panic among geese. They ran this way and that; they hid one behind another; they filled the newspapers with their squawkings; they reproached, implored, accused each other. At last they ran to their master—Morgan. And he negotiated with Carnegie."

But the negotiations came later. They were preceded by a bankers' dinner, at which were preached the joys of industrial peace. This famous dinner also grew out of a previous incident connected with Mr. Frick.

Somewhere about the time of the purchase of the Moore

option, Mr. Frick invited a number of prominent bankers to Pittsburg, to show them the armor-plate vault that had just been built for the Union Trust Company. Incidentally they were given an opportunity of seeing the extent of the iron and steel works at Pittsburg. Up to that time the resources of the Iron City were but imperfectly known in Wall Street. This visit showed that it was the busiest place in the world, and the centre of its greatest industry. Duly impressed, the bankers returned to New York; and the courtesies they had received as Mr. Frick's guests were now treated as an outstanding asset of the Carnegie Steel Company. Through the influence of Mr. Albert C. Case, credit agent of the Carnegie Company, and that of Mr. Charles Stewart Smith, an intimate friend of Andrew Carnegie, arrangements were made with a prominent banker of New York, who had been among those entertained by Mr. Frick, to give a return dinner, ostensibly in honor of Mr. Schwab. This dinner was duly given; and, as a spontaneous outburst of enthusiasm for Mr. Frick's earlier protégé, it has been much written about and discussed.

Mr. Morgan attended the dinner, and listened with great interest to Mr. Schwab's views on industrial combinations—"views apparently so large, so wise, and so interesting that Mr. Morgan was strongly impressed by the speech and the speaker. Then there began a series of interviews which eventually led to the founding of the United States Steel Corporation, to the realization of Mr. Carnegie's desire to retire from the control of the business,"* and to the sale and absorption of the Carnegie Company. It was the most masterly piece of diplomacy in the history of American industry, and formed a fitting climax to Andrew Carnegie's romantic business career.

The further story of the merger has been told a hundred times and need not be repeated here. The part of the Carnegies in it is indicated in the following letter to stockholders, now first published:

---

* Prof. Henry Loomis Nelson.

THE CARNEGIE COMPANY
Offices; Carnegie Building,

Pittsburg, Pa., 9th March, 1901.

Personal and Confidential.

DEAR SIR:

To facilitate the exchange of the Stock of The Carnegie Company for Stock of the United States Steel Corporation, the undersigned, at the request of a majority of the Stockholders, have agreed to act as a Committee, on behalf of their Fellow Stockholders, to receive Certificates of Stock of The Carnegie Company, and to make the exchange for shares of Preferred and Common Stock of the new Company.

You are therefore requested, if you desire to exchange your stock and to have this Committee act for you, to deliver the Certificates of Stock of The Carnegie Company held by you, to W. W. Blackburn, who will deliver to you the receipt of the Committee therefor. Such Certificates must be endorsed in blank (or may be accompanied by separate powers of attorney), with the names of the undersigned inserted as attorneys in fact, with power to them or any two of them to transfer the said Shares upon the books of the Company; proper revenue stamps to be attached. The receipt appended hereto will then be signed.

The basis of exchange is as follows:

One share of the Carnegie Company stock (par value $1,000) to receive of the United States Steel Corporation Stock 15.3558 Shares of Seven Per Cent. Cumulative Preferred, par value $100—$1,535.58; 14.1061 Shares Common, par value $100—$1,410.61. No scrip will be issued for fractional Shares, but exchange will be arranged at the rate of $100 per Share for Preferred and $50 per Share for Common, viz.:

Where a depositor is entitled to less than one-half of one Share of Preferred or Common Stock, he will receive cash for same; and where entitled to more than one-half of one Share of Preferred or Common Stock, he will be allotted and required to pay for the fractional Share at the above rate.

A deposit of Stock with the Committee will constitute an acceptance of the above terms by the depositor.

Yours respectfully,

C. M. SCHWAB, }
L. C. PHIPPS, } Committee.
W. W. BLACKBURN, }

Had all the stockholders been subject to these terms it would have meant that the $160,000,000 of the Carnegie Company's stock would have been exchanged for the United States Steel Company's stock as follows :

```
Seven per cent. cumulative preferred............$240,569,280
Common stock ..............................  225,697,760
                                            ─────────────
                                            $466,267,040
Add $160,000,000 bonds exchanged for the same
    amount of Carnegie bonds.................  160,000,000
                                            ─────────────
            Total.........................$626,267,040
```

As a matter of fact, however, Andrew Carnegie, Mrs. Lucy C. Carnegie, and George Lauder were paid entirely in United States Steel Company bonds, at the rate of $1,500 per share. Thus for 96,000 shares of stock in the Carnegie Company they received $144,000,000 in bonds of the United States Steel Corporation. . The balance of the $304,000,000 bond issue of the latter, or $160,000,000, was exchanged at par for the $160,000,-000 bond issue of the Carnegie Company.

For the balance of the stock of the Carnegie Company, i.e., 64,000 shares, was issued $98,277,120 in preferred stock and $90,279,040 in the common stock of the United States Steel Corporation.

At the time of purchase the bonds and the preferred stock were considered worth par and the common stock 50; making the total amount paid at that time $447,416,640. Since that time the stocks have declined; but the enhancement in the market value of the bonds has more than made up the difference. The present value of the securities issued for the Carnegie properties, computing bonds at 114, preferred stock at 84½, and common stock at 35, would make a total of $461,-201,830. Add to this the $22,000,000 dividend paid to Carnegie stockholders the previous year in adjustment of values in the consolidation of the coke and steel properties, and we reach the total cash value of the business to which Kloman's little forge had grown in forty years.

THE END.

APPENDIX

THE EQUITY SUIT

Some extracts from the pleadings of Henry C. Frick

On the 14th day of January, 1889, your orator was elected chairman of Carnegie Brothers & Co., Limited, and continued to act as such chairman until the new association of the Carnegie Steel Company, Limited, was formed. He was then elected chairman of the latter, and continued to act as such until December 5th, 1899.

On January 11th, 1895, with the assent of those interested and with a view to enable your orator to perform duties which were believed to be of more value to the firm than those then imposed upon said chairman, the office of president was created. Upon said officer was placed the details of the duties your orator had theretofore performed as chairman.

Your orator continued as chairman with general supervisory power until December 5th, 1899. About that date Carnegie without reason, and actuated by malevolent motives, demanded his resignation of said position. Recognizing Carnegie's paramount influence as the holder of a majority interest, and desiring to prevent the evil which might result from discord, your orator acquiesced in the demand and gave his resignation.

As chairman of said companies your orator had participated largely in and directed the business conducted by them and, until the time of his enforced resignation, said business was conducted to a large extent under his personal supervision, management, and direction. Carnegie lived in New York City. He spent much of his time abroad, remaining there continually, at one time, for over eighteen months. Of course he was consulted about important matters, but he rarely participated in the current management of the business.

For various reasons, none just, not necessary now to be stated, but which will appear hereafter in the taking of testimony, Carnegie has recently conceived a personal animosity towards your orator. This partly arose from the failure of your orator, in connection with others, to avail of an option given by Carnegie in consideration of the sum of one million, one hundred and seventy thousand dollars ($1,170,000), to Carnegie paid, and now retained by him, as a forfeit to purchase his (Carnegie's) interest in said Steel Company, Limited, for the sum of about one hundred and fifty-seven million, nine hundred and fifty thousand dollars ($157,950,000), which sum Carnegie insisted should be so preferred and secured that he would virtually have a first mortgage on all the partnership assets and thus gain a preference over all his partners.

As has been heretofore said, on the 4th day of December, 1899, without good reason, and from malevolent motives towards me, Carnegie demanded the resignation by your orator of his office of chairman of said company. This resignation, in the interest of harmony, was tendered. Since that time Carnegie has secured control of the whole association and of its affairs, and has compelled the co-partners, other than Henry Phipps, Jr., F. T. F. Lovejoy, and Henry M. Curry, and perhaps others, who refused to carry out his orders and desires, to pass such resolutions and do such acts as he dictated, without regard to their conformity to their real wishes,

365

or to their judgment, as to the true policy of the association. Many of the partners were unable or unwilling to incur his animosity, lest he might attempt to forfeit their interests in the association. Some of them were practically unable to resist his will because of their large indebtedness thereto.

In order that he might injure your orator, whilst benefiting himself, Carnegie conceived a scheme to forfeit the interest of your orator in the association, worth upwards of fifteen million dollars ($15,000,000), in such way as would not oblige him to pay therefor one-half of its real value and would enable him to make payment therefor in small instalments at very long intervals of time.

As part of this fraudulent scheme, Carnegie, who had rarely attended the meetings of the Board of Managers of the Steel Company, Limited, theretofore held, presented himself at a meeting of the said board, held on the 8th day of January, 1900, after the resignation by your orator of his chairmanship, and when he was not present. Carnegie then presented to said Board of Managers resolutions by him previously prepared, which he caused to be adopted. Many of the statements in said resolutions were false. The whole of the resolutions were misleading. In them he referred to a certain so-called iron-clad agreement. Carnegie followed up his action in this respect by obliging the Board of Managers to instruct the secretary to receive signatures to this so-called iron-clad agreement, which, for the first time, he called a supplemental iron-clad agreement, of July 1st, 1892. No such agreement had ever been executed by Carnegie. Many other members of the firm had never executed the same. This so-called agreement was inoperative and void. Carnegie knew that it was void and inoperative. He knew that neither he nor the Carnegie Steel Company had any power to compel any person to sell his interest in the firm in pursuance thereof; yet, knowing this, without your orator's knowledge, secretly, after said resolutions had been passed, he signed for the first time said so-called iron-clad agreement of July 1st, 1892. At the same time, or shortly after, he caused, directly or indirectly, other persons to sign the same, with a fraudulent intent thereby, and without your orator's knowledge or consent, to make a contract for him under which he, Carnegie, could seize your orator's interest in said firm. All these acts he carefully concealed from your orator, his partner. Subsequently, in person, Carnegie threatened your orator when he called upon him, that unless he would do what he, Carnegie, desired, he would deprive your orator of his interest in the firm. In pursuance of his fraudulent intent and in furtherance of his said scheme of fraud, Carnegie caused to be served on your orator on the 15th day of January, 1900, a notice purporting to be given under and in pursuance of said so-called iron-clad agreement. In this demand was made, in the name of Carnegie and in that of other persons who had been forced by him to sign the same, that your orator should transfer his interest in said Carnegie Steel Company, Limited. Having failed to secure this transfer, Carnegie persuaded Schwab, one of the defendants, who was acting as president of said association, to transfer, on the first day of February, 1900, on the books of the company, your orator's interest in said Steel Company, Limited, as if he were entitled to make said transfer as attorney in fact of your orator. After Schwab had made this pretended transfer, Carnegie pretended, now pretends, and many of the partners under his compulsion pretend, that the Carnegie Steel Company, Limited, owns all your orator's interest in said firm. Carnegie, being the owner of 58½ per centum of the entire capital thereof, is now pretending to be the owner of over 60 per centum of your orator's said interest, thus pretended to have been acquired. Carnegie further pretends that he need not and will not pay for your orator's interest what it is fairly worth, but that he can only be compelled to pay a price which will be determined by himself, and by the partners he controls. This price, he contends, can only be demanded by your orator in such small instalments during a term of years of such duration as will, probably, not only enable the company to entirely pay for your orator's interests by using the share of the profits applicable to them, but have a surplus left to the company. Thus, it is part of Carnegie's scheme not only to seize your orator's interest, but to make it pay for itself out of the profits, and thereafter leave Carnegie, in large part, the owner of said interests, with a large surplus of money besides. Though Carnegie pretends that he had thus secured a large part of your orator's interest in a way which will inure to his benefit, he denies all individual liability whatever for its payment, and claims that the only party who will be obliged to pay the price he will determine to give will be the Carnegie Steel Company, Limited, which he will use for that purpose.

The exact manner in which Carnegie will seek to depreciate the value to be paid for your orator's interest cannot be stated by your orator in detail with certainty; but he believes and therefore avers that although Carnegie's attention and that of the defendants have been called by him to the fact that the values of the company assets on its books were wholly inadequate, and although he and the defendants have been requested to make said values conform with the truth, he, the said Carnegie, will use figures put upon the books years ago, which are obsolete, and are not by any of the defendants pretended to be correct; will fail to put any valuation upon assets of immense value; and will resort to other illegal and unfair devices.

Your orator shows to your Honors that this attempt of Carnegie to expel him from the firm and seize his interest therein at but a mere fraction of its real value, is not made by him in good faith and for the best interests of the Carnegie Steel Company, Limited. It is not actuated by honorable motives on his part, nor for the future good of the firm, but is a determination to punish your orator, principally, because of the failure of the scheme by which Carnegie was to realize over $157,000,000 for his interest, and, also, in part, to make gain for himself by seizing your orator's interest at very far below its real and fair value.

In order that the business of the firm of the Carnegie Steel Company, Limited, might not be jeopardized by inharmonious relations between the partners and that its enormous business might be carried on by united and harmonious action, your orator was willing, upon ascertaining the animosity of Carnegie towards himself, and his determination to drive him from the firm, to dispose of his interest therein at a fair value. This fact was stated by your orator to Carnegie when the latter called, in January, 1900, at his office, in an endeavor to coerce the making of a sale by your orator at a price below what was fair. An offer was then made by your orator to Carnegie that in case a fair price could not be agreed upon for his interest, which the latter insisted upon securing, that your orator would agree to refer to the arbitration of three disinterested men, the determination and fixing of a fair value. This offer Carnegie refused, doubtless because he hoped to acquire such interest at much less than the fair value thereof by means of his fraudulent scheme hereinbefore set out, which scheme he was then, though without any intimation of that fact to your orator, secretly perfecting and determined to carry into effect.

Your orator still is willing, in order that harmony may be preserved and that the great interests involved may not be subjected to jeopardy, to sell his interest in the Carnegie Steel Company, Limited, at a fair value, to

be ascertained by three disinterested business men.   He now tenders his
willingness so to do.

Notwithstanding the fraudulent actions of Carnegie, your orator also is
willing, in order that the enormous business interests of the Carnegie Steel
Company, Limited, may be protected, without injury to any of its partners,
to continue the business of the said firm in accordance with the true spirit
of the articles of agreement of July 1st, 1892, creating the same.

If, as your orator is advised and believes, the said articles created a
general, and not a limited, partnership, he is willing, and now tenders such
willingness, to have such action taken by the firm and by the partners
thereof as will make the said firm strictly a limited partnership, as originally intended.   Your orator is further willing, and now tenders such
willingness, to continue the Carnegie Steel Company, Limited, as a general
partnership, if he is allowed, as one of the partners, to participate in the
management thereof, claiming no other or further right than that of a
general partner in a general partnership.

Your orator is not willing, however, to continue the general partnership
under the sole control of Carnegie, without being allowed to have any participation therein.   Carnegie is so engaged in other occupations and diver-
sions that, were he otherwise able so to do, he cannot properly manage
and carry on said business.   Your orator believes and avers that the
financial prosperity of the firm will be impaired by the exclusive management and control of the same by Carnegie.

All of the defendants excepting Henry Phipps, F. T. F. Lovejoy and
Henry M. Curry, and possibly others, at the instance of Carnegie, now
claim that your orator has no interest in the Carnegie Steel Company,
Limited, and that his only right is to demand from said company, at long
postponed periods, such amount in compensation as Carnegie shall be
willing to concede him.

Your orator thus by the fraudulent acts of Carnegie and the acqui-
escence therein of the defendants, other than those above named, has been
ejected from the Carnegie Steel Company, Limited, and has been and is
now denied any participation in its business.   Your orator's interest therein
has been taken possession of by the defendants, and they at the instance and
under the domination of Carnegie, are now carrying on the said business,
alleging that they will continue to carry it on as if your orator had no interest therein.

Your orator alleges that the whole effort which has been made, and
which the defendants are now seeking to make effectual, is in pursuance of
said fraudulent scheme of Carnegie to practically seize your orator's interest
in said firm.   This attempt is being made, although Carnegie knows, and
all the defendants know, that the prosperity of the firm, in considerable
part, is the result of your orator's continuous and close personal management of the same, from the time of its organization.

Your orator denies that there is or was when said notice was given any
contract under which the defendants have acquired, or lawfully can acquire,
his interest in said firm.

He avers that the attempt to acquire the same and said pretended
transfer thereof by said Schwab, are illegal and void.   Schwab was not the
attorney in fact of your orator to make said transfer nor did he have any
lawful authority so to do.

Wherefore your orator needs equitable relief, and prays as follows:

First.   A decree that the pretended transfer of your orator's interests
in the Carnegie Steel Company, Limited, was and is null and void.   .   .   .

Second.   An injunction, now special, hereafter to be made final, restraining the defendants from any interference with your orator's interest in said Carnegie Steel Company, Limited, and from excluding him from a participation in the care and management of the assets and business.

Third. An injunction, special until hearing, and perpetual thereafter, enjoining and restraining the defendants from conducting the business operations of the firm called the Carnegie Steel Company, Limited, without permitting your orator to participate therein.

Fourth. An injunction, special until hearing, and perpetual thereafter, enjoining and restraining the defendants from tranferring to the Carnegie Steel Company, Limited, or to any person or persons, or corporation, your orator's interest in the said Carnegie Steel Company, Limited.

Fifth. A decree ordering the defendants to cancel upon the books of the said firm, any assignment or transfer heretofore made, or pretended to be made, to said association, of your orator's interest in said firm, and all further assignments, if any, to any other persons, of your orator's said interests.

Sixth. A decree ordering the defendants to join with your orator in conducting and managing the affairs and business and properties of the Carnegie Steel Company, Limited.

Seventh. A decree ordering the defendants to cancel and erase all entries upon the books of the firm of the Carnegie Steel Company, Limited, of insufficient, unfair, and improper valuations of its assets and of your orator's interest therein, and to cause the said books so to be kept as to fairly and fully show the real value of the Carnegie Steel Company, Limited, as a going concern and your orator's interest therein.

Eighth. In case the defendants shall refuse the offers hereinbefore by your orator made, . . . that your Honorable Court will thereupon allow your orator to declare the said firm of the Carnegie Steel Company, Limited, dissolved, and that you will thereupon appoint a receiver to take charge of all the business and assets of the said firm, permitting said receiver to fulfil unperformed contracts and to do whatever shall be necessary in and about the proper liquidation of its affairs, and that, after the conversion of the entire assets of the company into money and the payment of the debts of the said company, your Honorable Court will then distribute the balance thereof among the partners in proportion to their interests.

Ninth. That an account be taken between Carnegie and your orator, whereby Carnegie shall be charged with all the losses, expenses, and damage he has caused your orator by his illegal and fraudulent conduct hereinbefore stated; and that if Carnegie persists in his said fraudulent scheme and refuses the offers hereinbefore made, and thus causes the actual dissolution of the firm, all losses incurred by your orator by reason of the said dissolution and forced winding up of the firm shall be charged against him, and that he shall be decreed to make good and pay to your orator the difference between what his interest was fairly worth on or about February 1st, 1900, and the amount he shall receive through the decree of this court in final liquidation and settlement of the said firm.

Tenth. That all entries Carnegie or any other person has caused to be made on the books of the Carnegie Steel Company, Limited, in pursuance of said fraudulent scheme of said Carnegie, shall be erased and cancelled under the decree of this Honorable Court.

Eleventh. General relief.

JOHN G. JOHNSON,
D. T. WATSON,
WILLIS F. McCOOK,
 Solicitors for Plaintiff.